D1272935

Collin College Library
SPRING CREEK CAMPUS
Plano, Texas 75074

WITHDRAWN

D   Black, Jeremy.
521
B57   The Great War.
2011

$29.95

The Great War and the Making
of the Modern World

The Great War and the Making of the Modern World

JEREMY BLACK

continuum

Published by the Continuum International Publishing Group

The Tower Building
11 York Road
London
SE1 7NX

80 Maiden Lane
Suite 704
New York
NY 10038

www.continuumbooks.com

Copyright © Jeremy Black 2011

All rights reserved. No part of this publication may be reproduced or transmitted in any form or by any means, electronic or mechanical, including photocopying, recording or any information storage or retrieval system, without prior permission from the publishers.

First published 2011

British Library Cataloguing-in-Publication Data
A catalogue record for this book is available from the British Library.

ISBN: HB: 978-0-8264-4093-8

Typeset by Fakenham Photosetting Ltd, Fakenham, Norfolk NR21 8LQ
Printed and bound in India

For James Chapman

About the Author

Jeremy Black is Professor of History, University of Exeter. Graduating from Cambridge with a starred first, he did graduate work at Oxford, before teaching at Durham from 1980 to 1995, eventually as Professor, and then moving to Exeter. His books include *War and the World, 1450–2000*, *The Age of Total War* and *Naval Power*.

Contents

Contents

List of Abbreviations

Add. = Additional Manuscripts
AWM = Australian War Memorial, Canberra
BL = Department of Manuscripts, British Library, London
DRO = Devon Record Office, Exeter
LH = Liddell Hart archive, King's College, London
LMA = London Metropolitan Archives
NA = London, National Archives (formerly Public Record Office)
WO = War Office papers

Preface

I sent for all officers, w.os [warrant officers], c.s.ms
[company sergeant majors] and sergeants to our
apology of a mess and explained the dire necessity
of stopping the Germans and told them that it must
be 'so far and no further', and then asked every one
present to drink to the health of the regiment, and to
take a solemn oath that wherever I gave the order to
stand, they would stand, and then to sign their names
… we kept our word and never gave way …. There
must have been few who really could have expected
to survive and stop the German advance which had
made steady progress for 8 days as reports of the
incoming tide were ominous.

Lieutenant-Colonel Percy Worrall, 1918[1]

It is always unexpected. You read in the archives for weeks, taking
notes, thinking, reading, taking notes, thinking, and then there is a
passage across the years that leaves you with a lump in the throat,
unless, for me, it was the research for my book on the Holocaust,
research during which I had a perpetual violent headache. For this
book, the lump came twice, uniquely on the same day. First, it was the
account above by Lieutenant-Colonel Percy Worrall about his battalion's response to the German Lys offensive in April 1918. In the event,
a brave and well-conducted defence that out-thought the German

infiltration tactics by employing all-round defensive positions was successful and 'the casualties were marvellously slight';[1] although, located too far forward, the sister battalion was largely wiped out soon after in the storm of shells on the opening day of the German Aisne offensive.

An hour later, another letter, from Viola Southcomb, written on 20 June 1987, in an envelope containing the 1917 letters of a young officer to his Aunt Connie. Noting that his grave was untraced, Viola wrote 'I have therefore decided to erect a tablet this autumn, in Rose Ash Church, from my sister Daphne and myself, in memory of our brother Edward: he was the last male Southcomb of this family'.[2] A simple truth of fighting typed out by the faltering hand of an elderly lady.

It is normal for authors of books on the Great War, especially British authors, to make reference to family members who served, and in particular died in the war, and indeed, the underage service of one of my grandfathers on the Western Front was part of family lore, while a grandmother could remember Zeppelin (airship) raids on London. Such references are designed to underline a link across the generations, one that can be seen more generally in war memorials across Britain. This is a link in which scholars play a major role as we owe it to others to understand, as well as to remember.

The Great War was also unprecedented in scale, as was noted around the world. Writing for a Japanese women's journal, Shioda Utako, a high-profile educator, observed:

> Everyday we read with amazement the press reports
> of the war. There surely cannot have been a confla-
> gration as great as this since history began ....
> Previous wars were fought on the surface. Today's war
> is fought on the surface, in the air and under the sea.
> Its violence and its cruelty are beyond comparison
> with any war to date.[3]

Made in October 1914, this comment showed just how quickly people even on the margins of the world war were able to recognize it as something unique. It may also help to stress the point of how the modern media made the facts and nature of this war immediately known around the globe, that is, it was a world war both in the geography over which it was fought and in the (potential at least) universal knowledge of its daily progress.

The First World War was the Great War for its leading participants, for example *La Grande Guerre* for the French, except for the Germans, for whom it was *Der Weltkrieg*, a suitably apocalyptic title.[4] This book sets out to provide an account of the Great War, of its key place in military history, and of its consequences for the making of the modern world. As such, it is not simply a narrative account. Indeed, the key perspective is that of a military historian with longer-range interests, not least in the Second World War, and also of a concern with how, with that later and also great struggle, the Great War became the First World War and, more generally, contributed to the making of the modern world.

In writing this book, I have benefited, in funding archival work, from the support of the University of Exeter, and also from the work of many other scholars. The papers of Alan Thomson are used by permission of his great-granddaughter and of H. J. Orr-Ewing by permission of his grandson. I would also like to thank Kristofer Allerfeldt, Ian Beckett, James Chapman, Robert Gerwarth, Bill Gibson, Blake Goldring, Richard Hall, Paul Herbert, Patrick Kelly, Stewart Lone, Sara Moore, Mike Nieberg, Gervase Phillips, George Robb and Dennis Showalter for commenting on an earlier draft and Katharine Timberlake for her first-rate copy-edit. They are not responsible for any errors that remain. I have also profited from discussions with John Derry, Richard Overy and Harvey Sichermann. This work, moreover, benefits from many years lecturing on this subject at Exeter and in part is intended for students as well as general readers. This purpose affects its character, not least the referencing to works in English. It is a great pleasure to dedicate this book to James Chapman, at once a good friend, a jovial companion, a wise counsellor and a perceptive historian. What more is there to say for any man.

Introduction

After dinner they took us into the garden and after pulling up flowers and rose bushes we dug up, by the light of a lantern, 16 bottles of rare old burgundy and a dozen of white port which had been buried there since 1914! So we got a great celebration and did not get to bed until 1am. We had to put out the lanterns once whilst we were digging as a Hun aeroplane flew over but it did not lay any eggs [bombs] thank goodness!

Alan Thomson to his wife Edith, 11 November 1918

For Lieutenant-Colonel Alan Thomson of the British Royal Artillery, the last night of the war was spent pleasantly at the Chateau Quévy-le-Grand in Belgium, half way between Mons and Mauberge. As he noted next day, he had 'been through such stirring times', and survived without injury, although very poor health led to his evacuation from Gallipoli to Egypt at the start of December 1915.[1] However, he returned to active service in 1916, first in Egypt and then on the Western Front. Many others, of course, both soldiers and civilians, had a far less bearable war, and for millions it proved fatal. The suffering and loss of the Great War proves part of its resonance and significance, but this book seeks to throw light on further aspects, not least in asking how it ended in the victory recorded by Thomson and others.

The exposition and significance of the Great War (1914–18) are now overshadowed by the Second World War (1939–45), not only because it is more recent and because the Germany of the Second World War appeared such a greater enemy than that of the Great

1

War, both more potent and more sinister, but also because the Second World War was won by the great powers of subsequent decades, with America, in particular, playing a far larger role than in the Great War. For European countries, the Home Front of the Second World War came to overshadow that of the Great War. Moreover, the key powers of East and South Asia, China, Japan and India, played a larger direct role in the Second World War, and that conflict was also more important for the public histories of states around the globe, notably those affected by decolonization.

Yet, significance changes with time, and not only with the loss of first-hand testimony.[2] As we move further into the twenty-first century, so the respective weight of the two world wars will probably alter, a process that will accelerate when the last of those who fought in the Second World War die. Nevertheless, the extent to which Hitler was such a distinctive enemy, whereas Kaiser Wilhelm II, the ruler of Germany in the Great War, appears banal and mediocre, if not weak and ridiculous, will remain an important difference.

In time, scholars and others may discuss the two world wars as a unit or together with a weighting that is less focused on the Second as a different and distinct struggle. This process will encourage a reconsideration of the Great War, a reconsideration that leads to a greater degree of attention but as part of an assessment of how the modern world was made and, notably, the role of the two world wars. That is one of the intentions here, but so also is the attempt to position the Great War in a narrative and analysis of military history that makes sense today, rather than those offered during the post-1945 Cold War between Communism and the West, when the devastating potential of modern warfare appeared clearly prefigured by the total and industrial warfare of the Great War, a conflict that was understandably seen in those terms. Exposition and significance therefore take on meaning as part of the process by which history is understood, recorded, written and constructed; words with greatly differing connotations.

There is no intention here to suggest that this account is *the* way to write the war, and, whenever I read accounts or reviews that pretend to such definitive status, I know them to be deeply flawed. Instead, there is an attempt, in the space permitted, to provide an intelligent discussion that focuses on many of the issues that were crucial both at the time and subsequently. There is a particular engagement with how and why the Allies, notably Britain (understood throughout as Britain, the Dominions and the colonies), France (and its empire) and America, won the war in 1918, as that issue tends to be under-played in general accounts that, understandably, focus on the horrors and impasse of trench warfare. The trench warfare was indeed both horrific and unprecedented in scale, but it was not new, having its origins in siege warfare, while the impasse of trench warfare on the Western Front was never static as new tactics were being developed all the time. Moreover, there is a clear parallel with the Second World War: each conflict was won by the Allies but there is a tendency to consider how and why the Germans lost the war and not why the Allies won. This is especially the case with the Great War, and the intention here is to focus on Allied victory.

There is not space for all the issues, nor for an equal weighting, which is appropriate given the scale of the conflict. Nevertheless, in considering the long-term significance of the Great War, there is an intention of honouring the many millions who died, suffered and served.

CHAPTER 1

Causes

At this crisis of our destinies, there is no great dead Englishman to whom the nation's thoughts turn so surely and so proudly as to Nelson. Final victory or defeat for us is always and inevitably at sea, and the mere name of Nelson sums up all we have ever achieved there in the past, all we hope to hold and win in the present ... men and the sea are unchanging.

E. Hallam Moorhouse, *1588 to 1914. Album-Atlas of British Victories on the Sea. 'Wooden Walls to Super-Dreadnoughts'*[1]

E. Hallam Moorhouse's book was a tribute to British heroism produced in the flood of wartime patriotism of 1914. The book included an autograph portrait of Winston Churchill, the First Lord of the Admiralty, and, on the inside page, 'Signatures of the Brave. A Place for the autographs of officers and men who served Britain by land and sea in the Great War of 1914', above William Shakespeare's lines from *Richard II* 'This happy breed of men ... this England'. Such a sense of national destiny and continuity with a glorious past was important, psychologically, culturally and in terms of mobilizing patriotism, to the bellicosity that contributed greatly to the outbreak of conflict in 1914. While bellicosity alone does not cause wars, a sense that war was acceptable, if not desirable and necessary, was important to the outbreak of the Great War.

The prospect of major war was discussed and planned for by many in the decades that closed for good with the beginning of fighting in July and, even more, August 1914, but the nature and, still more, consequences of the resulting conflict were understood by few. War seemed likely because both experience and assumptions led in that direction. The experience of the previous century had been that key issues were settled by conflict, whether the two overthrows of Napoleon I of France by a European alliance (1814 and 1815), the Unification of Italy (1860), the maintenance of the American union in the face of the Civil War (1861–65), the transformation of Prussia into the German empire thanks to repeated triumphs in the Wars of German Unification (1864, 1866, 1870–71) or the rise of Japan with victories over China and Russia (1894–95, 1904–05). This process was also true for other, lesser, states, such as Serbia, Romania and Greece, all of which traced their independence and expansion to success in recent warfare.

Conversely, those states that had failed in such warfare, for example the Ottoman empire (Turkey for short) or Bulgaria, both of which had been defeated in the conflicts of 1911–13, saw such defeats as an encouragement to reverse failure through subsequent struggles. Movements that lacked statehood, such as Irish and Polish national-ism, also looked to past defeats, notably unsuccessful rebellions against British and Russian rule in 1798 and 1863 respectively, as a call for fresh valour, and they saw war between the major states as an opportunity to press their claims.

War and victories as a measure of national success constituted a key ideological and practical predisposition to struggle. This predispo-sition had a variety of bases, including the intellectual conviction that such struggle was a central feature of natural and human existence and development as well as a cultural belief that struggle expressed and secured masculinity, and thus kept both society and civilization vital, a view, for example, that both the nationalists and the Futurists could share in Italy. Belief in war as an expression of a martial spirit and an ideology of masculinity was sustained by the popular liter-ature in Europe. In Britain, those who volunteered in 1914–16 were the generation who would have grown up reading storybooks like

Union Jack, Captain and *Chums* in the 1890s. Although Britain was not bellicose as far as other European powers were concerned, these populist working-class rivals to the *Boy's Own Paper* had promoted popular militarism, especially in an imperial context.[2]

Linked for some to these views was a sense of anxiety based on belief that the present situation was necessarily unstable and also prone to decline, decay and degeneration. Such a fate apparently could only be avoided by vigilance, effort and sacrifice. This cultural anxiety was accentuated by concerns about the alleged consequences of industrial society, urban living and democratic populism, concerns that were focused in some cases, notably Germany, by an opposition to the left-wing politics believed to flow from these developments. Socialism was seen on the Right as a threat to Germany's ability to fight.

There were also doubts about the strength of masculinity in the face of cultural and social changes, and these doubts were related to worries about national degeneration in a context of a belief in a Darwinian competition between nations and races, a competition that was seen as inherently violent.[3] This approach in fact rested on a false understanding and a corruption of Darwinian theory from 'survival of the fittest', which, as originally conceived, did not apply to states or peoples or groups within society, but to species and adaptations within species, for which the dynamics were different. Thus, Darwin's arguments were misused to justify aggression and domination.

These factors were accentuated by the apparent exigencies of an international system in which the only choice seemed to be between growth and decay, empire and impotence.[4] To fail to act was, allegedly, to be doomed to failure. Furthermore, the territorial expansionism of the imperialism of the period gave a tone of greater compe-tition to international relations, with alliances of mutual restraint being replaced by alliances focused on securing additional power.[5] Moreover, the imperial hopes, dreams, anticipations, expectations, anxieties and nightmares of the great European powers affected, and were affected by, the fate both of the non-European world and that of South-Eastern Europe. In particular, anxieties in and about the Balkans were to press directly and strongly on competing European alliance systems, ensuring that the limited wars and compromises at the expense of others, that were seen with European expansionism outside the continent, could not be sustained as a system within Europe itself.

These factors encouraged bellicosity, or at least an acceptance that war might be noble and strengthening as well as necessary; but they did not explain why large-scale conflict seemed more of a risk in the 1900s and early 1910s than earlier, nor why it broke out in 1914. Such explanation in part rests on contrasting assumptions. In particular, there is a tension between a 'systemic' account of the outbreak of war, which would trace it to the nature of the competitive international system, or, alternatively, one that places greater weight on the agency (actions) of particular powers. The latter is a more convincing account as it makes greater allowance for the extent to which individual leaders and specific policy-making groups took the key decisions including the crucial decisions of how, and when, to act.

In particular, it is apparent that the leading factor was the encouragement provided to Austria (short for Austria-Hungary, the empire ruled by the Habsburgs) by German policy makers, notably the Kaiser (Emperor), Wilhelm II (reigning 1888–1918), and his military advisers. This conservative German elite was worried about domestic changes, including left-wing activism, as well as by international challenges. Reflecting the atavistic roots of much militarism and imperialism, and the prejudices of a traditional elite who felt threatened by change and modernization and who used militarism to entrench as well as reflect their privileges, the German regime, like others, was operating in an increasingly volatile situation, in which urbanization, mass literacy, industrialization, secularization and nationalism were creating an uncertain and unfamiliar world. There was a particular spatial dynamic in Germany in that the wealth and political activism of industrial advance was concentrated in the west, notably the heavy industry of the Ruhr valley, but much of the military elite based their position on landholdings in the agrarian east.

Faced by international and domestic challenges, the temptation, both in Germany and Austria, was to respond by the use of force, to impose order on the flux or to gain order through coercion.

Germany was affected by pressures for welfare and education reform and by religious divisions. Militarism, in contrast, appeared to offer a source of unity and agreement. A growing sense of instability both encouraged the use of might to resist or channel it, and provided opportunities to do so. In large part, militarism fed itself in Germany, particularly after the failure of the liberal revolutions there in 1848, for, instead, German nationalism was focused on the more authoritarian political culture of Prussia. By means of defeating Austria in 1866 and France in 1870–71, Prussia, which had earlier been one of the weaker and, due to its central position, one of the more vulnerable of the major powers, created the German empire, and the Hohenzollern kings became emperors.

German strength in a central position in Europe created a new set of geopolitical tensions. In part, this was because the annexation of most of Alsace and part of coal- and iron-rich Lorraine from France as part of the peace settlement in 1871 left, as Otto von Bismarck, the German Chancellor, had been warned by the French emissary, a long-term sense of French grievance that posed a security challenge to Germany on its western border.[6] This challenge was greatly mitigated, however, by Germany's far larger population, and therefore army, and her stronger economy; while France, moreover, was weakened by its competition with Britain in imperial expansion, especially, but not only, in sub-Saharan Africa. Indeed, the two powers nearly came to war over control of Sudan in the Fashoda Crisis of 1898. Instead of fearing France alone, German policy makers saw danger in the possibility of French co-operation with other powers overshadowed by Germany's rise to power, both Austria, defeated in 1866, and Russia, which had lost relative strength with this rise.

Bismarck, one of the key figures in German unification, secured his achievement by means from 1871 of alliance with Russia and Austria, the *Dreikaiserbund* (League of Three Emperors) of 1881. However, this achievement was neglected by his successors, notably because the arrogant Wilhelm II, who parted company with Bismarck in 1890, was scarcely risk-averse and, instead, was committed to expansion, not stability. Wilhelm also viewed Russia with suspicion, and regarded it as a racial threat. The non-renewal of the German-Russian Reassurance

Treaty represented a clear strategic deviation from Bismarck's foreign policy and his overriding strategy of keeping France isolated.

More generally, expansionism also rose from a belief that there was a simple choice of growth or decline. This belief encouraged a concern with relative position, and, repeatedly, a perception of the reality, or potential, of relative loss was crucially important in helping centre anxieties and of a need for action, in particular conjunctures. Existing pacts, such as the Triple Alliance of Austria, Germany and Italy in 1882, pacts that had often restrained by joining together powers with different interests, appeared inadequate in the 1900s and 1910s as anxieties grew about shifts in international geopolitics and national politics.

This process was particularly apparent with both Austria and Germany. The Austrian elite worried that the breakdown of Turkish power, notably as a result of Turkey's defeat by the Balkan powers in the First Balkan War of 1912–13, was leading to a degree of nationalist assertiveness in the Balkans, especially by Serbia. This assertiveness threatened the cohesion of the Austrian empire, not least because Serbia encouraged opposition to Austrian rule in neighbouring Bosnia which Austria had occupied in 1878 and annexed in 1908. Whether Austria was itself overstretched in the face of rising nationalism within the empire, which included the modern states of Croatia, Slovenia, Bosnia, Slovakia and the Czech Republic and parts of Poland, Romania and Italy, is a matter for controversy, but political disputes related to this nationalism some of which was separatist in character made it difficult to pursue policy initiatives. Moreover, these disputes helped create a destabilizing sense of the enemy within. In Austrian eyes, this enemy would be neutered by reordering the Balkans in a way that served Austria's interests and demonstrated its superiority, and specifically by weakening Serbia. Ironically, an equal, or more serious, danger to the Austrian empire came not from Slav nationalism, but from a bellicose nationalism on the part of much of the ruling Austrian elite, and this bellicosity accentuated both domestic and international weaknesses.

In Germany, there was concern about the problems of the Austrian ally and, as a result, of the problems of having Austria as an ally. In the event, neither Germany nor Austria was to restrain the other sufficiently in 1914, a key instance of the manner in which, with this war, the geopolitical logic of alliances drew powers into actions that were highly damaging and, in the end, destroyed the logic of the alliances. Yet, although Austria helped cause the war, Austria was not the crucial element for Germany, for there was fear of Russians, not Serbs, in Berlin. The negotiation of a Franco-Russian military agreement in 1894 had led Germany, fearing war on two fronts at once, to plan to achieve by speed the sequential war-making (fighting enemies one after another) that had brought victory to Prussia in 1864–71 over Denmark, Austria and France and to Napoleon I of France in 1805–07 over Austria, Prussia and Russia. However, it appeared difficult for Germany to achieve a knock-out blow against Russia, the frontier of which had moved west to include much of Poland as a result of the major role of the Russians in victory over Napoleon I in 1812–14. This westward movement provided the defence of depth which indeed was to enable Russia to survive considerable territorial losses to Germany in the first three years of the Great War. This defence of depth led German planners to focus pre-war, first, on defeating France before turning against Russia. Unlike Moscow, Paris was within reach of German forces, as had been shown (successfully) in 1870 and was to be nearly shown again in 1914, 1918 and, finally successfully, 1940.

This strategy depended, in 1914, on a key capability gap which had uncertain operational results and strategic consequences: the contrast between rapid German mobilization and its slower Russian counterpart. As a result of the significance of this gap, there was German concern as Russian offensive capability improved. This was a capability financed by France, not least in the shape of railway construction in Russian Poland, construction designed to speed the movement of Russian troops westward towards the Austrian and German borders, for each power had benefited from the three partitions of Poland in 1772–95 in order to seize much of the country.[7] The Russian military programme announced in 1913 caused particular anxiety in Berlin, which encouraged Count Helmuth von Moltke (Moltke the Younger, nephew of the Moltke of the Wars of Unification), Chief of the German General Staff from 1906, to press for war in 1913–14. He feared that Germany would increasingly not be able to win later and, by 1916, he thought, Russia, with its larger population, would be in a position to start attacking effectively before the Germans had had an opportunity to defeat France. In Moltke's view, Germany's existing strategy could not operate after 1916.

Had Moltke been open to other ways of thinking, matters might have been different. Ironically, although the Russians had built up an army superior to that of Austria and had quickly recovered from defeat by Japan in 1904–05, the Russian attack on Germany was to be defeated easily and rapidly in 1914, and much of Russian Poland was conquered by the Germans in 1915. The Germans, both military and politicians, had consistently overestimated Russia's military potential, in part because they exaggerated the quantitative indices of army strength at the expense of qualitative criteria. There is nothing to suggest that this overestimate was deliberate, but the misperceptions proved very powerful. German overestimation of Russian strength was also born of irrational fears which overshadowed practicalities and which also satisfied aspirations and concerns focused on promoting war.

The defeat of France, in contrast, was regarded as probable because the Germans, encouraged by the example of victory over France in 1870–71, assumed that their better-prepared forces would win regardless of French actions. Although Moltke knew that the German army was not inherently superior to that of France, German commanders were very much in the shadow of expectations created by the successes of 1864–71, just as British naval commanders were affected by the Nelson legacy. The majority and, after 1906, all the British service attachés in Berlin reported that the German armed forces were preparing for attack and 1913–15 was seen as the likeliest period for this aggression.[8]

Moltke's predecessor, Count Alfred von Schlieffen, had changed the General Staff when he was its head from 1891 to 1906, allowing its members to become military specialists at the expense of more general, non-military knowledge. Non-military problems were consciously excluded from General Staff thinking. Military decision makers were therefore allowed to conduct their planning in a vacuum, with scant regard for the political situation around them. In 1914, by stressing future threats and affirming that Germany was still able to defeat likely opponents, the General Staff helped to push civilian policy makers towards war, although, in practice, civilians were not greatly consulted by the military. Moltke hoped that the resulting conflict would be the short and manageable war for which the Germans had been planning, but he feared that it could well be a long war, a struggle indeed for which Germany was unprepared. Because Moltke did not develop an alternative plan (instead deciding to scrap one in 1913), the option of deploying troops only in the East against Russia no longer existed in 1914.[9] Planning focused on France, and neither Germany nor Austria prepared adequately for war with Russia, which was an aspect both of how poorly they worked together and of the short-term nature of most military planning.

Alongside anxiety about Russia, there was an ambition on the part of German leaders that was more clearly a case of wishful thinking and strategic overreach. This ambition was for becoming not simply a great power but a world power, able to match Britain in this, and thus to overthrow and replace her imperial position. To do so, Germany sought a navy able to contest that of Britain, a drive which, in practice, was unnecessary to Germany's goals within Europe. Moreover, naval ambition was likely to alienate Britain and, therefore, to ensure that these goals became unattainable, as indeed was to be the case. The assumptions that Britain's differences with France and Russia would remain insoluble, and thus would lessen Britain's concern about Germany and make alliance with these powers unlikely, proved greatly mistaken. Moreover, the Japanese elimination of Russia as a naval power in 1905 at the battle of Tsushima (a decisive naval victory of the type not seen in the Great War) undermined Germany's calculations as it helped the British to focus on the German challenge.

Fear of German intentions, and particularly of her naval ambitions, encouraged closer British relations with France from 1904. The Anglo-French entente of 1904 led to military talks in part because defeat in the Russo-Japanese war of 1904–05 weakened Russia (France's ally) as a balancing element within Europe, thereby exposing France to German diplomatic pressure and creating British alarm about

German intentions, as in the First Moroccan Crisis of 1905–06. This crisis, provoked by Germany and an instance of how a struggle for primacy in a peripheral area could lead to warlike moves, was followed by Anglo-French staff talks aimed at dealing with a German threat. In 1907, British military manoeuvres were conducted for the first time on the basis that Germany, not France, was the enemy, while, also that year, fears of Germany contributed to an Anglo-Russian entente which eased tensions between the two powers, notably competing ambitions and contrasting anxieties in South Asia. Germany, with its great economic strength, naval ambitions and its search for a 'place in the Sun', was increasingly seen in Britain as the principal threat.

The economic statistics were all-too-present to British commentators, not least because they enabled Germany to pursue its naval race for battleship strength with Britain from 1906. The annual average output of coal and lignite in million metric tons in 1870–74 was 123 for Britain and 41 for Germany, but by 1910–14 the figures were 274 to 247. For pig iron, the annual figures changed from 7.9 and 2.7 in 1880 to 10.2 and 14.8 in 1910; for steel from 3.6 and 2.2 in 1890 to 6.5 and 13.7 in 1910. In 1900, the German population was 56.4 million, but that of Britain excluding Ireland only 37 million and including her still only 41.5 million.

In December 1899, the rising journalist J. L. Garvin, whose son was later to be killed in the war, decided that Germany, and not, as he had previously thought, France and Russia, was the greatest threat to Britain. Rejecting the view of Joseph Chamberlain, Secretary of State for the Colonies, that Britain and Germany were natural allies, their peoples of a similar racial 'character', Garvin saw 'the Anglo-Saxons' as the obstacle to Germany's naval and commercial policy. Imaginative literature reflected, and contributed to, the sense of crisis. A projected German invasion of Britain was central to *The Riddle of the Sands* (1903), an adventure novel by Erskine Childers which was first planned in 1897, when indeed the Germans discussed such a project.

Yet, political opinion was divided. There were British politicians who sought to maintain good relations with Germany. Moreover, the ententes with France and Russia were not alliances, and Britain failed to make her position clear, thus encouraging Germany to hope that Britain would not act in the event of war, which was also Hitler's mistaken belief when he invaded Poland in 1939. In 1914, the British certainly failed to make effective use of their fleet as a deterrent, restraining Germany from hostile acts.

Germany had won the Franco-Prussian War of 1870–71, despite French naval strength. In any future struggle, if Britain remained neutral, Germany could hope to trade both with her and with America, thus deriving an economic benefit that would make it easier to pursue her goals within Europe. Instead, the competitive naval race with Britain from 1906 was based in large part on a feeling of inferiority towards her, in part arising from the serious psychological issues of the maladjusted Kaiser, whose mother was the daughter of Queen Victoria.

Nevertheless, despite this competition, there was a lack of effective German planning for a naval war with Britain, and the priority placed on the German army, notably with the Army Bill of 1913, was such that by 1914 naval tensions between the two states had lessened. The concern of Theobald von Bethmann-Hollweg, who became Chancellor in 1909, about naval costs was matched by the army's emphasis on the needs of a two-front war on land, and the commitments in the Army Bill of 1913 represented, in effect, a unilateral German declaration of naval arms limitation, albeit at a high level of competition and annual completion of warships. The Germans were also deterred by the pace of British shipbuilding, which increased greatly from 1908.[10]

Naval interests also led in a different strategic direction to those of the army, which reflected and sustained the seriously dysfunctional character of German inter-service war preparations. The army and the navy had two completely different approaches. The army wanted to invade Belgium and leave Denmark alone, the policy followed in 1914, whereas the navy wanted precisely the opposite in order to leave Belgium and the Netherlands, especially the major port of Rotterdam, as a windpipe for German imports in anticipation of the British blockade of Germany, while strengthening the German position in the North and Baltic seas by conquering Denmark. There was no effort, on the part of Wilhelm II or anyone else, at the slightest semblance of joint planning, and, at the beginning of the war, long-range economic planning was completely ignored in Germany where it was treated as heresy against the confident belief in a short war.

European tensions rose in the years after 1910 with the respective alliances increasingly concerned about the real actions and supposed intentions of their rivals. For example, the visits of President Raymond Poincaré of France to Russia in 1912 and 1914 seemed to underline the danger to Germany posed by their alliance. The French increase in army spending in 1912, a response to the German move of the previous year, in turn led to a German rise in expenditure on the army. These increases and other moves encouraged a sense of instability and foreboding and helped drive forward an arms race on land. In turn, this greater military capability, by lessening earlier weaknesses, made armed diplomacy more plausible while, at the same time, increasing a sense of vulnerability to the armed diplomacy of others. As deterrence appeared weaker, so it seemed necessary to identify and grasp windows of opportunity for action which, in turn, weakened deterrence.

The Germans obtained further evidence of closer links between Britain, France and Russia in May 1914, with espionage information on Anglo-Russian talks for a naval agreement. The Germans increasingly felt encircled and threatened, but, as a reminder that there were also failings in analysis elsewhere, British strategy was affected by an inability to grasp the consequences of closer diplomatic relations with France and Russia. In the sense that they, together, could make war with Germany more likely, this outcome was appreciated, but not sought. Moreover, the British government failed to use the deterrence represented by its fleet and financial strength, in large part because of the German conviction that quick victory was possible thanks to rapid success on land whatever threat the British fleet posed in the long term. This conviction proved totally misplaced.

Russia sought to recover from its defeat by Japan by building up its military anew with resources that came from economic growth and French loans, notably that of 1905, which gave Russia access to French capital markets. Total Russian expenditure on the military rose greatly in 1907–13; although the majority of Russian officers remained unable to put men and equipment to good use and, indeed, encouraged by the conservative Nickolas II,[11] the Russo-Japanese War led to a conservative reaction in Russian military circles against attempts to reform operational practice.

From 1911, when the Prime Minister, Peter (Pyotr) Stolypin was assassinated, Russia was under a more interventionist and aggressive government, one that was less willing to subordinate geopolitical goals to domestic issues. Russia became Serbia's protector, although they were not formally allies as the relationship was based upon Russia's implicit support for the Bulgarian and Serbian alliance of March 1912 and her explicit agreement to settle any ensuing disagreement over the disposition of the region of Macedonia when it was conquered from Turkey (the Ottoman empire). There was a religious dimension as Russia, Bulgaria and Serbia were all Orthodox states opposed alike to Islam and Catholicism, the latter the religion of the Austrian and Hungarian elites. In the autumn of 1912, international tension over Serbian policy led Austria and Russia to deploy troops in mutually threatening positions, but these forces withdrew in the spring of 1913. The 1914 crisis, however, had a very different outcome.

Visiting Sarajevo, the capital of the province of Bosnia, Archduke Franz Ferdinand, the nephew and heir to the elderly Emperor Franz Joseph of Austria, and his wife Sophie were assassinated on 28 June 1914 by Gavrilo Princip, a Bosnian Serb, leaving black-and-white photographs of violence in hot streets. The terrorist group was under the control of the Black Hand, a secret Serbian nationalist organization pledged to the overthrow of Austrian control in South Slav territories, notably Bosnia. 'Apis', Colonel Dragutin Dimitrijević, the head of Serbian military intelligence, was a crucial figure, able to ignore his government's efforts to contain the activities of the Black Hand, which he had founded in 1911. Apis sought both to create a Greater Serbia and to overthrow the Serbian Prime Minister, Nikola Pašić. Indeed, Apis and two allies were to be executed in June 1917 on charges of conspiring against the then Serbian government-in-exile.

When the news of the killings in Sarajevo reached Vienna, there was shock and the customary response, not least by a militaristic state, to an unexpected and dramatic event, a sense that a display of action and power was needed. This sense interacted with an already powerful view that war with Serbia was necessary, and this new situation apparently provided the excuse to take care of Serbia, a policy already discussed in 1912 and 1913. Believing that German backing would deter Russia, the Austrians sought not agreement with the Serbs, who, in fact, were willing to make important concessions and prepared to accept binding arbitration on the points to which they objected, but a limited war with Serbia.

This policy was pushed by a key advocate of the value of force and the necessity of war, Franz von Hötzendorf (referred to as Conrad), the self-absorbed head of the Austrian General Staff. In addition, aside from the conversion of Leopold Berchtold, the Foreign Minister, to a military solution to the challenge apparently posed by Serbia to Austrian rule, the aristocratic culture of the Austrian diplomatic corps did not favour compromise. Instead, the South Slavs were generally viewed with contempt, and there was a strong cultural preference supporting the alliance with Germany. At the same time, military decision makers, not diplomats, played the vital role in pushing for conflict with Serbia.[12] Alongside a number of other Austrian policy makers, Conrad believed that war was the best way to stabilize the Habsburg monarchy in the face of serious nationalist challenges from both within, notably Czechs and Poles, and without, especially Italy and Serbia. The killings at Sarajevo thus provided him with the opportunity to carry out his belief in preventive war.

German support to Austria meant crucial encouragement. This support reflected the belief in Berlin that a forceful response was necessary, appropriate and likely to profit Austrian and German interests at a time when an opportunity for success existed. The Serb response of 25 July to a deliberately unacceptable Austrian ultimatum of 23 July was deemed inadequate and, on 28 July, without pursuing the option of further negotiations, the Austrians declared war. The Russians, meanwhile, responded to the ultimatum to Serbia by beginning military preparations on 26 July. They were confident of French support and believed it necessary to act formally in order to protect Serbia. On 30 July, Russia declared general mobilization, a step that the Germans had already been preparing to take. As a

WITHDRAWN

SPRING CREEK CAMPUS

result of Russia acting first, the Germans were able to present their step, in a misleading fashion, as defensive which helped lessen potential domestic opposition, notably in the *Reichstag*, to the voting of necessary credits for war. German mobilization was, in part, a question of timing in the knowledge that Russia was about to mobilize.

The German military was convinced that it must win the race to mobilize effectively and to use the resulting strength, and notably before the Russians could act against both Germany and its ally Austria. This concern encouraged the Germans, if they could not use the crisis to divide France and Russia, to attack both. In part, they were led by their strategic concepts and operational concerns, notably how best to ensure victory in any war that broke out, but, throughout, German leaders opportunistically sought to use the Balkan crisis to change the balance of power in their favour. They were willing to risk a war because no other crisis was as likely to produce a constellation of circumstances guaranteeing them the commitment of their main ally, Austria, and the support of the German public.

Thus, it is too much to say, as has been argued for Germany, that the war plans of 1914, with their dynamic interaction of mobilization and deployment, made war by timetable (a reference to the railway timetables that guided and registered the pace of mobilization) difficult to stop once a crisis occurred because such an argument underplays the extent to which politicians were not trapped by circumstances. Instead, their own roles, preferences and choices were important. An underplaying of the importance of choice reflects an anachronistic, later, sense that no one could have chosen to begin the Great War; but in fact, in 1914, decision makers believed that war was necessary and could lead to a quick victory.

The role of choice is illustrated by the extent to which an awareness of likely risks had helped prevent crises since 1871 from leading to war, while, moreover, alliances did not dictate participation: despite being their ally, Italy chose not to join Germany and Austria, instead declaring neutrality on 3 August. America, which was not allied to any of the combatants, also opted for neutrality, President Woodrow Wilson telling the Senate on 18 August that the country 'must be neutral in fact as well as in name'. He had ignored pressure from Theodore Roosevelt, a former President, to go to war in response to the German violation of Belgian neutrality. In Europe, the Scandinavian states, the Netherlands, Portugal, Spain, Switzerland, Greece, Romania and Bulgaria all declared neutrality. Reasons varied. Some powers, such as Italy, Romania and Bulgaria, had territorial goals, but did not think the situation sufficiently clear and propitious to encourage them yet to take sides in order to pursue them.

In 1914, the key element in leading to war was that Austria and Germany chose to fight and Russia to respond. All three were empires with constitutionalism held in check by practices of imperial direction, the latter providing characteristics that were autocratic and that ensured that small coteries of decision makers had great influence. As with Japan, these states were happy to see war with other major powers as a tool of policy, rather than as a means of distant overseas colonial expansionism that had only limited consequences for their societies, the position of the British, French and American elites.[13] Foreign offices and diplomats played only a secondary part in the policies of the autocracies, as the prospect of war led military considerations to come to the fore, while the rulers and their advisers took the key role in arbitrating between contrasting attitudes and policies.

The aggressive and ambitious views of Kaiser Wilhelm II were certainly important to the serious deterioration in Anglo-German relations.[14] There was a clear contrast between the commitment of the British elite, including the monarchs, Edward VII (reigning 1901–10) and George V (reigning 1910–36), to parliamentary democracy and Wilhelm's antipathy to liberalism and parliamentary government. The right-wing nationalists who looked to Wilhelm also despised parliamentary limitations, while Wilhelm's authoritarian position in the governmental system ensured that the extent to which such right-wing views were not, in fact, held by the bulk of the public could not determine policy. The moves to war in 1914 were not taken by the elected representatives of the German populace.

Similarly, in 1915, the demand by opposition leaders in Bulgaria that the *Sübranie* (Assembly) be summoned before any decision for war be taken was ignored by the king, and Aleksandar Stambolïski, the agrarian leader, who called on the people and the army not to act, was imprisoned. In contrast, in 1914, Carol I of Romania, a German by birth and marriage, wished to fulfil treaty commitments and support Germany and Austria, but the backing of most political leaders for neutrality led him to accept the constraints of his position as a constitutional monarch, and Romania initially stayed out of the war.

For the Germans, Russian mobilization provided an opportunity to advance their interests by demanding its cancellation, a step that would have identified Russia as an inadequate ally, and thus have wrecked the Franco-Russian alliance. When this demand was refused, war on Russia was declared on 1 August. Russia's ally, France, then became the key element for the Germans. They issued an ultimatum that France could not accept, that France declare neutrality and provide guarantees for this neutrality, steps that would have destroyed the alliance with Russia and made France appear a worthless ally for any other power. The guarantees included their forts at Toul, Verdun and elsewhere, which would have left France highly vulnerable. These forts provided France with protection from German attack across their common frontier and also provided bases from which to anchor any French attack on German-held Lorraine. France's refusal to accept the ultimatum led the Germans to declare war on 3 August.

This declaration did not exhaust the bellicosity of those early August days. Operational factors dictated strategy for the Germans, for the heavily defended nature of the Franco-German frontier, and the German need for speedy advances if sequential victory was to be obtained, with France overcome before Russia was defeated, had led to a decision to attack France via Belgium. The flat terrain of much of Belgium north of the River Meuse was more appropriate for a rapid advance than the more hilly terrain of eastern France, while the Franco-Belgian frontier was poorly fortified. Belgium, however, rejected a German ultimatum to provide passage, and this step ensured that the Germans would launch a violent invasion, instead of mounting an occupation.

Belgian neutrality was guaranteed by the major powers, including Britain as well as Germany. The Germans hoped that Britain would not respond to the invasion of Belgium, but, if it did, Britain, with its small army which had done conspicuously badly in 1899–1900 in the early stages of the Boer War against the Afrikaners of South Africa, anyway was a minor concern to German army planners. This view proved very foolish. There was even less concern about the possibility of American intervention, which, indeed, could have had little immediate military effect. 'Necessity knows no law', declared Bethmann-Hollweg, the German Chancellor, when speaking in the *Reichstag* on 4 August about the invasion of Belgium. 'Necessity' had ensured that the German army had equipped itself with heavy howitzers and mortars before the war specifically to deal with the Belgian forts.

The British government was far from keen on war, and, because of competing interests in Asia, there were serious tensions in Anglo-Russian relations.[15] Nevertheless, the government was unwilling to see France's position in the balance of power overthrown and was concerned about the implications, if so, for Britain, while Germany's naval build-up had left the British profoundly distrustful of her expansionism. Indeed, this aggressive expansionism was regarded as more threatening than any particular calculations of the balance of power.

That concern did not necessarily mean war with Germany on behalf of France, which, in fact, was distrusted by many British strategists, as the debates in the Committee of Imperial Defence on a projected tunnel to France under the English Channel made clear.[16] However, British military planners had long been concerned that war between France and Germany would lead to a German invasion of the Low Countries that had to be stopped.[17] In 1914, it was unclear until late whether Britain would join the conflict, but the invasion of Belgium united most British political opinion behind the war. National honour was an important factor in the political culture and international realities of British politics,[18] a point that is not adequately appreciated by those scholars who argue that Britain could, and should, have stayed out of the war.

As in other states, different British political groups had particular views, with the governing Liberal Cabinet focused on the issue of Belgian neutrality, as was public opinion, while the leadership of the Conservative opposition was particularly concerned about maintaining the Anglo-French entente. Some Conservative pressure groups, such as the National Service League, were more clearly anti-German.[19] On 4 August, an ultimatum demanding the German evacuation of Belgium was issued. It was unanswered and led to British entry into the war, which thereby became a more wide-ranging conflict, and one that was to be far longer than the Germans had envisaged.[20]

The flawed treatment of Britain, which anticipated the total misjudgement of Britain in both 1939 and 1940, was an aspect of the wider German failure to address the political aspects of any conflict. As the Germans sought, planned in great detail for, and anticipated, a swift and decisive victory, in order to avoid the military, political, economic and social complexities of a large-scale and lengthy war between peoples, the political dimension was not significant for their military planners, who, in any case, underestimated their opponents' power and resolve. An absence of rational assessment, as well as calculations that in fact suggested to some that the planned short war was improbable, resulted, in Germany, in a countervailing attempt to control anxiety as well as risk, an attempt which led to a focus on planning that deteriorated into dogma and failure to note wider strategic and political parameters.[21]

Across Europe, cultural factors helped support the willingness of governments to declare war. Fatalism encouraged the resort to conflict, as did the potent cult of honour of the period,[22] and a militarism, seen even in its widest senses in Britain, which did not have conscription, but which was a proud and confident nation at that time.[23] In Britain and elsewhere, pride led to enthusiasm for war in 1914 alongside a powerful sense of duty to fight.

The likely nature of a major war was one that had long attracted commentary, with correspondence in *The Times* about the industrialization of warfare as early as 1870. Initially, a small number of European thinkers had anticipated the horrific casualties that developments in military methods and the expansion of army size were likely to produce. Frederick Engels had argued that the American Civil War (1861–65) indicated the likely destructiveness of future conflict between European powers, and he thought that this destructiveness would undermine existing state and class hegemonies and make revolution possible. In his *War of the Future in its Technical, Economic and Political Aspects* (1897), part of which was published in English as *Is War Now Impossible?* (1899), the Polish financier Ivan Bloch suggested that the combination of modern military technology and industrial strength had made great power warfare too destructive to be feasible, and that, if it occurred, it would resemble a great siege and would be won when one of the combatants succumbed to famine and revolution. Bloch argued that the stalemate on the battlefield that came from defensive firepower would translate into collapse on the home front.

Bloch was often cited by later commentators, but one of the problems with his apparently prescient view of trench warfare in the Great War is that such warfare had already occurred in the last stage of the American Civil War (although only in part of the zone of conflict) but without it resulting in prolonged stalemate. More significantly, the idea that destructiveness alone was the cause of the stalemate on the Western Front is misleading, since it was firepower, tactics and operational considerations in combination which contributed to stalemate and also, crucially, to its resolution. This resolution was partly due to better technology and to better use of technology than was available when Bloch was writing.

The elder Moltke, the Chief of the Prussian General Staff in the Wars of German Unification (1864–71), himself had become increasingly sceptical about the potential of the strategic offensive after 1871, and, presciently, was fearful that any major war would be a long one.[24] However, concerns about the consequent impact on casualty figures and military morale, and emphasis on the dangers of battlefield stalemate and of breakdown on the home front, only encouraged a focus on preventing the stalemate by winning the initial offensive. Indeed, in 1914, the dominance of thinking about the attack, rather than anything else, persuaded armies that the war could be won quickly.

That view suggests a degree of folly that was apparently to be underlined by the subsequent conduct of the war, but, in practice, military planners were well aware of the challenge of defensive firepower and some of the remedies that were to be employed during the conflict were already in evidence. For example, German planners emphasized infantry–artillery co-ordination in the attack, as well as minimizing exposure to artillery fire by advancing in dispersed formations that coalesced for a final assault. As a consequence, when the autumn manoeuvres of the Saxon army, part of the German army, were reviewed in 1909, the thickness, and thus vulnerability, of the infantry firing lines was severely criticized.[25] Furthermore, it was observed that defensive strength could be challenged by field artillery operating in support of the attacking force.

A British observer at the German manoeuvres in September 1897 was impressed by the methodical character of German operational art, by the the high morale of the troops and by the

> most extensive latitude left to individual commanders ... with the result that an attacking line when opposed resolves itself, as a rule, into a succession of minor tentative assaults, rarely by a brigade ... more often by a battalion, and still more often by a company. The actual formation adopted is left to the idea and caprice of the original commanders and the total assault is carried out as circumstances seem to indicate.

Given the extent to which such attacks, albeit in a flexible open order, were to play an important role in 1918, it is worth noting the problems seen with them 21 years earlier: 'It is open to question whether such a system of individual, spasmodic, and unsupported effort is sound against anything but a weak and indifferently disciplined enemy ... the frequent weak attacks in close formations give the impression that a terrible loss of life must be entailed.'[26]

Planning encouraged an emphasis on discipline. Another British observer, Captain Birkbeck, commented on the German manoeuvres of 1896: 'It is impossible not to be deeply impressed by the smoothness and ease with which the German military machine works ... a well-trained and thoroughly practical staff ... The German army corps is no collection of units hurriedly collated for a time'; and Captain Holland in 1898 wrote about 'a system by which losses of smaller units are ignored, provided the main object is gained, the great aim being to train the soldier to carry out his orders regardless of consequence.'[27] Indeed, the Germans devoted more attention to training than other armies, and this attention doubtless helped in 1914 when their troops were exposed to the shock of war. However, the training of German reserves was much less developed than that of the regular units, and this problem helped explain the failures of 1914 for German war planning counted on the reserves to do much more than they were trained to do. Moreover, a major problem with the German military manoeuvres was posed by the need to satisfy the expectations of Wilhelm II, so that the defensive effect of machine-guns, for example, was often underplayed while the effect of the assault was overplayed. The manoeuvres were contrived to show the strength of cavalry against infantry or machine-guns, while the flexible open-order attack described by the British observer in 1897 was not encouraged and was sometimes described as cheating.

Despite such deficiencies, the disciplined military systems of the period were far from being inflexible, and, instead, were responsive to the pace of technological advance. Indeed, it was relatively easy to introduce innovations, as with the abandonment of volley firing in favour of individual fire.[28] On land and at sea, all powers sought to integrate new weapons, as well as improved weaponry, such as new artillery, and organizational means and systems, into their militaries, their manoeuvres and their plans, as part of the process by which they responded to advances and to apparent deficiencies.[29]

Yet, while great technological advances were made in artillery, small arms and ammunition, the advances were not necessarily recognized. Thus, the Germans did not take up the machine-gun until 1890, ten years after the British, while the firepower of quick-firing guns, as exemplified by the French 75-mm during the suppression of the Boxer Rebellion in China in 1900, created a new logistical problem, of providing sufficient shells, which was not addressed in any army prior to the Great War. This problem provided an instance of the need to understand technological advances in weaponry in order for them to be used effectively, rather than simply employed as bigger versions of their predecessors. To a large extent, armies acquired bigger and better guns because they were told they needed them by arms manufacturers who had to cover escalating research and development costs. Thus, commercial factors from about the 1850s became ever more powerful in what weapons equipped which armies. This situation did not mean that the armies knew how to use the weaponry to advantage and there was often ambivalence about new technology due to the cost.

The major war in the decade prior to the Great War was that between Russia and Japan in 1904–05, and it was followed carefully by foreign observers. They saw the war as a triumph for Europeanization in the form of Western military organization: the Japanese, whose army was modelled on the German and navy on the British, won by employing European military systems and technology more effectively than the Russians. Yet, the Japanese victory also came as a shock, in part because of Western racialist assumptions. The fighting featured many elements that were also to be seen in the Great War, including trench warfare with barbed wire and machine guns, indirect artillery fire, artillery firing from concealed positions, a conflict that did not ease at nightfall and a war waged with continuous front lines. Advocates of the offensive argued that the Russians stood on the defensive in Manchuria and lost, while the Japanese took the initiative, launched frontal assaults on entrenched forces strengthened by machine guns and quick-firing artillery, as at Port Arthur and Mukden in 1905, and prevailed, despite horrific casualties.

Most commentators focused on tactical and operational factors, and overlooked the strategic dimension, notably the extent to which the land battles had not been decisive but only caused the Russians to fall back in Manchuria, while the Japanese had been put under great pressure by the continuation of the war, which they could not afford.[30] Japanese victory in practice owed much to political weakness in St Petersburg in 1905, notably a revolution there, in part fostered by Japanese military intelligence, rather as German sponsoring of the Bolsheviks played a role in 1917. However, this strategic dimension behind Japanese victory was neglected, while Japanese success on the battlefield and in the war ensured that the tactical superiority of the defence was underplayed. Given contemporary racist attitudes, European experts concluded that the infantry of the superior races of Europe would be capable of at least similar deeds, albeit at heavy cost, maybe a third of the army.[31]

European army leaders assumed that troop morale and discipline would enable them to bear such losses, but the expectation of them provided the impetus for programmes to expand army size, including discussion in Britain about the need for conscription or more volunteering. The expansion in army size across much of Europe took forward the example created by the German army in the Wars of Unification (1864–71), and also drew on the major growth in the population of the West and Japan. The military, however, failed to anticipate how long a major conflict might be, or anticipated it but omitted to tell civilian politicians for fear that, if they knew, they would never contemplate war as an option.

Pressure for more men interacted with an increase in armaments.[32] Links developed between centralized state procurement of substantial quantities of weaponry and the foundation and development of large industrial concerns, such as Krupp's in Germany and Vickers in Britain, that invested in the capacity to do so.[33] However, the failure to appreciate the length of the likely conflict and the rate of artillery fire led to serious shell crises in the Great War as ammunition ran low.

Nevertheless, the large numbers of troops, notably those that stemmed from the measures of 1912 to increase military service and army size, posed problems of effective management and use. Indeed, for the British Expeditionary Force sent to France in 1914, systematic training did not begin until training schools began to be set up from mid-1915, and it took until 1916 for this practice to become universal. Enhanced preparedness was a matter not only of more men and *matériel*, but also of improved organizational means and systems that permitted their integration and increased their effectiveness. These included railways,[34] steamships, lorries, telegraph lines, telephones and, eventually, radio, and they were incorporated into war plans and military manoeuvres. Major naval powers responded to the transforming potential offered by radio which had developed rapidly since Marconi sent radio signals across the Atlantic in 1901. Radio networks were created, the Germans, in 1912–14, building a network of radio stations in their colonies, at Duala, Windhoek, Dar es Salaam, Kanuina, Tsingtao (Qingdao), Yap, Apia, Rabaul and Nauru.[35]

Increasingly, military leaders and thinkers also felt obliged to recognize air power. By 1914, the European powers had a total of over 1,000 aircraft in their armed forces: Russia had 244, Germany 230, France 120 and Britain 113. In 1910–13, the British army had rapidly responded to the possibility of airpower and had integrated it into manoeuvres,[36] while by 1914, the Eastchurch naval air station had created a defensive system in which British aircraft fitted with radios co-operated with ground observers. Meanwhile, in 1910, the American Eugene Ely piloted the first plane off a ship.[37]

Range, however, was more clearly displayed with the increased cruising capability of warships. By 1909, American battleships were being designed with larger coal bunkers allowing a steaming radius of 10,000 nautical miles, which was a major increase on the situation in the 1890s.[38] Such capability made it easier to think in terms of global policies, notably German *Weltpolitik*. Indeed, the American navy was planning war with an increasingly threatening Germany. The American fleet's circumnavigation of the world in 1907–09 revealed serious shortages in American infrastructure in the Pacific, as well as a lack of fleet colliers, but again showed a capability not seen in the 1890s. The navies that entered the Great War did so as rapidly changing bodies, at least technologically, although not necessarily tactically nor operationally.

Colonies and sea lanes ensured that planning took place on a global scale, and the British hoped to organize the support of the Dominions (Australia, New Zealand, Canada, Newfoundland, South Africa) through an Imperial General Staff, although this was not realized in practice. However, the greater use of oil by the Royal Navy increased the global concerns of British power by enhancing the importance of the Middle East, more particularly the Persian Gulf, providing an additional reason for British concern about the security of the Suez Canal.

On land, sea and in the air, the Great War, however, was to expose the difficulty of predicting developments and thus the limitations of much pre-war planning and speculation. These limitations also reflected serious deficiencies in the mechanisms for strategic planning.[39] Preparations for conflict were also inadequate. For example, the machinization of the European armies should not be exaggerated. The lack of motor transport and the reliance, instead, on horse transport greatly limited mobility once troops had got out of their trains behind the front line, while, when the Great War broke out, there was an average of only two machine guns per thousand troops (or a battalion), either by sections or, in the German and Austrian armies, in a regimental company. In part, however, this low rate reflected the widespread assumption that a conflict would be mobile and that heavy machine guns would be an encumbrance as their value was in the defence, not the offence. Despite heavy pre-war expenditure on the military, there were still important equipment deficiencies, for example in the Russian army, while Serb communications in part relied on 192 homing pigeons.[40] The Romanian army lacked machine guns, heavy artillery and aircraft, while the deficiencies of the Italian army were such that the Chief of Staff notified the government that it was not ready for war. Indeed, the army entered the war in 1915 with only 618 machine guns and 132 pieces of heavy artillery. After heavy losses in the Balkan Wars of 1912–13, the Turkish army was in a poor state.

Yet, alongside their homing pigeons, the Serbs had very effective Mauser rifles purchased from Germany, as well as French and Russian rifles, and also had 328 modern Schneider Creusot field-guns, while Turkey had German-made artillery. Montenegro, a minor Balkan power that was rapidly overrun by Austrian forces in 1916, still had Italian-made artillery. Thus, purchase as well as alliances spread advanced weaponry. Nevertheless, despite the investment in advanced weaponry, planning on the whole did not adequately address the issue of improved organizational means and systems, and this failure was to create significant problems with operational effectiveness during the Great War.

More specific problems arose from the failure to cope with the major increase in army manpower from 1912. These increases posed problems for the provision of adequate equipment and training, and there were failings in both. Indeed, in August 1914, none of the major armies had adequately responded to the manpower increases, nor expected to do so before 1916–17.[41] Organizational issues were also posed by changes in technology, notably the introduction of quick-firing artillery which represented a formidable challenge for munitions supplies, especially of shells, but also of gunpowder.

Pre-war planning focused on the offensive,[42] which was seen as the sole way to secure success. This conviction arose from the analysis of the Franco-Prussian War (1870–71), in which the attacking Prussians had been victorious, analysis undertaken by the generation of officers ultimately to hold high command positions in the Great War. Most of these men, however, had had no experience of commanding large numbers in war and, thus, of the problems posed by managing a successful offensive.

The focus on the offensive was true not only of Germany and its ally Austria, but also of its opponents, particularly France. There, analysis of the failure of 1870 by officers such as Colonel François de Grandmaison, Director of Military Operations from 1908 to 1911, led to a doctrine of *offensive à l'outrance* (offensive at all costs), a doctrine which played a key role in the rewriting of the French regulations in 1913–14,[43] as well as in the strategy which General Joseph Joffre, Chief of the General Staff from 1911 and a veteran of the Franco-Prussian War, unsuccessfully sought to pursue in 1914. Anxious to co-ordinate operations with Russia, Joffre planned to mount an early offensive against German forces in Alsace-Lorraine before launching what was intended as a decisive blow against the German centre in eastern Belgium.[44] An emphasis on the offensive also seemed the best way to respond to the limitations of much of the French (and other) officer corps, as well as to answer to the preference for traditional and simple tactics.

There was concern about the practical consequences of offensive tactics. *The Times* responded to the British field manoeuvres of 1903, in which victory was won by an attack culminating in an assault on artillery positions, by asking 'At what precise point will this principle of attack become applicable under modern conditions?'[45] However, drill books, such as the British *Combined Training* in 1905, continued to emphasize the offensive, so that fire action was to remain secondary to the movement of troops, and the firing line was expected to advance.[46] The British 1909 Musketry Regulations set down the role of a fire fight in deciding the battle.

Tactically and operationally, there was no single form of offensive, and much of the discussion across the West revolved around the form which was to be adopted, not least in terms of the balance between arms. This balance included not simply the role of artillery but also the place of cavalry, because cavalry generals tended to put an emphasis on moral superiority, not on firepower.[47] There were also differences between plans that favoured the envelopment of opposing forces, the German preference, with reference to Hannibal's victory over the Romans at Cannae in 216 BC, to be tried in 1914, and those that focused on breaking through opponents at the weakest point, the French alternative.

An emphasis on the offensive was seen as the best way to express and sustain the nation's martial fervour and to encourage and hold the enthusiasm of the troops, and thus to ensure superior morale to that of the defenders. Better morale appeared necessary to offset the killing character of defensive firepower, to provide a crucial capability gap between similarly armed forces and to offer the prospect of a short war, and therefore of victory, without the need for social and economic mobilization and transformation.

The Balkan Wars of 1912–13 provided important signs of what was to come, including the unsuccessful Bulgarian attacks on the entrenched Turkish positions at Chataldzha on 17 November 1912, in which Turkish artillery and infantry, unsuppressed by Bulgarian artillery, inflicted considerable casualties. In addition, aeroplanes were used by all participants bar Montenegro, mainly for reconnaissance, although Turkish-held Edirne (Adrianople), besieged by the Bulgarians, was the first town on which bombs were dropped from an aeroplane.

Nevertheless, the Balkan Wars did not challenge contemporary military assumptions, any more than the American Civil War of 1861–65 or the Russo-Turkish War of 1877–78 had done. Because of difficulties in obtaining reliable information, the stress on strategy rather than tactics and the focus on success rather than casualties, observers did not see the wars as compromising their faith in the offensive, more specifically in massed infantry assaults, notably the Bulgarian victories over the Turks at the battles of Kirkkilese and Lyule Burgas in 1912. There was a general failure to note the degree to which rapid-firing artillery and machine guns might blunt such assaults, in part because of the assumption that events in regions of lesser development could do little to instruct the Great Powers.[48] The Great War was indeed unprecedented since 1815 in involving conflict on Continental Europe between all the major European powers. More generally, the Great War was to be unusual in its scale, the number of combatants ultimately involved, the role of industry and the degree of national mobilization on the Home Front.

At sea, pre-war, there was also a confidence in the attack, and a conviction that a war could be rapidly brought to a close. The Japanese victory at Tsushima in 1905, with six Russian battleships sunk and four captured, while the Japanese only lost three torpedo boats, appeared to vindicate the influential ideas of the American naval educator and writer Alfred Thayer Mahan on sea power, that a high-sea encounter would occur, that it could be a decisive battle and that the result would then affect the fate of nations. Japanese victory led many commentators and planners to conclude (correctly) that, due to new advances in range-finding and gun-fighting, future battleship engagements would be fought at great distance, and thus outside the range of torpedoes,[49] reinforcing the case for the heavily armoured, all-big-gun battleship.

This case was to be embodied by the British dreadnought, designed before Tsushima but validated by it and launched in 1906. With its ten 12-inch guns paired in five turrets, this was the first of a new class of all-big-gun battleships, as well as the first capital ship in the world to be powered by the marine turbine engine. Navalists, particularly in Britain, went into the war, confident that there would be a glorious victory, another Trafalgar and Tsushima. By 1912, the rapid expansion of the German battle fleet, combined with improved British relations with France from 1904, had led to a British strategic, operational and tactical emphasis on how best to win a battleship struggle with Germany in the North Sea.[50] The Great War, however, was to reveal the problems of waging successful war between great powers, both on land and at sea.

CHAPTER 2

1914

All trenches hereabouts were merely cast-up ridges
of earth held in place by stakes, wire, hurdles and
wooden framework. Underneath their floors of
planks and slats, water welled and stagnated, and an
indescribable nocturnal smell, mortal, greenweedy,
ratty, accompanied the tramp of our boots to and fro.
Edmund Blunden's autobiographical account.[1]

Henry Sinclair Horne, a somewhat dour Scottish artillery expert,
by then commander of the British First Army, was to reach the end
of the war on 11 November 1918 campaigning at Mons in western
Belgium. He had begun his war fighting there on 23 August 1914,[2]
and thus survived both that baptism of fire for the British and the
conflict as a whole. Although the vast majority of generals did survive
the war, Horne was one of a lucky few to survive conflict from Mons
to Mons. Yet, the unexpected intervention of Britain helped to wreck
the German gamble of 1914 and, even more, to doom the German
drive for mastery.

British entry into the war made it a world struggle. The German
military leadership did not seek such a struggle, instead favouring a
quick European war, like that successfully launched against France
in 1870. With the second largest navy in the world, and colonies in
Africa, China and the Pacific, Germany would have been able to wage
naval and colonial struggles against France had Britain not entered

the war. Such a conflict would have been assisted by the Austrian navy in the Mediterranean, for the Habsburg empire in 1914 possessed a long Adriatic coastline including major ports such as Trieste. Austria also had a navy of regional importance, one that was the eighth largest in the world. Germany might also have been supported by Italy could it have been persuaded to enter the war, in accordance with its alliance with Germany and Austria, in order to win territory from France as it was to do in 1940. Yet, as in 1870, when France's navy was larger than that of Germany, the German military leadership sought a campaign and a victory on land before the naval equation could kick in, and the territorial gains pursued by Germany were in Europe, not overseas. This attempt to direct the strategy of the war assumed that British entry would not matter, as Britain would be isolated by French and Russian defeat. It failed.

The crucial campaign in 1914 was that launched by the Germans in the west, but it has to be considered in the context of the failure of the plans of all the armies (bar the Serbs), plans that focused on the offensive. The political ambitions of the combatants drove their offensive strategies. The Germans sought to capture Paris, and the Austrians Belgrade, as key means to force France and Serbia respectively to surrender. The French advanced to regain Alsace-Lorraine, and the Russians to reduce pressure on their allies, to overrun much of Austria and to march on Berlin. The British hoped to take part in Germany's defeat and for their troops to return home by Christmas. The goals of the powers altered during the war, but substantially continued to rest on gaining or regaining territory, which helped to sustain the central role of the offensive in strategic, operational and tactical terms.

In 1914, the Germans sought to repeat Moltke the Elder's strategy of envelopment and to achieve victory even more rapidly than in the conflicts of 1866 and 1870–71, in each of which Prussia/Germany had had only one opponent. Relying on rail transport and forced marches, the Germans advanced on an open front through Belgium into northern France, in a modified version of the Schlieffen Plan. This route permitted them to avoid the heavily fortified frontier of eastern France, a strategy that had been predicted by some commentators.[3]

Belgian fortifications did not stop the German advance, mainly because the poorly prepared Belgians did not field a powerful field army. The Belgian population was small and in the Germans the Belgians confronted an opponent more powerful than Serbia faced in Austria, but more than relative strength was involved in Belgium's failure. In part due to Belgium's strict neutrality, there was a lack of adequate planning for war, and this failing helped the Germans as they took the initiative. The extensive fortress complexes (offering defence in depth and circling the cities of Liège, Namur and Antwerp) that had been designed by Henry Brialmont, the 'Belgian Vauban', all fell after bombardment by 305-mm and 420-mm heavy howitzers designed before the war specifically for this purpose. The latter fired 2,052 lb high-explosive shells able to penetrate ten feet of concrete.

Nevertheless, Liège took far longer to fall than the Germans anticipated – 11 days instead of two – and this operation delayed the provision of an adequate supply system to support the German advance across Belgium. The initial attacks on Liège were driven back on 5 August, but the fortification system depended on a powerful force to fill the gaps between the forts and, in its absence, the Germans were able to move through these gaps and to capture the city and undefended citadel of Liège. However, the forts continued to resist, those on the left bank of the Meuse holding out until 16 August.

Thereafter, the Belgians were not able to offer adequate resistance; they were greatly outnumbered by the Germans, who had sent 16 corps into Belgium. Most of the Belgian army fell back on Antwerp, which ensured that there was no real resistance to the German advance further south through Belgium towards France and the Channel ports. A Belgian division was committed to the defence of the fortress city of Namur, but it fell on 23 August. Brussels had already fallen on 20 August.

Due to the treatment of Belgium, this advance rapidly became highly contentious as an instance of war crimes used by the Allies to castigate Germany's war aims and methods, both for domestic audiences and for those in neutral countries, especially America. The Germans killed 5,521 civilians, including 674 in Dinant and 248 in Louvain, and destroyed about 25,000 buildings, notably the priceless university library of Louvain on 26 August. Violence by the German military against civilians looked back to a recent tradition of such action by German forces in both Europe and overseas, notably in 1870–71. Crucially, the Franco-Prussian War (1870–71) had not proved the swift and cheap victory the Germans had anticipated and that they had gained at the expense of Austria in 1866. Problems in 1870–71 included supply difficulties, continuing French resistance and opposition from a hostile population. The Germans responded harshly to the *francs-tireurs* – soldiers, deserters or civilians who fought back – and treated them as criminals, not soldiers.

Summary executions helped dampen opposition, but they were also part of a pattern of German brutality in the Franco-Prussian War, which included the taking of hostages, the shooting of suspects (as well as those actually captured in arms), the mutilation of prisoners and the destruction of towns and villages, such as Châteaudun. In part, this practice reflected the problems posed for the Germans by hostile French citizen volunteers, who did not wear uniforms and were impossible to identify once they had discarded their rifles. In response, the Germans treated every 'blue smock', the customary clothes of French workers, as a potential guerrilla.[4]

The context was different to Belgium in 1914, as were the brutal German counter-insurgency campaigns in Africa in the 1900s. Nevertheless, German atrocities in 1914 owed something to the fear of *francs-tireurs*. These atrocities in part appear to have reflected fury that Belgium unexpectedly resisted German attack and, therefore, affected the German advance. Hostility to Belgians was also to be seen in the forced deportation of 60,000 of them to work in Germany in 1916–17, a process accompanied by considerable harshness.

In 1914, German losses at the hands of Belgian regular units led to reprisals against civilians, who did not in practice mount guerrilla resistance, as well as to the killing of military prisoners, while a high degree of drunkenness, confusion and 'friendly fire' among German units contributed directly to their mistaken belief that they were under civilian attack. This belief encouraged their attitude that it was acceptable and, indeed, sensible, to inflict reprisals on the innocent. This policy was then defended by strategies of deception and propaganda, organized by the German army and government in 1914, deploying arguments that were to be repeated at the time of post-war trials.[5]

The German army's quest for a crushing victory in a battle of annihilation was also important. Civilians were dispensable in this view, while there was also an emphasis on the punitive treatment of German's enemies that was unconstrained by international law. In addition to German actions in Belgium, captured wounded French soldiers were killed in some cases in August, in fulfilment of orders from officers.[6] The harsh argument of necessity were readily employed, although such behaviour as much reflected an expectation of victory that did not encourage restraint. Fortunately, this conduct did not set the pattern for behaviour, on that front or on others, or indeed in occupied zones, although there were Austrian atrocities in Serbia and Russian ones in East Prussia. Moreover, the brutal treatment of prisoners was not uncommon on both sides, and prisoner escort parties sometimes failed to deliver their prisoners because they had dealt with them along the way.

The Germans were helped in their advance across Belgium by the positioning of most of France's army south of Verdun and by the latter's attack on the Germans in Lorraine. This attack, moreover, was not abandoned in response to the German invasion of Belgium, for Joseph Joffre, Chief of the French General Staff and a veteran of the German siege of Paris in 1870–71, sought to regain French territory and to force the Germans to respond to his advance, and he did not believe that the main German offensive would be mounted through Belgium. Joffre continued in his belief even after German troops were known to have entered Belgium in large numbers.

Taking the offensive seemed to the French command to be the only way to deny the initiative to the Germans and was regarded as a counter to German numerical superiority; at the tactical level, it was also seen as a way to exploit the value of the bayonet. Instead, the attacking French forces were stopped by heavy German defensive fire. The Germans had prepared positions and Joffre had failed to understand the disposition of their forces. At the level of individual armies and corps, the French advance lacked cohesion, and thus there was an absence of mutual support. In particular, on 20 August, the French attack on the Morhange heights was smashed by German defensive fire.

The following day, the French Third and Fourth armies attacked in the Ardennes, as Joffre sought to hit the German centre, which he mistakenly thought weak as a result of a concentration of German forces on the Germans' left and also, as it now appeared, on their right in Belgium. The poorly prepared French fought the German Fourth and Fifth armies in an encounter battle in which the (heavier) German artillery proved superior, while, in what in effect was a series of struggles, the individual French divisions and corps suffered from a lack of mutual support that left them particularly vulnerable to flank attacks on their right. Heavy French casualties ensured that only the French Fourth Army resumed the attack on 21 August and two days later the French began to retreat.[7]

On the French left, Charles Lanrezac's Fifth Army had been ordered to attack on the River Sambre and thus, in concert with the Belgians and the British Expeditionary Force (BEF), to consolidate the Allied position in Belgium. The BEF, the British army sent to the continent, had landed in France from 9 August and, by 20 August, had concentrated near Maubeuge on the River Meuse to the left of Lanrezac's army. However, with information coming in on the real size of German numbers in Belgium, Lanrezac decided to remain on the defensive. Contact with the advancing German Second Army began on 21 August and successful resistance was mounted the next day.

The BEF had been asked to advance to Lanrezac's left, protecting the latter from German envelopment on the open flank, but the German offensive exposed the BEF to attack by the more numerous First Army under the energetic Alexander von Kluck, a veteran of the Franco-Prussian War. With Lanrezac now on the defensive, the BEF also took up defensive positions on the Mons-Condé canal; these positions gave the British an advantage when they were attacked by German forces that were not expecting to find them. The Germans were checked in bitter fighting at Mons on 23 August, but the British took heavy casualties in repelling the attacks and then fell back as a result of Lanrezac's decision to retreat. The Germans pressed closely, which led the British Second Corps to fight a rearguard action at Le Cateau on 26 August, although they again took heavy casualties.

In the face of German defensive successes on the French right and centre, and advances on the French left, Joffre, on the morning of 23 August, acknowledged the need to remain on the defensive until the Germans had been worn out. The Germans, meanwhile, were slowed down by the need to transport food and ammunition for their formidable numbers. Furthermore, the greater power of artillery posed logistical problems as guns, especially but not only heavy ones, really needed to be moved on paved roads. Thus, advance by such roads had become an adjunct to mobilization by railway. Aside from serious faults in planning and execution, there were also problems with equipment and discipline which qualify the usual historiographical picture of total German competence, a point also valid for the Second World War.

German problems gave the French a better opportunity to regroup, while German war-making, with its emphasis on surprise, speed and overwhelming and dynamic force at the chosen point of contact, was not effective against a French defence that had depth and that retained the capacity to use reserves by redeploying troops by rail during the course of operations. Interior lines and railways provided opportunities, from 26 August, for moving troops between fronts, from the French right wing to the French left, a shift in the centre of gravity not matched by the Germans. These opportunities were grasped because, although the government, as in 1870 and 1940, left Paris, moving to Bordeaux until December, the French did not lose their nerve. There were episodes of panic and of a collapse of discipline in the army, and many troops ran away, but swift executions without trial steadied the situation, and the bulk of the army remained resilient.

So, crucially, did Joffre and this resilience ensured that decisions were taken carefully even as the direction and seriousness of the German advance became more apparent. The highly active Joffre also used the crisis to dismiss many commanders, notably those who were elderly. In replacing them, he put the focus on professional competence rather than on the pre-war prerequisite of republican loyalty. This steadiness on Joffre's part was important because, for all the powers involved in the war, the pace and scale of operations on an unprecedented scale were putting considerable pressure on command systems that were overly dependent on personal relationships, and were also greatly affected by problems arising from casualties and the even greater inexperience of replacements.[8]

The Germans made a crucial mistake when they mishandled their advance near Paris, leading to a deployment, especially a gap between the two armies on the advancing German right, that was vulnerable to counter-attack. Kluck's First Army had departed from the original plan to advance to the west of Paris, as part of a grand envelopment of the French forces. Instead, on 30 August, he decided, with Moltke's agreement, to move south, so as to advance to the east of Paris and thus maintain contact with Karl von Bülow's Second Army on his left. This axis, however, made Kluck vulnerable to the forces Joffre was building up near Paris and these forces, the French Sixth Army, under Michel Maunoury, were sent on 3 September to attack Kluck's right flank on the River Ourcq. Maunoury, who had been wounded in the Franco-Prussian War, had been moved with many of his troops from the Army of Lorraine on the French right.

In response, Kluck, on 7 September, turned to the west to meet this attack, only to create a gap between his forces and those of the mediocre Bülow by moving two corps which had been on the latter's right. British and French forces advanced into this gap on 8 September, threatening both the German First and Second Armies. The French seized their opportunity in what became known as the Battle of the Marne, although their execution did not match the plan. In particular, the British and French forces moved too slowly to exploit this gap, in large part because the subordinate commanders did not seek a major battle.

The Germans were not defeated, but, in the face of this Allied advance, the German high command, which had earlier failed to maintain a tight grip during the advance, suffered a failure of nerve and on 10 September Kluck was ordered to pull back.[9] The Germans withdrew from the River Marne to the River Aisne in what became a key failure of impetus. That is not the same as arguing that the Germans had overextended themselves with their offensive, for such an overextension was more a matter of the contingent execution of the plan than an element inherent to the outcome. Advancing as the Germans withdrew, British and French forces fought their way across the Aisne on 12 September, but German counter-attacks sealed the front next day.

Here and elsewhere, the opening campaign of the war in the west was instructive for all concerned as pre-war plans fell apart, a product both of their deficiencies and of mistakes in implementation. These failures partially reflected the strength of the defence, particularly in the case of the French defeat in Lorraine by the Germans, but more was involved, not least because some of the invasions were checked by counter-attacks within manoeuvre warfare, as with the Serbian and German successes against Austrian and Russian invasions respectively.

The limitations that invading powers faced in manoeuvre warfare were serious, especially in sustaining mass and maintaining the tempo of attack, and these limitations helped to cause the failure of the German offensive on the Western Front. On the other side, whatever the German deficiencies, the maintenance of the French army in 1914 was a fundamental Allied strategic achievement, one that ensured that Germany would have to fight land wars on two fronts, unlike in 1918 and 1941. France's survival also ensured that Germany was deprived of Italian support, whereas in 1940 Mussolini joined in on the victorious German side.

The Germans had weakened their forces on the Western Front by sending two corps to East Prussia to counter the Russian advance, launched on 15 August. The first general mobilization of Russian reservists, which involved 3,915,000 men over two weeks, was successful and, quicker than anticipated by the Germans, the Russians took the initiative.[10] The initial success of the Russians, including a victory by Pavel Rennenkampf's First Army over attacking German forces at Gumbinnen on 20 August, led to wild talk by the German commander, Max von Prittwitz, of possibly abandoning East Prussia and withdrawing west of the River Vistula. Such an outcome was totally unacceptable as far as the German leadership was concerned, although it was better than that of failing against France in the west. In the event, Moltke replaced Prittwitz on 22 August.

A new command team, Paul von Hindenburg and his Chief of Staff, Erich Ludendorff, proved able to rally the defence and to take advantage of the serious command faults in the inadequately co-ordinated Russian invasion of East Prussia: Rennenkampf, invading from the east, had very poor personal relations with Aleksandr Samsonov, the commander of the Second Army, who was invading from the south, although the feud has been overblown and does not alone explain German success in 1914. The Russians were heavily defeated at Tannenberg on 27–30 August in a battle reminiscent of the successes of the Elder Moltke, especially Sadowa in 1866, and then at the Masurian Lakes from 10 to 13 September. The lack of co-ordination between the invading Russian armies permitted the Germans to use their Eighth Army with the advantages of interior lines of communications and without facing the danger of concerted actions by the two Russian armies. In fighting the Russian forces separately, the Germans also benefited from their ability to adapt more rapidly to opportunities, and thus to seize the advantage.

At Tannenberg, Samsonov's Second Army was encircled and attacked from different directions; the Russian commander was unable to mount a coherent response, while the First Army provided no support. Defeated, Samsonov committed suicide. In turn, the First Army was routed at the Masurian Lakes, although, unlike the Second Army, it was able to fight a rearguard action. In these battles, the Russians lost over 130,000 prisoners.[11] There was to be no repetition of the damaging pressure on the Prussia of Frederick the Great exerted by Russia during the Seven Years' War (1756–63). German success was important because the Russians, not the British, were at this stage the key adjunct to the French war effort on land.

In strategic terms, moreover, the Russians had made a major mistake in dividing their resources between separate offensives against Austria and Germany. That against Austria from 26 August to 26 September proved more successful than the invasion of East Prussia. Attacked in southern Poland from the east and the north, the Austrians were put under considerable pressure and their Third Army was heavily defeated in the attack from the east in the Battle of Gnila Lipa of 26–30 August. The subsequent Austrian retreat exposed the rear of their Fourth Army which had initially thrown back the attack of the Russian Fifth Army from the north in the Battle of Komarow of 26 August to 1 September. The Austrian Fourth Army turned to engage the Russians advancing from the east in the indecisive Battle of Rawa Russaka of 8–10 September, but was then threatened from 9 September by the renewed advance of the Russian Fifth Army which threatened to outflank it to the west. From 11 September, the Austrians fell back to the west toward Cracow, although they left 100,000 troops to garrison the fortress of Przemysl on the River San.

The loss of much of Galicia (southern Poland) by the Austrians exposed the flank of the German position in Silesia (south-west Poland). Unrelieved, Przemysl itself surrendered the following March which greatly increased the number of prisoners held by the Russians. However, it was difficult for the Russians to sustain this success, especially as the Germans came to the assistance of their Austrian allies by moving troops to south-west (German) Poland from 22 September 1914 and invading the Russian part of Poland from 4 October. The Russians mounted a powerful counter-attack on the German Ninth Army, driving it back from near Warsaw, but the Germans, benefiting from their use of rail movements, regrouped and mounted a new offensive on 11 November that put great pressure on the Russians near Lodz in late November.

The Russians sought to resume their offensive in December, advancing on Cracow in order to threaten Silesia, and also capturing the Carpathian passes, through which it would be possible for them to advance into Hungary, a major part of the Austrian empire. The fighting centred south of Cracow with the Russian advance flanked by Austrian forces under Roth in early December, leading the Russians to move their troops to face the new threat. In turn, the Russians moved troops from their Eighth Army on the Carpathian front in order to threaten Roth's flank. This move left the Eighth Army weak and it was attacked from 8 December by the Austrian Third Army which recaptured the passes lost at the end of November. Combined with renewed German pressure further north near Lodz, the Austrian advance led the Russians to fall back. The highpoint of their December advance into the Austrian empire was not to recur.

Further south, the Austrians had done very badly against the Serbs, mounting an offensive from 12 August that was rapidly defeated by a successful Serbian counter-attack. A subsequent Austrian advance led to the capture of Belgrade on 2 December, but the Serbs mounted another successful counter-attack from 3 December and regained Belgrade on 15 December. This was a considerable humiliation for the Austrians, albeit on a secondary front.

On the Western Front, after the battle of the Marne, both sides unsuccessfully sought to outflank the other to the north-west in order to avoid the high casualties of frontal attacks and to gain the advantage of the open flank. The Allies also wanted naturally to retain as much of France and Belgium as possible, to protect a route to Antwerp and to hold the Channel Ports. Antwerp, however, was exposed by the German advance and was abandoned on 6 October, which shortened the eventual front line.

The last opportunity for open mobile warfare on the Western Front, before the closing stage of the war in 1918, occurred in Flanders in October and November, as the Germans struggled to break through to the English Channel. They were hit, however, by exhaustion after the initial advance as well as by harsh weather and serious shortages of shells. The fighting, in the resulting First Battle of Ypres from 30 October to 13 November, with minor operations thereafter, was transitional, with hand-to-hand combat still taking place and with riflemen proving as important as artillery. Compared with what was to come later, this was a mobile and fluid battle. Moreover, the Germans came close to success, and might have done so had they mounted another push, but the British held them off, although much of the pre-war army was destroyed in the process with the British losing 54,105 men and the Germans about 80,000: there were also Belgian and French losses. Both sides were exhausted by mid-November.[12]

Such high casualties reflected the peril of the modern battlefield, a peril that owed much to enhanced technology. In particular, the potency of artillery was increased by better sights, new propellants and fuses, steel-coated projectiles, high-explosive fillings and new recoil/recuperator dual systems whereby one part allowed the barrel to recoil without moving the carriage and the other part allowed the barrel to return to its original position on the carriage. This hydro-pneumatic and hydromechanical system was essential to quick-firing guns.

The enhanced accuracy of artillery helped make the open battle-ground dangerous to an unprecedented degree, affecting tactics and uniforms. Prior to the outbreak of the war, there had been changes in uniforms in order to make troops less conspicuous. The Germans adopted field grey and the French had decided on horizon blue, but the French troops who went into combat in 1914 still wore bright red trousers. However, these were swiftly covered with blue overalls and, by the end of 1915, French troops had blue uniforms as well as Adrian helmets which provided some protection against head wounds. Exposure to firepower also encouraged entrenchment, much of it in the sticky cold mud that became central to the new experience of war by the soldiers. Field fortifications had long been a feature on battlefields, and entrenchment was scarcely new, but the danger from artillery in the Great War very much ensured that entrenchments played the major role in field fortifications.

By November 1914 there was a stalemate on what had become a fixed Western Front, with the front line stretching all the way to the North Sea and 'the chief need ... for infantry and as many of them as possible', so that cavalry units were dismounted and sent into the trenches.[13] The Allies had the Channel Ports of France (Boulogne, Calais and Dunkirk), but the Flemish coast of Ostend and Zeebruge had been won by Germany, as in October, after a siege, had Antwerp, which increased the German threat to British control of the North Sea.

The manoeuvre stage of the war in the West, with its emphasis on a strategy of envelopment, and on a battle of annihilation in order to secure total victory, was now over. Generals were to try repeatedly to recreate this early flexibility, and, in particular, to seek to reopen a war of movement by breaking through their opponents' front line, but this goal was to prove elusive year after year.

It is unclear how far manoeuvre warfare as conceived prior to the war was, in fact, a real possibility for the industrialized armies of major European powers fighting each other in a confined space in this period, or whether it was an illusion, so that a quick victory from out-manoeuvring the enemy was not plausible. In short, was trench warfare inevitable, or could it have been avoided by better planning, better generalship or better tactics? Trench warfare certainly had not been avoided in Manchuria in 1904–05 nor in the Balkans in 1912–13.

Germany's failure in 1914 threw the wider war into sharper perspective and notably Britain's role. Without a conscript army and with imperial forces, for example in India, Australia and Canada, at a distance, Britain was unable to take a leading part on the Western Front in 1914, but the wider significance of British power was readily apparent both at sea and in the colonies. In the opening months of the war, there were two surface actions in the North Sea, the key area of conflict between the British and German surface fleets, although neither saw a clash between battleships.

In the battle of Heligoland Bight on 28 August, British battlecruisers played the decisive role in an engagement that started as a clash between British and German squadrons of light cruisers and destroyers. The Germans lost three light cruisers and one destroyer, while, although one British light cruiser and two destroyers were badly damaged, the fact that none was lost helped ensure that the battle was presented to the Allied public as a striking victory. In practice, it was not so much a coherent, highly structured battle, but rather a series of individual ship engagements conducted in poor visibility. The British were hindered by the general lack of co-ordination in the Admiralty, the force composition for the raid, the limitations on gunnery and torpedo skills (which ensured that the heavy use of ammunition and torpedoes brought few successes), and the quality of British shells: many failed to explode.

Given these and other deficiencies, it is unsurprising that the British did not inflict heavier losses on the Germans, but all the latter's warships were outgunned by their British counterparts, while the German torpedo boats were outclassed. The Germans were also affected by serious tactical problems and communications were an issue, while there was a poor command response to the British raid, and, in particular, a lack of co-ordination and inaccurate assessment of likely and actual developments.

The battle reflected and strengthened a sense of psychological inferiority on the German part, confirming their cautious use of the fleet. The belief that the British would not send heavy units into the Bight had proved misplaced, while the Germans were both properly, and yet overly, anxious about risking their better ships, which greatly affected their response to the raid. Wilhelm II felt justified in his instructions that battle was to be sought only under the most favourable circumstances. These restrictions were now underlined with particular limitations with respect to the Bight.[14] The battle certainly gave the British a powerful psychological advantage, which was underlined on 17 October when, in the Battle of Texel, four German destroyers were sunk.

In 1914, the loss of ships to German submarines and mines cost the British more men and major ships than the Germans lost in battle, but the impact of these British losses was less dramatic in terms of the perhaps crucial sense of relative advantage. Indeed, submarines and mines appeared to be a means only to snipe at the British naval advantage, rather than an effective counter to it. Moreover, Wilhelm's restrictions helped ensure that the surface war at sea would probably be lost by Germany through limited contest. After the battle of Heligoland Bight, Wilhelm's tight rein on the fleet was frequently in evidence, and the defence of the island of Heligoland thereafter was essentially entrusted to minefields. This, however, was no way to challenge the British blockade of Germany. In the event, the British were to win the war on the Western Front in 1918 but, had the conflict continued for longer, the blockade would have proved even more important, although it would not necessarily have proved a war-winning strategy, especially once Germany was able to exploit the resources of Romania and Russia.

In the early stages of the war, British naval operations suffered from the weaknesses of the Naval Staff, not least inadequate numbers and a poorly developed planning system.[15] Nevertheless, the strength derived from the Royal Navy, a strength confirmed by the pre-war shipbuilding programme, was significant. Thanks to the navy, the British retained control of their home waters and were, therefore, able to avoid blockade and serious attack, to maintain the flow of

men and munitions to their army in France unmolested, to retain
trade links that permitted the mobilization of British resources and
to blockade Germany, declaring, on 3 November, that the North
Sea would be a military area with shipping subject to Admiralty
control. Neutrals were prevented from re-exporting their imports
to Germany, with particular pressure on the Dutch not to re-export
food to Germany. British actions breached the Paris (1856) and
London (1909) agreements on wartime trade, but seemed necessary
if economic warfare was to work.[16] Blockade was supported by a
system of pre-emptive purchasing that was important to the international control of raw materials as well as greatly influencing neutral
economies. In particular, cutting off trade with Germany lessened
American economic and financial interest in its success.

Alongside resources, naval, maritime, financial and economic,
geography was a key factor, with the Germans bottled up in the
North Sea by Britain's location athwart their routes to the oceans.[17]
There was periodical German interest in sending cruisers out into the
Atlantic in order to harry British trade but, aside from the problems
of coaling such ships once at sea, the location of British bases was a
key problem. The German route to the Atlantic was threatened by the
major base of Scapa Flow in the Orkneys, which anchored the British
naval position, while, in 1909, a new base at Rosyth on the Firth of
Forth, in east Scotland, had been begun. It was designed to help the
Grand Fleet contest the North Sea, and included three dry docks able
to take dreadnoughts. The lack of a comparable base further south on
the east coast, however, was a major problem for the British, both in
protecting the longer coastline from attack and in responding rapidly
to German naval moves. German naval bombardments of east coast
ports, starting with Great Yarmouth on 3 November 1914, outraged
British public opinion. Hartlepool, Scarborough and Whitby were all
bombarded on 16 December. Such attacks contributed to the highly
negative impression created by German atrocities in Belgium.

Alongside location and naval strength, came the use of Intelligence,
notably as a result of the British control of long-range communications, including the transatlantic cables. This control made it possible
to gather information on German attempts to evade the blockade,

and thus to take counter-measures.[18] The British also benefited from the Russian seizure of the signal book of a German warship that ran aground in the Gulf of Finland as that gave them access to German naval codes.

Britain's supply system was that of a country that could not feed itself: nearly two-thirds of British food consumption was imported. Britain also had an imperial economy which relied on global trade; and a military system that required troop movements within the vast empire. All of this was challenged by German surface raiders, such that the New Zealand government was concerned about the dispatch of its troops overseas. However, these raiders were hunted down in the early stages of the war. The East Asia squadron under Vice-Admiral Maximilian Graf von Spee was the leading German naval force outside Europe at the outset of the war. It sailed to Chile where a weaker and heavily outgunned British force under Rear-Admiral Sir Christopher Cradock was defeated off Coronel on 1 November with the loss of two cruisers. Spee then sailed on to attack the Falkland Islands, a British colony with, at Port Stanley, a naval base including crucial coaling facilities, but Sir John Fisher, the First Sea Lord, had already sent two battlecruisers and six light cruisers there to hunt Spee down, and Spee was defeated on 8 December with all but one of his ships sunk, although only after a prolonged chase which practically exhausted the magazines of the British battlecruisers. This engagement also indicates the importance of values in war, especially the sense of justice and nationalism. Among the autobiographical records of sailors, Henry Welch of HMS *Kent* reported vividly on the sinking of SMS *Nürnberg* in the Battle of the Falkland Islands:

> we have avenged the *Monmouth* [sunk off Coronel].
> I really believe it was in the *Nürnberg*'s power to have
> saved many of the *Monmouth*'s crew. Instead, she
> simply shelled her until the last part was visible above
> water. Noble work of which the German nation
> should feel proud. Thank God I am British.[19]

Thereafter, the Germans only had individual warships at large and these were eventually hunted down, although not before SMS *Emden* had inflicted some damage (and more disruption) on shipping in the Indian Ocean and had shelled Madras in east India. The *Emden* was lost to the combination of naval fire and a reef in the Cocos Islands on 9 November 1914. In East Africa, the light cruiser SMS *Königsberg* supported the unsuccessful German attack on Mombasa that September, only to be sunk by the British in the Rufifi River the following year.

The threat to the Allies from German surface raiders was essentially restricted to the opening months of the war. Indeed, Allied success in blockading the North Sea, the English Channel and the Adriatic, and in capturing Germany's overseas colonies, ensured that, after the initial stages of the war and despite the use of submarines, the range of German naval operations was smaller than those of American and French privateers (licensed private commerce raiders) when attacking British trade between 1775 and 1815.

On 6 August 1914, Britain and France signed a naval convention under which the French navy was responsible for much of the Mediterranean and the British for the rest of the world. As a result, there were no French warships in the North Sea. With British as well as French warships present, German and Austrian naval power was outclassed in the Mediterranean, which enabled the French safely to move troops from North Africa to support their forces in France. The small German squadron in the Mediterranean, the battlecruiser SMS *Goeben* and light cruiser SMS *Breslau* shelled the ports of Philippeville and Bone in the French colony of Algeria on 4 August, evaded British attempts to intercept them and took shelter with the Turks later in August. The ships entered Turkish service and their actions against the Russians in the Black Sea helped bring Turkey into the war against the Allies at the end of October.

Turkish entry opened up an important prospect for Allied naval action, and greatly extended the geographical range of the Central Powers, giving them a new front with Russia, in the Caucasus, as well as the possibility of land conflict with the British, for the British and Turkish (Ottoman) empires had a common border on the Egypt–Palestine frontier, while Turkish rule of Iraq threatened the British position in the Persian Gulf. Thus, the strategic problems facing the Allies increased greatly, notably the problems posed by Russia no longer having access to the Mediterranean and thereby a safe supply route.

The Turkish decision owed much to the concern of its ruling elite that the war threatened further subordination to outside powers, a concern also (correctly) seen in Persia (Iran) and China, as well as to a belief that it was necessary to join a major international alignment in order both to preserve independence and prevent a continuation of the process of territorial loss seen most recently in 1911–13 at the hands of Italy and the Balkan powers. Alliance with Germany seemed the way to win support and military *matériel* and, in particular, to gain backing against Russia which had longstanding territorial ambitions in the Caucasus as well as a determination to control the route from the Black Sea to the Mediterranean.[20]

In 1914, Allied sea power supported operations against German colonies, with the Japanese capturing undefended German possessions in the north-west Pacific as well as Germany's base of Tsingtao on China's upper east coast. Under the Anglo-Japanese treaty of 1902, Japan was not obliged to enter the war, but the Prime Minister, Shigenobu Ōkuma, was ready to do so in order to gain German possessions and to strengthen Japan's position in China. The Germans in Tsingtao were heavily outnumbered, and, despite a stubborn resistance, were outfought by a successful British-supported Japanese use of combined operations, surrendering on 7 November.[21] This operation provided Japan with a foothold on the Chinese coast, but its seizure of the colony led to an upsurge of Chinese nationalist opposition, which continued and grew in the following decades, as well as to American criticism of Japanese expansionism.

Attacks on German colonies did not always achieve success. Thus, the costly and unsuccessful British amphibious assault on the port of Tanga on 2–3 November, the first major clash in East Africa, exposed the sometimes amateurish nature of British planning and command, suggesting that there was an absence of adequate co-ordination between army and navy and, more generally, that the peacetime system of planning and controlling operations was unable to cope with the strains of war. A path can be traced from Tanga to the unsuccessful amphibious campaign at Gallipoli in 1915,[22] but the margin between success and failure is always close and another British expeditionary force captured Basra from the Turks on 22 November 1914. Moreover, although failure is generally readily explained, it is necessary to give due weight to the problems facing all operations and to remind ourselves that the far-better-prepared Germans did not win in 1914. The British were certainly able to destroy the articulation of the German empire. The seizure or destruction of German wireless stations played a major part with the attack on East Africa beginning with the shelling of the wireless tower at Dar es Salaam. Other British forces that year destroyed German wireless stations in the Pacific and cut German cable routes, a New Zealand force supported by Australian and French warships seizing Western Samoa on 29 August.

Albeit without its later range, air power came to play a greater role in 1914. Reconnaissance was a key capability and, despite the constraints of the weather, aeroplanes came to replace the reconnaissance functions of cavalry. Over land, they reported the change of direction of the German advance near Paris and helped the Germans in the Tannenburg campaign. On water, Admiral Sir John Jellicoe, the commander of the British Grand Fleet, warned that 'the German airships will be of the greatest possible advantage to their fleet as scouts'.[23]

Aerial bombing was one of the most modern and terrifying aspects of this war. German Zeppelin (hydrogen-filled) airships attacked Antwerp and Warsaw, and Liège, on 6 August, was the first city to be bombed during the year, Paris following on 30 August. In response, in September and October, before having to withdraw from Antwerp, aircraft of the British Royal Naval Air Service conducted effective raids thence with 20-pound bombs to strike Zeppelin sheds at Düsseldorf, destroying one airship.

As yet, the scale of activity was still modest. At the start of the war, the Royal Aircraft Factory at Farnborough could produce only two air-frames per month, but its artisanal methods were swiftly swept aside by mass production with existing factories converted to war uses, so that the Birmingham and Midland Carriage Company built Handley Page bombers, while Sunbeam, Wolverhampton's car-makers, manufactured aero-engines.[24]

On 9 September, Bethmann-Hollweg announced German war aims including territorial gains, notably the Longwy-Briey iron ore basin from France, dominance of Belgium and colonial gains in Africa. These, however, were not acceptable as the basis for negotiations and already, on 5 September, Britain, France and Russia had agreed by the Pact of London not to negotiate separately. Particular German lobbies had their own goals. Thus, naval commanders were keen on obtaining bases on the coast of Belgium and, if possible, France.[25] Tirpitz, the administrative head of the navy and a bitter opponent of Britain, suggested to Moltke's replacement, Erich von Falkenhayn, on 15 November, that Germany focus on the Western Front and pursue a separate peace with Russia on the basis of the pre-war positions of Germany, Austria, Russia and Turkey in Eastern Europe, but there was no dynamic behind such a proposal, not least because of German interest in territorial gains in the region.

Herbert Asquith, the British Prime Minister, in turn, declared that Britain would fight on not only to secure Belgium and France but also to destroy 'the military might of Prussia', by which he meant Germany. The alleged support of the Angel of Mons, the angel that helped British troops at Mons, encouraged a feeling that Britain's task was a holy one, a theme also adopted, for example, by Horatio Bottomley in his recruiting speeches. Whereas there was a reluctance among many to join up initially, there was a flood of volunteers after Mons. Other participants in the war also advanced bold claims, the Serb government declaring that it would liberate and unite in one state all Serbs, Croats and Slovenes,[26] as indeed was to happen after the war with the creation of Yugoslavia. Austria sought Russia's share of Poland, as well as a stronger position in the Balkans. Turkey's entry into the war enabled Russia to add control of the Straits (the Bophorus and the Dardanelles) between the Black and Mediterranean Seas to its gaol of control over the German and Austrian portions of Poland. President Woodrow Wilson of America was encouraged in a different direction by the realization that the war would be long. He felt that neutrality would provide economic opportunity and that a long war would increase the weight of America's economic muscle.

It was clear that war was going to be not only on an unprecedented scale but also lengthy and maybe of an unusual character and length. Both governments and publics gritted themselves to the task. Thus, in Britain, the more urgent need for troops led to an increase in volunteering for service. Many who did so, however, were to be killed in 1916 with the Somme campaign being the first major commitment of the New Armies.

CHAPTER 3

1915

I lit a cigarette and tried to pretend I wasn't frightened to death. And just then a man ran by with his arm nearly off. I was so afraid he would bleed to death that I lost my fear for a minute or two and followed him, stood in the trench and dressed him. Lewis my corporal was cowering down by my side in a small scoop. I wouldn't let him come out, as I told him one of us was enough at a time, when suddenly a shell exploded on him and blew him to pieces, knocked me over and broke the leg of a stretcher bearer who was 2 yards further off than I was. I don't know why I wasn't killed. My nerve went and I would have bolted only I heard the poor beggar hit in the leg calling for me so I groped my way to him and dressed him. I have never been so shaken .... Found Lloyd of A Company – his servant had had one of his legs blown off. I got down and dressed him, how I don't know, and was absolutely literally sick from shock, then dressed 2 others and then had a very stiff brandy then I am afraid I broke down.

Captain Hugh Orr-Ewing, Medical Officer, to his fiancée, 28 September 1915, written from battle of Loos.[1]

The basic strategic fact of the war in its second year was that Germany had seized much of Belgium and part of France and, without any offensive plan for the Western Front to supersede that employed in 1914, had dug in to protect its gains. This situation forced Britain and France to mount offensives in order to regain the lost territory. Another necessity was provided by the wish to reduce German pressure on Russia and to prevent it from being knocked out of the war. Similarly, the German offensive in Poland in 1915 was aimed at helping Austria and giving it time to recover from its defeats in southern Poland. Furthermore, there was a conviction that, only through mounting an offensive, would it be possible for the Allies to gain the initiative and, conversely, deny it to the Germans, and that both gaining the initiative and mounting an offensive were prerequisites for victory.

More specifically, in early 1915, it was widely believed that the stalemate of the winter was due to the exhaustion of men and supplies in the previous autumn's campaigning with its unexpected demands; and that it would be possible, with fresh men and munitions, to restart a war of manoeuvre. Trying to do so, however, required a difficult, and perhaps impossible, reconciliation of the bold operational planning by General Staffs with the supply management of war ministries trying to adapt to unprecedented demands. Britain was not alone in facing a shell crisis, but organizational factors were particularly serious there as the War Office had placed contracts with the armaments firms which were entirely ad hoc and without regard to lead time or capacity. British ammunitions production prior to the establishment of the Ministry of Munitions in June 1915 was not geared to mass production on the scale required, and a new organizational structure was needed.

Seeking to restart a war of manoeuvre by breaking through opponents' front line was to prove elusive on the Western Front and, in trying to do so, generals risked losing large numbers of troops without causing comparable casualties to the enemy. It was not generally appreciated by the Allies, nor among all German generals, that stalemate and trench warfare reflected the nature of modern industrial war once both sides had committed large numbers of troops and lacked the ability to accomplish a breakthrough. There were organizational, operational and tactical dimensions to this stasis. At the interrelated organizational and operational levels, the logistical burden of supporting large forces encouraged a position warfare that reduced the options for manoeuvre. At the tactical level, trenches were the means to protect troops from artillery fire, and, as Alan Thomson, a British artillery officer, noted in Gallipoli in 1915, troops were never more vulnerable than before trenches could be dug.[2] In conflict, trenches remained vulnerable to plunging shell fire, hence the need for rifle grenades, howitzers, mortars and rifle grenades to attack trench positions, but the men who moved above ground were far more exposed to both machine guns and artillery. This meant that artillery became the key equalizer to support attacking infantry by suppressing defensive firepower.

The Great War fitted into a continuum in which, as small arms and artillery became more powerful during the nineteenth century, so the role of trenches for protection increased. Moreover, trenches had always figured into the siege of fortresses in order to protect the attackers, and the role of the trench in attacking an entrenched enemy was highlighted in the Russo-Japanese War of 1904–05 when the Japanese employed trenches in assault operations.

Generalship was also an important factor in the failure to stage successful offensives. The Allies, especially in 1915, did not understand the strength of the German defensive positions, and Joffre continued to seek a strategic breakthrough that did not match the possibilities on the ground. Such efforts encountered the tactical and operational drawbacks that German lines were carefully located on favourable terrain, while Allied lines were sited against those of the Germans, which greatly hampered Allied offensives. 1915 saw somewhat ad-hoc British and French attempts to obtain a strategic breakthrough on the Western Front by frontal attacks, with key assaults by the British at Neuve Chapelle and Loos and, deploying more troops and suffering greater casualties, by the French in Artois and Champagne. These costly failures proved particularly devastating for the French, affecting the manpower they would have available in 1916.

The 1915 battles revealed the defensive strength of trench systems. The concentration of large forces in a relatively small area ensured that any defender was able to call on plenty of reserve troops to stem an infantry advance. The difficulties for the attackers were exacerbated by the intrinsic defensive strength of trench positions, a strength that had more than tactical consequences. While trenches protected troops from artillery, especially the field guns most in evidence, such as the French 75-mm and the British 18-pounder, the trenches also enhanced defensive capability by freeing troops for offensives elsewhere. The strength of trench positions also owed much to the weaponry available for their protection and which they could protect, especially quick-firing artillery and machine guns with their impressive range and rapidity of fire. Barbed wire[3] and concrete fortifications also enhanced defensive positions, while German reserves provided defence in depth.

Furthermore, even if such positions were breached, it was very difficult for an attacker to make substantial gains. Local superiority in numbers could not be translated into decisive success. Although it was possible to break through at least some of the opponents' trench lines, it was difficult to exploit such successes, in part because the attacking army generally had exhausted itself in the first stage. This was seen at Neuve Chapelle on 10 April, where, despite a weak bombardment that did not cut all the German wire, the British had sufficient mass to break through German trenches which did not yet display the sophistication they were to show by later in the year. In such a context, frontal attacks could prove amazingly successful. Indeed, although the German defence was assisted by the British lack of heavy guns and ammunition, as well as by a British loss of control of the battle because of poor communications (a loss not peculiar to the British), the British nearly succeeded at Neuve Chapelle and, indeed, came closer than in many subsequent battles.

However, at Neuve Chapelle, the Germans quickly brought up reserves by train and established a fresh front line, for which the British artillery was entirely unprepared. Success, therefore, evaporated, and additional attacks failed. Private Stanley Green commented on the stunned nature of the surviving attackers: the operation proved very different to the 'visions of thrilling charges and hand to hand combat' he and others had anticipated.[4] The French also failed in attacks that spring, with their artillery outclassed by the heavier German guns. Advancing French troops took serious losses and made only limited gains.

Renewed attacks in May against Aubers and Vimy ridges, in the Second Battle of Artois, also failed with heavy casualties. Supported by inadequate artillery, the British attack on 9 May was defeated by deadly fire from well-dug-in machine guns. The French attack, a week later, was initially successful, and troops rapidly advanced three miles, but the gap was sealed by the Germans before the French reserves could arrive to exploit it.

On 25 September, the British attacked in the coal-mining area of Loos and the French in Champagne. The British employed gas (which the Germans had first used on a large scale at Ypres on 22 April), but with scant effect, the wind blowing it back in their face. The British used heavy artillery with more success. The German lines were breached in the attack at Loos. Captain G. D. Robert of the 8th Devons described the attack under the cover of smoke and gas that 'produced a very passable imitation of a bad London fog'. There was savage German fire from artillery, machine guns and rifles, and casualties, as he noted, 'were at once very heavy and before reaching the first German trench all but two officers were either killed or wounded'. British instructions were to press on across the trenches and to leave following troops to deal with the remaining Germans. The troops crossed two trenches and reached the guns which, 'when taken were red hot ... 750 men went over the parapet and about 130 came back ... though of course many of the wounded were very slightly hurt and gassed and have since rejoined'.[5]

The exploitation of this success, however, was mishandled by the British commanders. Sir John French, the commander of the BEF, did not entrust the reserves to Sir Douglas Haig, whose First Army mounted the attack, and, when they arrived on 26 September, they could make no impact on the German second position which provided a crucial defence in depth. The issue of British reinforcements not being fed into the battle was blamed for the failure and helped discredit French. He was replaced by Haig as commander of the BEF in December.

A failure to benefit from initial success was also the case for the larger-scale French breakthrough in Champagne on 25 September. The French, with good artillery support, broke through the German front line that day, but could not breach the German second line the next day. Further attacks were no more successful. The Germans proved able again to seal the gap, and the failed offensive contributed to French wartime military fatalities of a million men by the end of the year.

As yet, aeroplanes and motor vehicles had not been effectively harnessed to help the offensive and exploit any breakthrough. Motor vehicles would still have been restricted to roads. Cavalry was the only arm of exploitation available, and its potential was limited by the shell-damaged terrain and especially because of defensive firepower. Moreover, once troops had advanced, it was difficult even to recognize, let alone reinforce and exploit success: until wireless technology improved in late 1917, communications remained primitive, and this stultified control of forward operations. This problem was part of a more widespread limitation in command structures, specifically poor communication and, often, cohesion between front-line troops and more senior command levels. In addition, the devastating impact of modern shell fire ripped up the terrain to such an extent that it was difficult to bring up supporting artillery behind any advance, which meant that the impetus of the critical attack could not be sustained unless the enemy had already been substantially weakened. Shell fire also cut the telephone wires from observers on which artillery depended for information on targeting and accuracy, affecting Alan Thomson, for example, in Gallipoli in November 1915.[6]

Although much of the popular discussion of firepower focuses on machine guns, artillery was the real great killer of the war: estimates suggest that high explosive fired by artillery and trench mortars caused up to 60 per cent of all casualties, compared with 15 per cent in the Russo-Japanese War. The relative stability of the trench systems made it worthwhile deploying heavy artillery to bombard them as the guns could be brought up and supplied before the situation changed, as it did in manoeuvre warfare. It was also necessary to provide artillery support in order to batter an enemy's defensive systems. Maurice Hankey, Secretary to the British Committee of Imperial Defence, presciently suggested in 1914 that 'one of the lessons of the present war appears to be that the German infantry are not very formidable unless supported by their highly efficient artillery'.[7] The trenches provided plentiful targets for such bombardment, whether the motivation was attritional or breakthrough. There was also the need to knock out opposing artillery in order to protect one's own troops.

The tactical reasons for a stress on artillery were matched by operational factors. Without often appreciating the difficulties of its effective use in the circumstances of trench warfare, artillery came to be seen as the method to unlock the static front, indeed as a substitute for, or complement to, the offensive spirit of the infantry that had been emphasized in the opening stage of the conflict. J. F. C. ('Boney') Fuller, later a prominent military thinker, but then a British officer on the Western Front, wrote to his mother in August 1915, 'One salient fact stands out throughout history ... whichever side can throw the greatest number of projectiles against the other is the side which has the greatest chance of winning'.[8]

The heavy casualties suffered on all sides by the infantry in the 1915 offensives accentuated the stress on artillery. Confronted by a shortage of ammunition, the Allies used successively more heavy guns (and troops) in their offensives on the Western Front that year, although each was unsuccessful. The French had not envisaged trench warfare and, at the outset of the war, lacked the heavy guns necessary to destroy trenches. Their 75-mm field gun could fire over 15 rounds a minute and had a range of 9,000 yards, but it was designed for the open field, and its flat trajectory and light calibre were unsuited for the conditions of trench warfare. The lack of heavy artillery greatly hindered the French attacks in 1915. However, the numbers of guns increased and, as an instance of the weight of firepower available, the Italians, not the strongest or most industrialized of powers, deployed 1,200 guns for their attack on the Austrians in the Third Battle of the Isonzo in October 1915.

Mass alone did not suffice for artillery. It was also necessary to confront the problems posed by trench warfare, specifically a focus on indirect fire as well as the need for accuracy. Heavier, high-trajectory pieces capable of plunging fire were more effective in trench warfare, but the lack of howitzers in general led to the widespread use of medium and heavy trench mortars which were a cheap alternative. Shrapnel was ineffective against well-entrenched troops, and only high explosive could deal with them. Thus, it was the increase in high-explosive shells, especially of higher calibres, that made artillery more deadly. The spread of steel helmets offered only partial protection, although they were useful against medium and low velocity projectiles and significantly reduced head injuries. In contrast, in Spain, which did not take part in the war, steel helmets were not issued until 1935, and it was only then that the Spanish army was provided with any significant number of medium and heavy guns.

In Western Europe, where the ratio of troops and firepower to space was particularly high, frontal attacks remained costly, as had been the case from the outset of the war. On 8 September 1914, Hankey had written about 'the absolute disregard of human life by the Germans in the recent fighting. Time after time prepared positions have been captured on land in frontal attacks by sheer weight of numbers notwithstanding terrible losses'.[9] These losses in the early stages of the war, like those in the closing campaign in 1918, reflected the large number of troops involved and the advance across the killing zone along an extended front. In intervening campaigns, the front of attack was more compressed, and, as a result, total casualties were reduced, although not the rates of casualties to men engaged.

Frontal attacks were the conventional tactical form in the period, for example, also used across the Atlantic in the Mexican Revolution, especially by the revolutionary general Francisco 'Pacho' Villa. They won him victory at Torreón in 1914, but the tactic was costly even there, and also could be unsuccessful, as with Villa's defeat by Álvaro Obregón in 1915 at Celaya, a battle in which trenches, barbed wire and machine-guns thwarted the attack. In Western Europe, where the ratio of troops and firepower to space was far higher than in Mexico, such methods were much more costly.

The nature of most contemporary European generalship, with its preconceived, usually outdated, ideas and tactics of slogging forward, did not help. Some generals were slow to adopt different approaches, and this failure was to lead to serious criticism as part of the post-war depiction of the conflict. Yet, the criticisms of generalship had a strong political component, both in the 1920s and 1930s, and again in the 1960s when anti-Vietnam War sentiment stoked the fires. In fact, the generalship of the opening stages of trench warfare was not notably worse than at the beginning of other wars, but the fact that the stalemate of the Western Front remained unresolved for so long created the impression that not enough was done to break the deadlock, whereas in practice, the tactics of attack and defence evolved from the outset of trench warfare and continued to do so into 1918 and afterwards. The tactics of 1918, indeed the armies of 1918, were entirely different from those of 1914.

In the case of the British, there was a key change of command in December 1915. Sir John French, the commander of the BEF since the outbreak of the war, was replaced, as a result of his indifferent not to say hostile relations with the French as well as the poor use of his reserves at Loos, by General Sir Douglas Haig, the commander since February of the First Army and a more determined leader than French. Able to give an impression of greater energy, Haig also had better relations with politicians, which proved an increasingly important skill as the war continued and casualties mounted. Duty and dedication played key roles for Haig, but he was less cautious than French, and his optimism was to have dire consequences for Allied troops when he persisted in costly offensives in which his belief in the value of determination could take precedence over the practicalities of the situation on the Western Front.[10] Yet this stubbornness was also to play a key role in enabling him to oppose the German offensive in 1918. Haig's reputation has been very mixed. His faults helped cost many lives, and his management of subordinates was often flawed, not least because he used favouritism to promote those who supported his values, but his willingness to back new technology helped make the army more effective in 1918.[11]

It would be wrong to assume that generals and politicians were entirely unable to appreciate the dilemma posed by the war or unwilling to think about new approaches.[12] In January 1915, Arthur Balfour, former (Conservative) British Prime Minister and a member of the Committee for Imperial Defence, wrote:

> I agree, and I fear everybody must agree, that the notion of driving the Germans back from the West of Belgium to the Rhine by successfully assaulting one line of trenches after another seems a very hopeless affair, and unless some means can be found for breaking their line at some critical point, and threatening their communications, I am unable to see how the deadlock in the West is to be brought to any rapid or satisfactory conclusion.[13]

Balfour sat on the Committee at Asquith's request but, that May, his position changed when he became First Lord of the Admiralty on the formation of the wartime coalition, a step taken in order to lessen the danger of Conservative criticism of the Liberal government. The Conservative party leader, Andrew Bonar Law, became Secretary of State for the Colonies.

1915 saw many attempts to end the deadlock, on land and at sea. Neither side was satisfied with the status quo nor willing to offer realistic peace terms. The Germans played the central role as the 1914 campaign had left them with significant gains, and in order to regain this territory, it was necessary for the Allies to drive the Germans out because the government in Berlin was unwilling to accept a compromise peace that did not include substantial gains.

The situation in 1915 thus underlined the political failure of the German 1914 offensive by obliging the Allies to set aside the defensive option and to try to regain the lost territories, at great cost. Indeed, David Lloyd George, a leading Liberal minister as Chancellor of the Exchequer, who had at first been unsure about Britain going to war, now pressed in a speech in February 1915 for 'a holy war' against German militarism.[14] The 1914 offensive also encouraged German expansionism, and therefore lessened, if not removed, the strategic option for the Germans of a good compromise peace, in the sense of a peace that would work. As a result, the German efforts were devoted to a goal that was not worth the costs and risks it entailed, one that ultimately proved fatal for German stability and territorial integrity, and those of their allies. Intransigence over war goals was scarcely novel, but its consequences proved particularly deadly, and the military and political consequences help explain why total war has been seen by some scholars as a development of the Great War, rather than its cause.[15]

Having gained so much territory, the Germans felt they not only had to hold it but to force their opponents to accept their peace terms. This was the strategic problem for Erich von Falkenhayn, who became Chief of the German General Staff in September 1914 when Moltke was replaced after the failure of the initial campaign. Appreciating that Germany did not have the resources to defeat its enemies in the rapid, decisive campaign required by pre-war doctrine, Falkenhayn, instead, sought a negotiated peace, albeit on terms favourable to Germany. This goal built on earlier discussion, by Moltke the Elder and the academic commentator Hans Delbrück, of the limitations of the concept of decisive victory and the doctrine of a war of annihilation cherished by the General Staff.[16] To develop a matching new operational method, however, proved difficult, not least because of opposition within the officer corps, an issue that revealed the difficulties of implementing policy.

In April 1915, Falkenhayn launched another attack on the Western Front, at Ypres. However, this attack, mounted on 22 April, did not bring any breakthrough even though the Germans used poison gas, a weapon prohibited by The Hague conventions. The chlorine gas caused panic and the Germans were able to gain territory, but they then dug in and proved unable subsequently to regain the initiative. Sir Horace Smith-Dorrien, the commander of the British Second Army, reported heavy German casualties: 'Artillery observing officers claim to have mown them down over and over again during the day'.[17]

Gas proved deadly for individual opponents and, initially, devastating at the tactical level, but it was also difficult to use consistently and only accounted for about four per cent of fatal casualties. Gas warfare was a complex business that required a mix of technical skill, scientific knowledge and tactical ability, as well as favourable weather conditions for operations to be successful. Aside from the problem of wind direction possibly blowing gas back into the faces of attackers, any attempt quickly to exploit the use of gas meant advancing into it; there was also the increasing resort to gas masks by defenders. At first primitive, these rapidly became more effective. Gas thus not only added to the horror of fighting. It also forced the pace of new equipment and tactics, as effective ways of employing gas and also anti-gas defences were adopted. Mustard gas, which harmed by contact (as well as by the ingestion that had proved fatal with the earlier chlorine and phosgene gas attacks), was first used in 1917, by the Germans at Passchendaele. Mustard gas was primarily an incapacitant, burning and blistering its victims, and so compounding the problems facing medical and support services.[18]

Despite the attack at Ypres in April 1915, Falkenhayn focused on remaining on the defensive in the West, while trying to force Russia into a separate peace. This policy was an admission of Allied strength on the Western Front, as well as of the difficulties of offensive warfare there. The legacy of the fighting in late 1914 was also significant, namely German failure at Ypres contrasted with the more promising situation in Poland. Attacking in Poland also drew on the prospect of Austrian support, as well as offering assistance to Austria against Russian attack and in the event of a deterioration of its strategic situation elsewhere. Such a deterioration indeed happened when Italy came into the war on the Allied side in May, and was further threatened by Allied pressure on Turkey. Italy's entry into the war put pressure on Austria, which, in turn, underlined the need to strengthen the German position in Eastern Europe. Thus, the strategic interrelationship of real and potential fronts was amply shown. The role of personalities in strategic decisions also emerged clearly with Falkenhayn pressed by Hindenburg and Ludendorff to send troops to the Eastern Front.

The leading German military success in 1915 was their major achievements in Poland. The Russians were defeated at Gorlice-Tarnów in May and large portions of Russian territory were conquered,

Warsaw falling on 5 August. Russian defeats, combined with Anglo-French failure at Gallipoli and the German offer of Serbian territory (once conquered), led Bulgaria to decide to join the Central Powers and it entered the war on 28 September. The activity in the Black Sea of the German warships under Turkish flag underlined the sense of comparative advantage between the two sides in Eastern Europe.

Nevertheless, it is understandable that the 1915 German campaign in Poland is not as famous as the Tannenberg campaign in 1914. Falkenhayn did not fulfil his goals in part because breakthroughs at the front did not produce strategic results, either in terms of the collapse of the Russian army or politically. Moreover, there was no encirclement of large Russian forces comparable to those seen with Operation Barbarossa in 1941. The Russians lost many troops in 1915, largely because there was a decision to stand and fight, rather than retreat, in the initial stages of the German offensive, but, once the decision to retreat had been taken, it was carried out with some success. Furthermore, the retreat and the resulting loss of Russia's Polish salient ensured that Russia had a shorter frontline, and, thus, one that could be more readily held.

Yet, pushed back by the end of September to a line from Riga along the River Dvina and then south via Pinsk, the Russians had lost much territory as well as many casualties. Although the German advance was slowed by logistical issues and the impact of autumn rains on a poor road system, they had captured more than the Polish salient. Brest Litovsk, taken on 25 August, had been followed by Grodno on 2 September and Vilnius on 19 September. Courland (western Latvia) had also been overrun. These were very substantial losses, although their distance from the centres of Russian power in St Petersburg and Moscow ensured that they did not have the strategic effect that comparable losses of territory in France would have had. Suffering over a million casualties greatly weakened the Russian army as did the vast quantities of *matériel* abandoned in the retreat.

German successes increased the pressure on the Allies to react by taking steps, both on the Western Front and elsewhere, to assist Russia where, amidst rising inflation, social discontent and political pressure for change, Tsar Nicholas II mistakenly dismissed and took the place of his more impressive uncle, Grand Duke Nicholas, as commander-in-chief. In June, Russian defeats led the French General Staff to conclude that the war was without direction on the Allies' part and required a co-ordinated strategic planning that France must provide.

The Germans also attacked at sea, although the plan to fall upon part of the British Grand Fleet with their entire High Seas Fleet, and thus achieve a superiority that would enable them to inflict serious casualties that affected the overall situation at sea, was not pursued. Instead, on 23 January, a German force of four battlecruisers and four light cruisers put to sea in order to lay mines in the Firth of Forth, threatening the British base at Rosyth, and also to attack the British fishing boats on Dogger Bank in the North Sea, boats which were seen as an Intelligence asset. The interception of a German naval signal led to a loss of surprise, but the British missed the opportunity to deploy their navy so as to cut off the German force. On the morning of 24 January, in the Battle of Dogger Bank, five British battlecruisers under David Beatty engaged the Germans, although it proved difficult to close, and this problem enabled the German ships to concentrate on his lead ship, the flagship HMS *Lion*, which took serious damage. By contrast, confused signalling, the fear of submarine attack and a lack of initiative by subordinate commanders ensured that the British force focused on SMS *Blücher*, a pre-dreadnought armoured cruiser, and this was sunk, but the other German ships were able to escape. The British were also affected by the contrast between the long-range at which shells could be fired and their limited number of hits. At sea, as on land, successful artillery tactics proved difficult to achieve. Yet, the British Grand Fleet was becoming both absolutely and relatively stronger, with five newly operational dreadnoughts added to it in the winter of 1914–15.

There was even less surface naval warfare elsewhere. Italy's decision to abandon Germany and Austria, with which it had agreed a naval convention in 1913, and, instead, to join Britain and France in May 1915, ensured that the Mediterranean was controlled by the latter, with Austria and Turkey unable to contest their dominance. A French squadron at Corfu and most of the Italian fleet at Taranto confined the Austrians to the Adriatic and prevented them from breaking out into the Mediterranean. This was a significant outcome as the Austrians had a series of bases on the Dalmatian coast as well as a large fleet which exerted considerable pressure on the Italians, not least by bombarding coastal towns on the Adriatic Sea.[19]

In the Black Sea, the Russians had more warships than the Turks, and, on 6 November 1914, mined the entrance to the Bosporus.[20] However, the following year, a Turkish naval attack on the Russian port of Odessa underlined the risk posed to any Russian amphibious operation to the Bosporus in support of the Gallipoli campaign. The Russians, in turn, used Black Sea routes to reinforce troops in Anatolia in 1916, landing them at Trebizon.

In the Baltic, the Russian fleet was weaker than the forces the Germans could deploy if they moved in some of their High Seas Fleet units from the North Sea via the Kiel Canal. This German capability encouraged Russian caution, which was also in keeping with long-established Russian doctrine and with the Russian emphasis in the Baltic on local operations. Defeat by the Japanese navy at Tsushima in 1905 was scarcely an encouragement for bolder operations. The Russians laid extensive minefields to protect the Gulf of Finland and staged raids into the Southern Baltic in order to mine German shipping routes, while the Germans, in turn, also laid mines.

The Atlantic trading system on which the British economy rested was the prime target for German naval warfare by 1915. Trade played the key role in mobilizing the capital and securing the *matériel* on which Allied war-making depended. Neither Britain nor France had an industrial system to match that of Germany which, by 1914, had forged ahead of Britain in iron and steel production. The Allies were dependent on America for machine tools, mass production plants and much else, including the parts of shells. American industrial output was equivalent to that of the whole of Europe by 1914, and the British ability to keep Atlantic sea lanes open ensured that America made a vital contribution to the Allied war effort before its formal entry into the war, although the cost of this contribution to Britain in particular was heavy. French and Russian transfers of gold to the Bank of England helped support sterling and the ability of Britain to raise loans and credits in America, while South Africa's role in the imperial war effort was greatly enhanced by its production of gold. Transoceanic trade and naval dominance also allowed the British and French to draw on the resources of their far-flung colonial empires.

Submarines were a new type of an old challenge, the commerce raider, and, in confronting it, Britain was helped once again by geography. Whereas France had many anchorages and an Atlantic coastline from which Britain could be readily attacked (which created serious problems in 1940 when France was conquered), Germany had only restricted access to the high seas. This situation reflected not only the limited number of German anchorages, but also the extent to which Britain could try to block the English Channel and the North Sea through anti-submarine measures, particularly minefields and by focusing interception efforts.

Nevertheless, German submarines proved a serious challenge. Submarines had not featured prominently in naval operations over the previous decade, for example, in the Russo-Japanese or Balkan wars. Indeed, their potential had been greatly underestimated by most commentators.[21] Tirpitz, the administrative head of the German navy (Wilhelm II was its Supreme Commander), was a late convert to submarines. Britain, which had only launched its first submarine in 1901, had the largest number – 89 – at the outbreak of the war, but had devoted insufficient thought to the defence of warships and merchantmen against submarines.

In September 1914, the first warships sunk by submarines included three British cruisers (all to the submarine *U-9* on 22 September) and one German cruiser. As a result of this threat, the British Grand Fleet was obliged to withdraw from the North Sea and from its base of Scapa Flow in the Orkney Islands in 1914 to new bases on the north-west coast of Scotland; it did not return to Scapa Flow until 1915, when the base's defences had been strengthened. That year, Admiral Sir John Jellicoe, the commander of the Grand Fleet, observed 'I am most absolutely adverse to moving the Battle Fleet without a full destroyer screen'.[22]

The Germans stepped up submarine production once war had begun, but relatively few were ordered, and most were delivered behind schedule. In part, this was because of problems with organizing and supplying construction, but it was largely due to a lack of commitment from within the German navy to submarine warfare (instead, its preference was for surface warships which required more maintenance in wartime), and, crucially, a longstanding concentration of industrial resources on the army, a pattern that was to be repeated in the Second World War. As a result, although submarines swiftly affected the conduct of operations, the Germans did not have the numbers to match their aspirations. In early 1915, only 29 submarines were available and, by the end of the year, only 59. Moreover, to move submerged, they were dependent on battery motors that had to be recharged on the surface where they were highly vulnerable to attack. In addition, submarines were slow which lessened their chance of hitting a warship moving under full steam.

Submarines, however, benefited over time from an increase in their range, seaworthiness, speed and comfort, from improvements in the accuracy, range and speed of torpedoes which, by 1914, could travel 7,000 yards at 45 knots, and from the limited effectiveness of anti-submarine weaponry. These improvements reflected the possibilities for war-making of a modern industrial society with its ability to plan, design, manufacture and introduce better specifications for instruments and processes. Submarines came to play a major role in naval planning, both operationally, in terms of trying to deny bodies of water to opponents, and tactically; in practice, merchant shipping, not warships, proved the most important target for German submarines and ensured that they were given a role in strategic planning. By attacking merchantmen, the Germans were demonstrating that the sea, far from being a source of protection for Britain, could in fact be a barrier to safe re-supply.

Operating commerce raiding by the well-established prize rules was restricted submarine warfare, and without regard to these rules, unrestricted. The prize rules were essentially to stop suspected vessels, search them for contraband, and, if contraband was found, to take them into port where the ship could be condemned by a court as a prize. If it was impossible to get the vessel into port, the prize rules stipulated that it was to be scuttled after provision had been made for the crew and passengers by allowing them into the lifeboats or holding them on board. This approach entailed the submarine coming to the surface to stop the vessel and, subsequently, sinking it usually by gunfire: submarines carried a deck artillery piece as well as torpedoes, and the former used less ordnance and was more accurate. However, coming to the surface entailed the risks of being detected and sunk.

In 1915, the Germans increased the threat and tempo of their assault on Allied shipping by declaring, on 4 February, unrestricted submarine warfare, which began on 18 February. This policy entailed attacking all shipping, Allied and neutral, and without warning, within the designated zone, RMS *Lusitania*, the largest liner on the transatlantic run, was sunk off Ireland by *U-20* on 7 May. Among the 1,192 passengers and crew lost, there were 128 Americans and there was savage criticism in America. In response, the Germans offered concessions over the unrestricted warfare, which was finally cancelled on 18 September in order to avoid provoking American intervention, which both Bethmann-Hollweg, the Chancellor, and Falkenhayn wished to avoid. Aside from the impact on neutrals, Germany anyway was unprepared for such a war as it lacked sufficient submarines, trained crew or bases to mount an effective blockade of Britain. The Germans sunk 748,000 tons of British shipping in 1915, but Britain and its empire launched 1.3 million tons.

The Germans were not alone in attempting to transform the overall stalemate by mounting a more vigorous attack. The Allies also sought to do so by attacking on land and by using their naval superiority. The former proved unsuccessful, not least as their armies had not mastered the problems posed by the numbers involved on the constricted Western Front, nor by the tactical strength of trench warfare. Neither factor was as pertinent on the Eastern Front, as the density of troops was lower on what was a more extended frontage, but the Russians were outfought by the Germans, and the British and French were unable to bring their troops to bear there.

Instead, there were attempts to combine alliance politics with military capability, by extending the Alliance and weakening the German bloc, with the Mediterranean serving as the key forum of

Allied activity and one in which they could employ naval superiority, both in itself and, by covering amphibious operations, as a force multiplier. This policy entailed attempts to bring Italy and Greece into the war on the Allied side and to support Serbia and Russia, while weakening Austria and knocking Turkey out of the conflict.

Naval power offered a chance to attack the centre of Turkish power, a policy which geography made inapplicable for Germany and Austria, and that appeared to its proponents to be a viable alternative to the effort required in any confrontation with the Germans on the Western Front. This search for the indirect approach appeared to conform to British strategic traditions, notably the focus on secondary theatres, especially Portugal and Spain, in the conflict with Napoleon. Such a focus would permit Britain to use its naval power and to achieve success with its relatively modest army without weakening the latter by attacking the main opposing force. This policy would also enable Britain to direct a campaign without relying excessively on France.

The plan to bring naval pressure to bear on the Turkish capital, Constantinople (modern Istanbul), was energetically pushed by Winston Churchill, the dynamic, but not always perceptive, First Lord of the Admiralty. This plan entailed first forcing a passage through the Dardanelles, the strait from the Aegean to the Sea of Marmara, on the other side of which lies the Bosporus, the passage to the Black Sea on which Constantinople lies. The Anglo-French naval attempt to force the passage on 18 March, however, was stopped by mines, shore batteries and an unwillingness to accept further losses after three battleships (two British and one French) were sunk and three more were badly damaged.

The naval experts had been aware of the hazards posed by the mines and shore batteries of the Dardanelles, not least because, before the war, the British naval mission to Turkey had provided advice on mine-laying,[23] but their caution was thrust aside by Churchill, although the First Sea Lord, Jackie Fisher, bears some of the responsibility for the debacle, not least because he and Churchill could not work together easily. The naval attempt on the Dardanelles was not renewed, a course that has been criticized, although the Turkish forts had not run out of ammunition (as was claimed later) and the problems of suppressing the defences remained acute.

The failure of this naval assault was followed that year by an attempt to gain control of the shores of the Dardanelles by landing troops on 25 April, the Gallipoli expedition, an attempt, however, that was flawed in both conception and execution. A lack of appropriate equipment was a serious problem. The British had been building powered landing-craft from 1914, but most of the British and French (both categories that very much included imperial units) troops that went ashore in amphibious operations along the Gallipoli Peninsula were landed from ordinary ships, in other words, steam-driven vessels that could not beach, although SS *River Clyde* was run aground at Cape Helles. As a result of this problem, troops were landed into dinghies, a vulnerable situation, or into shallows that in fact were far from shallow. Each method was difficult and left the troops gravely exposed to defensive fire.

The Gallipoli landings were further hindered by the extent to which the Turks had strengthened local defences under German direction, and by poor Allied generalship and planning. Despite a successful deception that confused the Turks as to the likely landing zones, the Allies failed to push initial advantages, with the result that their advances were contained. The initial assault was not pressed forward hard enough instead of digging in almost as soon as the men were ashore. This failure of initiative left commanding high ground to the Turks who quickly occupied it. Subsequently, Turkish fighting skills proved important, as was the general strength of defensive firepower particularly when unsuppressed by artillery fire. Aside from a failure to anticipate the numbers the Turks could deploy and the strength of the defence, the Allies' flawed assessment of Turkish fighting quality and skill was an issue, not least as it led to an under-rating of a resilience and bravery that drew in part on a strong Turkish nationalism.[24] The *Notes on the Turkish Army* published by the British army in March 1915 were misleading:

> The Turkish army, which suffered to a very great
> extent both in men and material during the last

Balkan wars [1912–13], have since then been reorganised, and … undergone a severe course of training under the supervision of German officers …. Although a great improvement has taken place during the last two years, it cannot truthfully be said that Turkish troops are even now in any way equal, except in courage, to those of the Balkan states with whom they were lately at war.

The guide did note the recent supply by the Germans of some modern quick-firing artillery, but it was this misunderstanding of Turkish troops which helped lead to disastrous tactical errors.[25]

The fighting at Gallipoli rapidly became static, with the tiny, exposed Allied positions made even grimmer by the heat, dysentery and, eventually, typhoid. In May, Lieutenant-General Sir William Birdwood of the Indian army, the commander of the Anzac (Australian and New Zealand) force, reported that deficiencies in the attacking force had ensured that he was pushed back onto the defensive and 'practically reduced to a state of siege',[26] in the face of repeated Turkish attacks. Moreover, mobility had been lost, Birdwood complaining in June: 'It seems quite ridiculous that we should be within ten yards of each other, and yet I am unable to get into their trenches'.[27] On the night of 6–7 August, the British made fresh advances and landings, but a combination of poor command decisions and firm Turkish resistance led again to failure.

The Gallipoli operation encapsulated much of the problem with the offensive during the war, whether mounted by the Allies or by the Central Powers. Allied failure at Gallipoli in part reflected a lack of experience of modern conflict, notably that the campaign occurred early in the war before the learning curve produced solutions to trench warfare. As a result, according to one scholar, 'tactics ate strategy at Gallipoli'.[28] Gallipoli, indeed, was an instance of how, repeatedly during the war, strategic conception was not matched by tactical and operational success, which was partially a matter of the absence of marked capability gaps in combat effectiveness between the combatants. This absence should not be seen as the product of military failure, but rather of the fact that there was no failure creating such a gap. This absence of marked capability gaps was related to the tactical and operational strength enjoyed by the defensive, especially the role of entrenched firepower.

There were also the specific problems caused by the British failure to develop an amphibious capability and strategy prior to the war, which ensured that the Gallipoli campaign rested on a political drive and suffered from inadequate preparation, specifically the lack of a relevant planning and command structure. The Allies also suffered from the degree to which the concentration of troops and *matériel* on the Western Front meant that insufficient munitions and high-quality troops were sent to Gallipoli. Major-General Sir Alexander Godley's explanation of failure underlined the need to consider both sides, although, in fact, he also showed questionable leadership:

> the lack of fresh reinforcements, both in April and in August, the strength and superiority of the enemy, in troops, guns and positions, were the true causes of why we did not get across the peninsula and it was not on account of bad plans, or failure of the troops, or bad orders, or want of water, or want of co-operation with the Navy.[29]

Gallipoli captured different aspects of military experience during the war, including the continual nature of exposure to the pressure of battle. This relentlessness was not unprecedented, as it had been seen in lengthy sieges, but the scale was far larger in the Great War. John Monash, an Australian brigade commander, wrote to his wife in May:

> We have been amusing ourselves by trying to discover the longest period of absolute quiet. We have been fighting now continuously for 22 days, all day and all night, and most of us think that absolutely the longest period during which there was absolutely no sound of gun or rifle fire, throughout the whole of that time, was ten seconds. One says he was able

on one occasion to count fourteen, but none believe
him.[30]

Others also noted the intensity of fire, Birdwood writing on 18 May:

> We have daily and nightly fights with the Turks, and,
> indeed, I do not think there has been a single half
> hour since we landed without a rattle of musketry or
> shrapnel fire. At night, the former constantly grows
> into a regular roar, the Turks expending thousands of
> rounds of ammunition.[31]

Monash also described the extent to which troops were part of an
industrial process, with a specialization of function and intensity of
organization that matched, and connected with, features of contemporary industrial society:

> We have got our battle procedure now thoroughly
> well organized. To a stranger it would probably look
> like a disturbed ant-heap with everybody running
> a different way, but the thing is really a triumph of
> organization. There are orderlies carrying messages,
> staff officers with orders, lines of ammunition carriers,
> water carriers, bomb carriers, stretcher bearers,
> burial parties, sandbag parties, periscope hands,
> pioneers, quartermaster's parties, and reinforcing
> troops, running about all over the place, apparently
> in confusion but yet everything works as smoothly
> as on a peace parade, although the air is thick with
> clamour and bullets and bursting shells, and bombs
> and flares.[32]

The Gallipoli campaign led British submarines to pass through the
Dardanelles and to operate in the Sea of Marmara against Turkish
supply routes, and also led to the arrival of German submarines in the
Mediterranean. They sank two British battleships taking part in the

campaign, challenging the Allied position off Gallipoli, and went on to attack Allied shipping in the Mediterranean, affecting, for example, the post to and from British and Dominion troops at Gallipoli.[33] In a world by then used to regular postal communications, the loss of postal deliveries could severely weaken morale. The submarine threat led the French and Italians to withdraw their major ships from the Adriatic and also led to the laying of mines in the Straits of Otranto at the entrance to the Adriatic, in order to keep hostile submarines in the Adriatic.

Aside from putting pressure on the Turks, it was also hoped that the Gallipoli operation would unlock the Balkans for the Allies. These hopes provided those who were not privy to strategic planning with a sense that the operation had great significance. Alan Thomson, a British officer, wrote to his wife Edith on 24 September: 'Don't worry about me sweetheart. I daresay we shall get Romania and Greece in and if that happens we may be able between us to hold up the Germans in Serbia …. If the Germans don't get through to Turkey, I think the latter will give in'. He returned to this theme on 7 October, noting the report that Russia and Greece were preparing to attack Bulgaria which had declared war on Serbia on 28 September, and again on 20 November.[34]

The Gallipoli campaign was finally abandoned after very heavy casualties, with the successful withdrawal of the invasion force in night-time operations on 18–19 and 19–20 December 1916 and 8–9 January 1917 the only impressive feature of the operation. British hopes from the campaign had been cruelly disabused and it was not to be repeated, although, paradoxically, failure at Gallipoli led subsequently to greater interest in amphibious operations. However, plans for a landing on the Belgian coast in 1916–17 were not brought to fruition,[35] while earlier pressure on Turkish communications in the Gulf of Alexandretta was not developed.

The Turks also proved a difficult foe elsewhere, notably when the British, in order to provide forward protection for the Persian Gulf and India, tried to conquer Mesopotamia, modern Iraq. A lunge toward Baghdad was stopped in November 1915 and the British force besieged at Kut had to surrender the following April.

Yet the German hopes from the Turks had also been disabused. They had planned to use them to further a policy of *Insurgierung* and thus to damage, if not overthrow, much of the empires of their competitors. The Turks were expected to fight both Russia and Britain and to provide the leadership for pan-Islamic revolts, which, in the words of the German diplomat, Rudolph Nadolny, were 'to light a torch from the Caucasus to Calcutta'. The German leadership planned through war, rebellion or revolution to extend hostilities, especially to Egypt, the Caucasus and India. This seemed a way to put pressure on Russia in the Caucusus and to threaten the strategic links and economic resources of the British empire.

In the event, most of the 270 million Muslims in the world did not respond to the declaration of *jihad* (holy war) on behalf of the Caliph, Mehmet V, the Turkish Sultan, on 14 November 1914. Within the Muslim world, pan-Turkism was widely considered an unacceptable part of pan-Islamism, a situation that was readily apparent in Egypt where German promises of independence from Britain required Turkish troops to make them real. However, there was no supporting rising in Egypt and the Turkish attack on the Suez Canal was repelled on 1–3 February 1915 by Gurkha and Indian units, supported by British and French warships. Turkish pressure on the Aden protectorate was also unsuccessful. In 1915, Indian forces helped maintain British power there, in Oman, and in the British sphere of influence in Persia, with attacks on Muscat, Jask and Chahbar all defeated. In India, both the Muslim League and the Indian National Congress supported the war effort.

In a 1920 discussion of the recent world war, General Hermann von Kuhl, Chief of Staff of Army Group Kronprinz Rupprecht, noted that the pre-war analysis of Britain by the General Staff had been mistaken in assuming that the Germans would be able to stir up Muslim opposition and that the British would face serious native uprisings in India and Egypt. Instead, Britain had been able to draw more troops from India than the Germans had anticipated.[36] In this sense, once again, failed judgements about other peoples had proved enormously costly. Yet, concern about the possibility of pan-Islamic subversion encouraged the British to take an active stance, as with the deployment of troops into Mesopotamia from November 1914.[37]

By February 1915, Turkish defeats ensured that German hopes of a holy war directed against their opponents remained a dream. The Turks fought well in defence, but were less effective on the offensive, in part because of poor leadership in the Caucasus by Enver Pasha, the Minister for War. In harsh winter weather, he led the Third Army through difficult terrain towards the city of Kars, only to be defeated between 23 December 1914 and 17 January 1915 at the battle of Sarikamish, suffering heavy losses. This defeat led to the Russians gaining the initiative, which helped create the background to the Turkish resort to what became genocide against the Armenian minority whom they saw as pro-Russian. Operations in the Caucasus also increased the importance of neighbouring Persia (Iran) which was unable to protect its neutrality. Turkish, British and Russian forces all operated in Persia, the Russians occupying the north in 1915 taking the important city of Tabriz after defeating the Turks at the battle of Safian on 26 January. The Turks were still useful to the Germans in that they engaged large Allied forces, rather like Italy in 1940–43, although in the Second World War there was no alternative Western Front to which to commit British and American troops until 1944. Whereas, in the Great War, most of Germany's colonies had fallen rapidly and ceased to absorb large numbers of Allied troops, this was not true of the war with Turkey.

This conflict was not the limit of the Allied commitments outside Europe as the Allies faced serious problems across much of the Muslim world. These problems were not so much due to Turkish encouragement, however, as to continuing resistance to European imperialism that had begun in response to the original attempts to extend European control. Thus, for example, the Italians faced ongoing problems in Libya, which they had invaded in 1911, as did the British in Somaliland. Italian firepower had defeated Libyan forces at Asaba in 1913, but the Libyans then resorted to guerrilla tactics and the Italians were untrained for such a conflict. In 1915, an Italian force of 4,000 troops was largely destroyed after its local auxiliaries turned against it, and the Italians were driven back to the coast. Italian pressure in Libya was dramatically reduced once Italy entered the war in May 1915, with troops moved to fight Austria. However, despite the efforts of German agents seeking wide-ranging Muslim action, fears of successful Turkish and German support for the Senussi sect which opposed the Italians proved exaggerated.[38] An invasion of Egypt by Senussi was checked by the British near the frontier.

In the Horn of Africa, the Royal Navy was used to block the possibility of Turkish support for opposition in Somaliland. The British struggle there with the Dervishes under Mullah Sayyid Muhammad 'Abdille Hassan (the 'Mad Mullah' to the British), who, in 1899, had declared holy war on Christians, had long been difficult. During the Great War, there was not the troops to spare for a major offensive against them, but there were British successes, including the capture of the Dervish fort at Shimberberis in February 1915. The naval blockade also became more effective, hitting the supply of arms and ammunition to the Dervishes. Furthermore, the Turkish failure to break through into Egypt in 1915, and their defeat in Arabia at the hands of the Arab Rising meant that the Dervishes did not receive the foreign assistance they sought. This defeat in Arabia owed much to the British encouragement of Sharif Hussein's revolt against Turkish rule, encouragement which reflected the skill of the Arab Bureau established by the British to organize operations in the Arab lands.[39]

Like Britain, France faced concerns about the impact of Muslim opposition in its North African territories. The French, however, suppressed a revolt in Tunisia that broke out in September 1915, controlling the situation from October 1916, and French fears that Allied failure against the Turks in 1915 might lead to serious trouble in Algieria, for which they had no spare troops due to the fighting on the Western Front, proved misplaced.[40]

The French faced opposition further south with the 1915–16 Volta-Bani War in modern Burkina Faso, then part of French West Africa. Beginning on 17 November 1915, in part in response to conscription by the colonial government, this was the largest military challenge the French had faced in the region since they had conquered it, and one that led to the deployment of a substantial French force: 5,000 men, mostly West African troops. Although lacking comparable firepower, with consequences seen in battles such as Boho (1916), the rebels sought to develop tactics in order to weaken the French columns, to reduce local support for the French and to limit the impact of their firepower. The French themselves employed brutal 'anti-societal' warfare: targeting their opponents' farms, herds, wells and families in order to destroy the environment among which they operated, an interesting comparison with German atrocities in France and Belgium. Once the rebels' centres had been subjugated, organized opposition to French rule ceased. About 30,000 of the local population had been killed.

The ability to suppress colonial opposition was an aspect of the successful articulation of the British and French imperial systems on a global scale. This articulation was unprecedented in scale and posed considerable political and organizational challenges. The French deployed imperial forces on the Western Front, in the Balkans, and in their operations against German colonies: Togo and Cameroon. Moreover, alongside the Volta-Bani War, the French benefited from massive support from their colonies. About 140,000 French West African troops were deployed on the Western Front,[41] and the French colonial authorities successfully introduced conscription in Senegal. Because they did not wish to divert national troops from the Western Front, the French deployed a considerable number of imperial troops at Gallipoli, their division in the original assault being part of the *Corps Expéditionnaire d'Orient* and including North African and Senegalese troops.

The experience of different military conditions established disruptive norms, Birdwood noting in Gallipoli that 'the Martinique and Guadeloupe troops [from French Caribbean colonies] are treated in precisely the same way as if they were Frenchmen, which from our Indian Army point of view strikes one as curious'.[42] At the same time, there were serious inequalities in the French treatment of African troops, with paternalist attitudes on the part of the officers linked to infantilization of the soldiers.[43] Colonial units were frequently committed to costly assault roles, notably with the use of Senegalese *Tirailleurs* in the unsuccessful Nivelle offensive on the Aisne in 1917.

The Indian army was in a poor state at the outbreak of the war and its operations were to be hindered by the division of military and political direction between Britain and India. Nevertheless, more than 800,000 Indian soldiers, all volunteers, fought for the British in the war, so that, far from the British having to garrison South Asia, it was a crucial source of manpower, both freeing up British troops for duties elsewhere and also providing a substantial number of effective troops. Large numbers of Indians were used on the Western Front at first, a corps arriving in October 1914, but the climate proved very damaging and many died or became ill as a result. The infantry were withdrawn to the Middle East in November 1915, although the cavalry remained. Indian troops were also used in substantial numbers in the Mediterranean and Middle East: they greatly reinforced Egypt in 1914, repulsing the Turkish advance on the Suez Canal in 1915, and were also sent to Gallipoli in 1915 and Salonica in 1916. In part in order to protect the British position in the Persian Gulf and further east, there was also a major commitment to Mesopotamia (Iraq) where five Indian divisions as well as cavalry and other forces played a major role. They captured Basra from the Turks in November 1914, protecting British oil interests in south-west Persia, and advanced into Mesopotamia the following year. The Indians were also active elsewhere. A force of over 10,000 troops was sent to Mombasa in October 1914 and the Indians took a major role in the East Africa campaign until the end of the year. The Indian contingent there was never larger than 15,000 men but the casualty level, largely due to illness, was such that over three times that number were sent from India by the end of the war. The impact of raising troops in the Punjab, the major region in India for recruitment to the British Indian army, was such that it became a virtual 'home front' for the British war effort.[44]

Australian and New Zealand troops played a key role in the Gallipoli campaign, although there were more British troops there than tends to be appreciated, especially in Australasia, while the French presence would surprise most British as well as Australasian readers. Australian, New Zealand and Canadian troops were sent to the Western Front, the Canadian 1st Division arriving in France in February 1915,[45] while South Africans captured German South-West Africa in 1915, resistance ending there on 9 July.

This conquest of German South-West Africa was a key success in the drive to conquer the German overseas empire. Far from being a footnote to the war in Europe, this was a difficult struggle. Whereas, prior to 1815, the British essentially had to capture a few bases, principally port cities, in order to secure the conquest of French colonies, now the German colonies enjoyed control of extensive interiors that posed a more serious military challenge to would-be conquerors, and one that amphibious operations were less obviously able to secure. Although invaded by British and French forces from August 1914, Cameroon did not finally fall until February 1916, when Mora, the major base in the north, was captured.

This point was made abundantly clear in the lengthy struggle to defeat German forces in East Africa, a struggle that continued to the end of the war, as, adopting a vigorous offensive campaigning, Lieutenant-Colonel Paul von Lettow-Vorbeck, the German commander, successfully avoided destruction by far larger Allied forces. In 1914–15, he launched raids into the neighbouring British colony of Kenya, making the railway there his particular target. In turn, a major Allied attack in the spring of 1916 led to an effective delaying retreat by the Germans in which disease hit the far larger Allied force. From December 1917, Lettow-Vorbeck took the war south into the Portuguese colony of Mozambique before raiding into the British colonies of Southern and Northern Rhodesia (Zimbabwe and Zambia). Undefeated, he surrendered on 23 November 1918 only as a result of the official end of the war.

A war hero, who subsequently took up anti-democratic far-right politics, although later opposing the Nazis, Lettow-Vorbeck's African career was to be the basis for a post-war legend. The idea of a brave and undefeated leader who fought off larger numbers, provided a posthumous defence of the German empire and it was claimed that his *askari* (African soldiers) were loyal to the end. This account ignored the extent to which (like the Allied African forces) many deserted (many did not), as well as the coercion involved in obtaining

African support in a conflict that led to maybe 700,000 deaths in East Africa.[46]

In Africa, the lengthy struggle also meant that Allied forces faced formidable logistical hurdles. Confronting them required the recruitment of large numbers of African porters, and this was an aspect of the acute disruption caused by the war: many porters died, while the process of recruitment itself was very disruptive.[47] The war in Africa was very different to that in Europe. The ability to cope with disease was critical, while, given the distances and the poverty of the transport links, the movement of supplies by land played a major part in capability and operations. Operationally and tactically, manoeuvre and surprise were crucial in Africa, while concentrated firepower, especially heavy artillery, was less important than in Europe. As a result, the Great War in Africa involved a 'traditional' form of warfare.

Alongside porters, many Africans were recruited to fight. For example, the impact of disease and an absence of new manpower, ensured that the all-white Rhodesia Regiment was supplemented from 1916 by the Rhodesia Native Regiment which also served in East Africa, although, in 1918, many of its members died in the great influenza pandemic.[48]

Imperial support was critical, even decisive for Britain. Without the empire, the British would have been unable to mount offensive operations in the Middle East, would have been largely reduced to the use of the Royal Navy against German colonies and would have been forced to introduce conscription earlier than in 1916 in order to support operations on the Western Front. The British use of imperial forces was helped by the absence of an enemy in East Asia, with the exception of the German base at Tsingtao in China, which was captured by Britain's ally, Japan, in 1914. The situation was to be very different in the Second World War.

The participation of the British empire also involved tensions and rivalries. In the case of South Africa, since 1910 a Dominion, the defeat of the Indian forces at Tanga in East Africa, combined with South Africa's victory over German South-West Africa, to reinforce white South African racial prejudices, while the war also served as an opportunity to push territorial claims. Thus, in return for its dispatch of troops to East Africa, where they arrived in January 1916, South Africa sought to obtain the strategic anchorage of Delagoa Bay in Mozambique from Portugal in exchange for part of German East Africa. The issue was confused by the claim of the British South Africa Company, which administered Southern Rhodesia (now Zimbabwe), that it be given control of Delagoa Bay and the Mozambique port of Beira, a key outlet for Southern Rhodesia. The Company's Directors argued in 1917 that the South African government was 'not progressive', but the British government did not take the issue forward.

Nevertheless, the South African government failed both to obtain the desired territory (Portugal refused) and to unite the white South African population in war. Instead, the Great War reinforced the division among the white South Africans, specifically between the Boers, many of whom were pro-German, some rebelling unsuccessfully in 1914, and the Anglos, and this division affected the national memory of the conflict, although other factors also played a role. Thus, whereas the South Africans who died at Delville Wood on the Western Front during German counter-attacks in the Somme Offensive in July 1916, and are remembered,[49] fought as a unit, those in East Africa frequently changed brigades and had scant chance to develop a level of fraternity.[50] As far as tensions among the Allies were concerned, a serious absence of co-ordination between Portuguese and other Allied forces in Mozambique in 1917–18 gravely hindered operations there against the Germans. This factor helped enable Lettow-Vorbeck to hold out.

Aside from mobilizing their empires, Britain and France also strengthened their alliance system by winning over Italy, which, moreover, was thus subtracted from Germany's potential system. Instead, the Central Powers would have now to man a new front along the long common frontier between Italy and Austria, which, from the Anglo-French perspective, was the prime strategic benefit to be gained from the alliance with Rome. In 1914, Italy had chosen not to come to the aid of Germany and Austria, its allies since 1882. Instead, it was won over by the Treaty of London, signed on 26 April 1915, by which Britain, France and Russia promised Italy extensive gains from Austria: the Trentino, South Tyrol, Trieste, Gorizia, Istria and northern Dalmatia.[51] This meant that these territories, presented in Italy to the public as the last stage of the war for independence from Austria, had to be conquered. Germany had bullied Austria into offering the Trentino to Italy, but Austria was not willing to match the Allied offer elsewhere.

Only the Socialist Party opposed the war when it was voted on by Parliament on 20 May. The rest of the political world wished to see Italy become a great power, and Antonio Salandra, the conservative Prime Minister, presented Italy's policy as 'sacred selfishness'. Benito Mussolini, the editor of the Socialist Party newspaper *Avanti*, was expelled from the Party because of his support for the war, which he saw as a reconciliation of patriotism and socialism. Instead, with support from Italian and French industrialists, Mussolini launched the interventionist paper *Il Popolo d'Italia* in November. Italy declared war on Austria on 23 May, and Turkey on 21 August, although not on Germany until 27 August 1916 as the government did not wish to provoke the Germans to send more troops to the Italian front.

The Italian forces were poorly trained, equipped, supplied and led, while the Austrians fought well. Successive Italian attacks on the Austrians on the Isonzo front, designed to open the way to Gorizia, Trieste and Istrica, were unsuccessful. On a concentrated front, where there were few opportunities to vary the axis of attack, Austrian defensive firepower prevailed, and the Italians suffered heavy casualties with very few gains. In the four Isonzo battles in 1915, respectively those of 23 June–7 July, 18 July–3 August, 18 October–4 November and 10 November–2 December, the Italians suffered about 250,000 casualties and the Austrians about 160,000. Thanks in large part to the advantages of the terrain, Austrian defensive positions were strong and the Italians lacked sufficient artillery or aerial reconnaissance.

In contrast, the overrunning of Serbia by Austrian, German and Bulgarian forces in 1915 demonstrated the ability of contemporary armies to achieve decisive victories in certain circumstances. Large forces were ably deployed and co-ordinated over difficult terrain. The heavily outnumbered Serbs were attacked on 6 October from the north by Austrian and German forces and from the east by Bulgarians who provided the largest contingent. By 9 October, Belgrade had fallen. The Austro-German advance to its south was delayed by firm resistance and dire weather, but the Bulgarians attacked west from Bulgaria, into the poorly defended Serb rear and overran southern Serbia and Macedonia. The Serbs had to retreat across the arduous terrain of Albania, and King Peter I, the government and army took refuge on the Greek island of Corfu. Part of the reason for overrunning Serbia was to improve supply links within the Central Powers' bloc. The Turks, for example, relied on German ammunition.

That November, the Allies landed an expeditionary force at Salonica in Greece, with a view to moving north into Serbia and coming to its support. They were too late to save Serbia, but other reasons for maintaining the expedition were advanced. In November, Herbert, Earl Kitchener, the Secretary for War, wrote of the French leadership: 'They simply sweep all military dangers and difficulties aside and go on political lines such as saving a remnant of Serbs, bringing Greece in and inducing Romania to join'.[52] Political factors, the equations of alliances, played a major role in such operations.[53] However, the Allied forces advanced slowly, in part because anticipated Greek help was pre-empted by the King's dismissal of the pro-Allied Prime Minister, Eleutherios Venizelos, and were blocked by Bulgarian forces in Macedonia. Subsequently, the Allied advance positions were driven in by Bulgarian attacks in December, the Allies retreating toward Salonica, but the Germans forbade the Bulgarians from pressing on there as they preferred to keep the expeditionary forces bottled up in the city rather than expelling them to fight elsewhere. The Serbs were not saved by this intervention, while the entire history of Balkan operations in the war indicated the strategic limitation of amphibious forces at that juncture, a lesson that was to be underlined anew by the failure of British hopes of the Balkans in the Second World War, both in 1941 and in 1943–44.

Nationalism and power-politics interacted, with control over territory serving as the bargaining basis for alliances. For example, Bulgaria's entry into the war had been pressed for by the Hungarian political establishment, which had resisted support from Wilhelm

II and Emperor Franz Josef for the Romanian offer of continued neutrality in return for autonomy for Transylvania, the part of the Habsburg empire with a Romanian majority, a part within the kingdom of Hungary. Instead, the Hungarian leadership argued that Bulgarian entry would isolate and neutralize Romania.

The entry of Bulgaria and Italy into the war on behalf of their respective allies reflected not a depth of commitment but the continued determination and perceived need for second-rank powers to make assessments of opportunity. Far from the perceived ideology of either alliance playing a role, the key element was the gain of territories – small in themselves but made important as a result of nation-alist public myths, and their gain seen as a sign of national success and regime justification. The Bulgarians were promised Serbian Macedonia and Serbian territory on the left bank of the River Morava by Germany and Austria, who also successfully pressed Turkey to offer Bulgaria territory. In contrast, Russia had supported Serbia in opposing promised gains for Bulgaria in Macedonia if it joined the Allies. However, for these lesser powers, late entrants, the war proved far more difficult than had been anticipated.

Bulgaria's entry into the war and Serbia's collapse did not end Anglo-French hopes in the Balkans, but it made them far less viable. On 9 November, Alan Thomson wrote to his wife Edith that he felt sure that Greece and Romania would join in eventually, and that he had heard that 200,000 Russian troops were being sent against Bulgaria. Such numbers, however, were totally unrealistic given Russia's defeat at the hands of Germany in 1915; still less the 500,000 Allied troops in the Balkans Thomson had mentioned on 3 November. The absence of the force multipliers that were supposed to come from Anglo-French intervention undermined Allied policy. This offers us an understanding of the argument, then and later, that the British should have directed more resources to this operation rather than to the Western Front, one officer writing from Gallipoli in July 1915: 'What people out here feel is that the army in France has nearly all it asks for while the Mediterranean Expeditionary Force gets little or nothing'.[54] Yet, supporting more troops in Gallipoli or elsewhere in the Balkans would have posed far greater logistical problems than in

France. Operational difficulties in the Balkans included formidable terrain, the climate, poor communications and disease, all being more serious issues than on the Western Front. Even when NATO forces had airpower in support, the prospect of an invasion of Kosovo in 1999 seemed very challenging to commanders and planners.

Further afield, the recently established Chinese republic attempted in 1915 to join the war on the Allied side, as it had earlier done in 1914. It was thwarted by Japanese opposition (the Japanese military being stationed at strategic points in China), as was also to be the case in 1916. Japan was the only industrialized state in Asia and it sought the benefit of sole regional identification with the Allies. By this, Japan also hoped to increase its power in China, which was still unstable after the 1911 revolution. Indeed, in 1915, Japan presented China with the so-called 'Twenty-One Demands' designed to ensure Chinese dependence on Japan.[55] In turn, to try to win Allied support against Japanese hegemony, the Chinese sent close to 150,000 workers, including many medical aides, to help in France, which serves as a reminder of the larger number of national narratives involved in the war and their marked contrasts.

Meanwhile, the major powers were confronting the challenges of conducting large-scale war against opponents armed as heavily as themselves and, specifically, of overcoming the constraints of trench warfare. Major difficulties included those posed, particularly for the British, by the large numbers of new officers and troops, most of whom were poorly trained. Writing from Gallipoli in December 1915, Birdwood emphasized the problem with new troops:

> I have only one regular division, viz. the 29th, which as you know came out here as a most magnificent force of old soldiers from India. I fancy that about 80% of these have disappeared for one reason and another, so it now consists of a vast proportion of young soldiers. With the exception of my own [Anzac] corps, the other divisions are Territorial and New Army, and I am sorry to say that the former include certainly one so-called division which is to

all intents and purposes, useless, while all are very short of artillery.[56]

Concerns about the Territorials, the reserve force established in 1907 to absorb both the yeomanry and the (pre-war) volunteers, were more widely expressed, one officer complaining 'The men fight gallantly enough, but to be honest the Territorials here have not all the soldierly instinct; officers and still more NCOs are diffident in giving *orders*. They ask men to do things'.[57] For all combatants, there were also the problems of providing enough of the appropriate equipment, especially the heavy artillery pieces required when bombarding opposing trench lines and the very large number of shells necessary to maintain continuous bombardments.

At the same time, difficulties were aspects of an impressive, but nascent, attempt to respond to the unfamiliar strains posed by this war. Various new measures and institutions reflected the extent to which governments extended their regulatory powers in order to ensure that resources were devoted to the pursuit of total war and to increasing economic effectiveness. Bread rationing began in Germany in January 1915 as the British blockade took effect. In Britain, the Ministry of Munitions was established in June in order to confront the shells crisis, and there were increased calls for the introduction of conscription. In the *Observer* on 5 December 1915, J. L. Garvin, a supporter of conscription, asked 'Shall our army be raised to higher standards or kept at a lower level as some statesmen prefer?'

There was also a major effort to mobilize scientific and technical expertise and resources,[58] although this could be a matter of trial and error. In 1915, Balfour wrote about 'The matter of Cambridge Laboratory ... There is one problem which, I think, is deserving of immediate consideration, namely the explosion of hydrogen in zeppelins. There is no doubt that the result of the recent air-fight between the zeppelin and our aircraft was very disappointing. The incendiary bullets were fired through and through but with no effect; and I gather our authorities are puzzled'.[59] Science was harnessed to find ways of making good optical glass and more high explosive, but the important inventions came from engineers, not scientists, and in

Britain practically all trench warfare munitions, notably the Stokes mortar and the Mills grenade, were, in a major engineering feat, invented by civilian engineers without being approached by the War Office. The hydraulic interrupter gear to enable aircraft machine guns to fire through their propellers, developed by the British in 1917, was also down to private enterprise, although the tank and gas munitions were the result of official research.

Air warfare, meanwhile, was becoming bolder in conception. From January 1915, Zeppelins attacked Britain while they continued to bomb French cities, being joined by planes. The material damage was relatively modest: 51 attacks (208 sorties) on Britain during the war dropped 196 tons of bombs, which killed 557, wounded 1,358 and caused £1½ million worth of property damage. Nevertheless, these attacks had some impact in terrorizing civilian populations, though they also inflamed British and French opinion,[60] providing a counterpart to atrocity propaganda about the Germans in Belgium.

These attacks also affected troops at the front, collapsing the distance between it and the Home Front. Alan Thomson was worried about his wife in London and wrote, with reference to the Zeppelins, about 'those infernal devils'.[61] Such bombing raids on civilians were a preparation for a new type of total war, in which the centres of opposing states could be attacked with increasing speed and scale. Having said this, while the sense of what air power could achieve expanded, many ideas were not feasible, as when the British Committee of Imperial Defence considered using long-range planes based in Russia and dropping incendiary bombs to destroy German wheat and rye crops.[62] This idea, nevertheless, indicated how quickly military planners began to envisage a war virtually without limits, as well as showing the importance attached to agricultural production.

While there were only limited changes in airships, the capabilities of aircraft improved. For example, their ability to act in aerial combat was enhanced. Increases in aircraft speed, manoeuvrability and ceiling made it easier to attack other planes. Engine power increased and engine size fell, while the rate of an aircraft's climb increased. Synchronizing gear, developed by Anthony Fokker, and modelled on a French aircraft shot down by the Germans, was used by the German military from April 1915. It enabled aeroplanes to fire forwards without damaging their propellers and gave the Germans a distinct advantage. In turn, however, this system was quickly copied by the British, showing once again how war accelerated technological development but, with equal speed, resulted in another stalemate of sorts.

Aircraft also took a greater role in reconnaissance. The Turkish columns advancing on the Suez Canal were spotted by British planes, while General Callwell remarked of the plans for Gallipoli, ' As a land gunner I have no belief in that long range firing except when there are aeroplanes to mark the effect'.[63] The value of reconnaissance encouraged chasing off other planes. Thomson recorded at Gallipoli a British plane chasing off a German one, and a German aeroplane flying low machine-gunning a sailor on a destroyer on patrol duty offshore.[64] Another officer at Gallipoli noted, 'The Germans have been dropping bombs and proclamations', although the former did little damage.[65]

The failures of both sides led to planning in late 1915 for different strategies in 1916, planning that encompassed the intensification of war economies as well as military schemes.[66] Aristide Briand replaced René Viviani as French Prime Minister in October 1915 on the platform of improving relations with France's allies so as to ensure a more co-operative war effort. For 1916, the Allies agreed at Chantilly a more coherent and ambitious grand plan than the essentially ad-hoc attacks mounted in 1915. Instead, there was to be a series of concerted assaults by the British, Italians and Russians mounted on all major German fronts, designed to inflict sufficient all-round damage on the German army to permit follow-up attacks by the French, with the goal of delivering the long-awaited breakthrough. This strategy, however, was to be derailed by the earlier launch of its German counterpart, an attempt to break the French will in an attritional battle at Verdun. As in 1915, both sides were to be unsuccessful.

CHAPTER 4

1916

Do not think that this is war. It is not war. It is the ending of the world. This is just such a war as was related in the *Mahabharata* about our forefathers.

Indian soldier writing home.[1]

1916 was the last year of the war before it was transformed as a result of the events of 1917: revolution in Russia and America's entry into the conflict. It was also the year of the most memorable, indeed, iconic battles: Verdun, the Somme, Jutland, the Brusilov campaign. 1916 witnessed both attritional and breakthrough strategies on land, and also saw the combatants benefit from the gearing up of their economies for war. Governmental control became more intense. Opposition to this was limited, and the most dramatic instances of hostility to state control occurred as anti-imperial risings: in Central Asia and in Ireland.

German strategy remained that of putting so much pressure on their opponents that they were persuaded to accept peace terms that yielded Germany an effective hegemony in Europe. In 1916, the point of pressure was shifted from East to West, with the Germans concentrating on France instead of Russia. At the same time, the German navy maintained its focus on Britain, and that led to the battle of Jutland, the leading naval clash of the war.

In 1916, Falkenhayn accepted that a breakthrough in the west was impossible given the nature of warfare on the Western Front, specifically the defensive strength of modern weapons and the possibilities of reinforcement. Instead, he sought in the Verdun offensive to break the French will by inflicting heavy casualties and creating what was termed a 'blood mill'. The alternative to the pursuit of the strategic breakthrough appeared to be a strategy of attrition, which focused primarily on killing large numbers of opponents. Falkenhayn regarded France as weaker than Britain, and hoped the offensive would knock her out of the war. Without France, he argued, with reason, that Britain would not be able to fight on the Western Front. Both sides believed that attritional conflict would be more successful if they could take the initiative, and thus chose both the terrain for attack and a battlefield where they had amassed artillery.

Falkenhayn planned to gain the advantage of the strategic offensive and the tactical defensive. He aimed to do this by advancing rapidly on the front of his choice to capture territory, which the French, rather than creating and consolidating a new front line, would then suffer heavy losses trying to regain. Verdun, a fortress in the Meuse Valley, had great symbolic significance for the French, notably for politicians who resolutely linked national glory to their presentation of the self-sacrificing dedication of the troops, and was also seen as important to the defence of Paris against attack from the north-east. In practice, the vulnerability of Verdun was such that the French might have strengthened their position by abandoning the Verdun salient, and, by doing so, would certainly have shortened their line, anticipating the course the Germans were to follow on the Western Front in 1917.

The nature of the front line gave the Germans many advantages as Verdun's communications were exposed to German attack and bombardment: these communications were largely restricted to one road. Thus, a successful German attack with limited objectives based on an understanding both of the ground and of the French psyche would, Falkenhayn hoped, be leveraged into a major outcome. In his plan, the tactical, operational and strategic dimensions of the war were in concert. The resources devoted to the attack reflected its importance to the Germans as did the decision to entrust the command of the Fifth Army to the Crown Prince of Prussia. Yet, as so often happens with planning, there was overdetermination, with everything depending on the Fifth Army achieving its goals and on the French doing exactly what Falkenhayn wanted.

In the event, after a delay from 12 February due to the weather, the Germans were unable to profit as planned from the offensive they launched on 21 February, Operation Gericht. As a reflection of the strength of their munitions industry, which was far stronger than that of France, they deployed 1,220 guns, the largest number hitherto used, but the Germans attacked on too narrow a front, and initially with too few troops: the emphasis, instead, was on the artillery. The narrow front of advance ensured that Falkenhayn exposed the German troops to artillery fire from the French on the other (western, left) bank of the Meuse, while, at the tactical level, artillery fire, though devastating in the nine hour bombardment at the outset, produced the cover of shell-holes for the defenders, which supplemented their trenches. Instead of a fast-moving advance and rapid results, Falkenhayn increasingly had to rely upon the effects of a steady haemorrhaging of the French army brought about by a near-continuous German offensive. This offensive, however, engaged most of the German reserve, and led to heavy German casualties, while French willpower remained strong despite serious losses.

The distinct benefit the Germans had gained from their use of Fokker Eindekker aircraft enabled them to seek the aerial advantage over Verdun. More generally, there was also considerable pressure on British aircraft over the Western Front. Harold Wyllie, a squadron commander, wrote 'sending out F.E.s [Fe-2bs, two-seater scouts with the gunner in front] in formation with Martinsydes for protection is murder and nothing else. But flying men are very cheap. And those who send them out get DSOs [Distinguished Service Orders] instead of a slip knot'.[2] Troops on the ground increasingly had to be mindful about the risk of air attack. The order of 26 October 1916 for the British 169th Infantry Brigade noted 'When hostile aeroplanes are in sight troops will halt and clear the road as far as possible'.[3] However, the French were able to drive off German reconnaissance airplanes from Verdun because of their eventually successful attempt to contest the German Fokker planes through their development of large groups of aircraft and because they now also had planes with synchronized forward-firing machine guns.

Given command of Verdun on 24 February 1916, Henri Philippe Pétain proved a resolute commander, being associated with the phrase '*Ils ne passeront pas!*' (They shall not pass!). Convinced of the value of the defensive, Pétain did not crack under the pressure and eased the bloody burden on his troops through the Noria system of replacements in which units were rapidly circulated through the front line, benefiting from periods in the rear. As a result of such circulation, much of the French infantry served for a period in Verdun. The patriotic dedication of many of the French troops helped ensure continued commitment to the bloody struggle.[4] The resolution of the French military was matched by that of the politicians, and this was seen across the spectrum of mainstream leaders with the right-wing President, Raymond Poincaré, and the left-wing former Prime Minister, Georges Clemenceau, both determined to defeat Germany.

Thus, as the offensive developed, it both cost the Germans heavily and served no strategic purpose. Fresh German attacks brought more gains, Fort Vaux falling on 7 June, but there was no breakthrough and German losses continued to be heavy. The offensive finally ground to a halt in July. It had failed, but German troops were also moved from the Verdun operation in July to confront the British attacks on the Somme. A sense of failure led to Falkenhayn's removal on 28 August. He was sent to the Eastern Front and replaced as Chief of the General Staff by Hindenburg. There was, however, a more basic strategic flaw in the German policy, namely that any peace on German terms involved territorial gains that, in fact, were politically unacceptable to Germany's enemies, while, at the same time, the Allies could afford the costs of wearing down the German army.[5]

Promoted on 1 May 1916 to commander of Army Group Centre, Pétain had been replaced as commander of the Second Army at Verdun by Robert Nivelle, who was seen by Joffre as more willing to mount attacks. After the German attacks on the Verdun front ended, Nivelle, indeed, regained the initiative and much ground, although the costs were heavy. The French were greatly helped in gaining and using the initiative by an effective use of artillery, including the creeping barrage (when gunfire falls just in front of advancing troops) employed to support the counter-offensive in October, as well as by an impressive logistical effort, which included the use of motorized supply columns, that was organized by Pétain.[6] The final French attack, launched on 15 December, took the front back to near where it had been in February. In the end, attrition affected both sides in the Verdun campaign and the French lost 378,000 men, the Germans 336,000.

The Allied grand strategy of concerted attacks agreed at Chantilly in late 1915 was derailed when the Germans got their blow in first at Verdun, because that battle soaked up many of the French reserves. The strain this placed on the French led the British government, on 7 April, to give its final approval for the offensive on the Somme where the two armies joined, and also led to a change in the balance between British and French forces. Instead of providing equal numbers, the French provided six first-line divisions, the British 19, and, more significantly, the Somme offensive was to help save Verdun and the French army. Douglas Haig, the British commander on the Western Front, would have preferred to delay until August when he thought his forces would be more prepared and more artillery would be available.[7]

Launched on 1 July, the initial assault, however, proved disastrous as the British troops advanced on a German line whose defences had not been suppressed by artillery fire. The British guns were spread too widely to be effective, there were not enough heavy guns to destroy German dugouts, some of which were very deep, and the seven-day preparatory bombardment lacked the accuracy that was to be achieved in 1918. The bombardment confirmed German Intelligence warnings of a British assault on the Somme. On 1 July, machine guns exacted a heavy toll on the long lines of slowly advancing British infantry, and the 120,000 attackers, from the finest volunteer army Britain had ever assembled, suffered 57,470 casualties, 19,240 dead, 2,152 missing and the others wounded, in what proved the bloodiest day in British military history. Individual units lost very heavily, with 32 battalions losing over 500 men that day. The circumstances of the casualties were harsh. Many soldiers were killed as they advanced in lines, a large number soon after they crossed their own parapet. Machine gun fire proved particularly deadly, but there were also many casualties from German shellfire behind British lines. The French attack on the British right was more successful, in part due to a more effective use of more numerous heavy artillery.

The reality of the conflict (the term 'fighting' implies a shared experience that may seem misleading) was kept from the British public. Dependent on official information which they failed to question, the press provided scant clue to the heavy cost at which limited success had been obtained and Arthur Child-Villiers noted 'the papers do not enable a very correct idea to be formed of modern warfare'. Indeed, by 1917, he could suggest the abolition of newspaper correspondents.[8] In the *Daily Express* of 3 July 1916, John Irvine claimed:

> the taking of the first line trenches was in some places comparatively easy – almost a walkover. It was only when our men bit deeper into the enemy's defences, that they were brought face to face with difficulties; but their indomitable pluck and perseverance have triumphed … one word of caution … it would be altogether premature … to assume that the offensive on which the British Army has now embarked is a movement which is going very soon to end the war.[9]

Irvine wrote of 'British Lions … let loose on their prey', while, that day, the *Daily Mail* referred to 'going over the top' as a 'gay, impetuous and irresistible leap from the trenches'. Its correspondent, Beach Thomas, wrote:

> The toll of blood-taking [1 July] has been fairly heavy, but I am glad to be able to state from reports received that it is by no means excessive, having regard to the magnitude of the day's operations – it is and for many days will continue to be siege warfare, in which a small territorial gain may be a great strategical gain and the price we must pay is to be judged by another

measure than miles or furlongs or booty. We are laying siege not to a place but to the German Army'.

Irvine, however, struck a more candid note in the *Daily Express* of 5 July:

> we are learning gradually how terrible this machine gun fire has been ... a hail of machine gun bullets which were simply terrible ... casualties were considerable on the first day of the advance.

The contemporary representation of the Battle of the Somme, and the extent to which the reality was kept away from the public, were also highlighted in the official film which was an enormous popular success as the public were hankering for images of the front. In practice, what they were shown was a re-enactment, both with troops going over the top and with them advancing across no man's land.[9] Yet, while the national press and the film did not convey anything regarding the scale of losses, the provincial press remained effectively uncensored and carried full lists of casualties, so that the loss on the Somme was certainly known in the localities from which units were recruited.

The offensive continued, not only for the strategic purposes of easing the pressure on the French (at Verdun) and the Russians, but also because of the conviction, strongly held by Haig, that it was necessary to persist in attacks. This conviction entailed a belief in the value of willpower, in providential support and in the possibility of gaining success with one more push. Indeed, Haig believed that the German error in 1914 had been to abandon their offensive prematurely, notably at Ypres. This commitment to pressing on may appear foolish in light of the resulting heavy losses, but there was a finer line between success and failure than is often accepted by discussion of this war, and indeed other wars. Yet, Haig's commitment to a breakthrough ignored the more prudent view of other senior British commanders that small-scale successes were more viable and would be less costly.

Casualties were certainly heavy. At the Somme, the New Zealand contingent suffered more than 6,700 men dead or wounded, 40%

of the strength of infantry units, in 23 days' operations. A British Quartermaster Sergeant noted in his diary:

> the whole place smells stale with the slaughter which has been going on for the past fourteen days – the smell of the dead and lachrymatory gas. The place is a very Hell with the whistling and crashing of shells, bursting shrapnel and the rattle of machine-guns. The woods we had taken had not yet been cleared and there were pockets of Germans with machine-guns still holding out and doing some damage. A sergeant sinks to the ground besides me with a bullet wound neatly drilled through his shoulder. Lucky man. It is not likely to proved fatal. It is too clean and it means a few months in Blighty [Britain] for him.[10]

Haig hoped for a breakthrough that would be exploited by cavalry, but this unrealistic assumption rested on a misreading of how the battle would develop, a misreading he failed to correct. Instead, the Somme campaign became attritional, and in 142 days the British advanced to a maximum depth of about six miles. Their attacks finished on 19 November, with the last major push, on 13–14 November, the Battle of the Ancre, being what the original attack should have been: well-planned, appropriately supported by artillery and focused on limited goals.

Subsequently, Haig was to argue that the Allied offensives of 1915–17 on the Western Front, were a crucial preparation for the final victory in that they wore the Germans down. The War Diary of the London Rifle Brigade for 1 July 1916 suggested 'It seems probable that although the actual attack was unsuccessful and was very costly, we killed a large number of Germans but undoubtedly the attack failed'. On 3 July, the General Staff of VII Corps claimed 'Although Gommecourt has not fallen into our hands, the purpose of the attack, which was mainly to contain and kill Germans, was accomplished'.[11] However, at the time, Haig wanted the offensives to be far more decisive: tactically, operationally and strategically. His failure was matched by that of the civilian politicians who had insisted that the Somme offensive be conducted with due regard to manpower issues, but were unable to ensure this goal. The Cabinet did not really understand what had happened and did not insist on a change in policy. The lack of responsive political oversight compounded Haig's mishandling of military planning.

There are 73,357 names on Sir Edwin Lutyens's powerful Memorial to the (British) Missing of the Somme at Thiepval,[12] and, given the heavy casualties involved (about 420,000 British and 200,000 French), to write of the benefits from the Somme offensive may seem highly inappropriate, but, nevertheless, they need noting. The impact of taking the war to the Germans was to thwart their plan for an offensive in the Arras area, while, alongside the German failure at Verdun, that of the Austrians in the Trentino offensive and the success of the Russian Brusilov offensive against the Austrians, there was a crisis among the leadership of the Central Powers. Although their casualty figures are controversial, the Germans certainly suffered very heavy casualties on the Somme, possibly half a million men, thus close to those of the Allies, as well as a bad blow to their optimism and morale, not least due to their realization of Allied material superiority and to the improvement of Allied performance during the Somme offensive. Moreover, as a consequence of the Somme, the initiative on the Western Front was wrested from the Germans and they did not mount a major attack there in 1917, while their 1918 offensives were dependent on troops transferred from Russia.

German casualties on the Somme reflected the pressure of numerous Allied attacks, as well as the frequent German counter-attacks mounted in order to regain ground. A lack of sufficient fire support was a major problem for the British there, but their artillery, nevertheless, killed many Germans. British artillery tactics improved greatly during the battle, which enhanced the effectiveness of their attacks. Horne, a corps commander on the Somme, who became commander of the First Army in September, used his guns in a methodical fashion, although in January 1917 he wrote: 'No truth in my *inventing* the barrage fire. We copied it from the French I think. Anyhow it came about gradually by the necessity of finding means of keeping down the German machine gun fire'.[13] On 13 September 1916, the order for the 169th Infantry Brigade noted that half the supporting artillery would be used for a creeping barrage and half for a stationary barrage. On 24 September, the order noted 'The attack in each stage will be carried out under cover of both a creeping and stationary barrage'.[14] Thomson was 'very busy. The booming of the guns never ceases day or night, and we give the Hun no rest at all', although, in early November, his position, in turn, was shelled for six nights in succession.[15]

Moreover, British fire-support for the infantry improved greatly, thanks to the use of the three-inch Stokes light infantry mortar, as well as the development of tactics using rifle grenades in support and suppression roles. Production rose rapidly to meet demand. In the last quarter of 1914, only 2,164 hand and rifle grenades were produced in Britain, and, although the figure had risen to 65,315 in the first six months of 1915, it was still well below demand. Only in October 1915 did the output of the Mills No. 5 grenade meet demand when it passed 300,000 a week. Already in 1915, the monthly demand for percussion grenades alone had risen to 252,000. British output of mortar ammunition rose from 50,000 rounds in April–June 1915 to 2,185,346 million rounds for April–June 1916. A total of 11,052,451 grenades were delivered from Britain in the second half of 1916 and, that year, the British output of hand grenades was close to 29 million.[16]

Other British improvements in capability included the use of aircraft in ground-attack roles. Yet, although the equations of respective loss altered as the campaign continued so that it was less against the British, the strain was still formidable, both for manpower and for *matériel*. Indeed, manpower losses encouraged the extension of conscription, for example in Canada in 1917. Equipment, moreover, suffered from wear and tear, particularly for the artillery, the mechanical difficulties arising from worn barrels, faulty recuperator springs lessening the chance of an easy recoil, and other defective results of heavy usage. These problems contributed to greater inaccuracy, which considerably reduced the effectiveness of massed artillery.[17]

The Somme and Verdun were campaigns rather than battles; otherwise Verdun has to be seen as the longest field battle in history.

Both were larger in scale than earlier battles on the Western Front, which reflected the success of the combatants in raising troops and concentrating resources, especially their ability to sustain large numbers of men in the same area for long periods, as well as the pressure on commanders to break through. Yet, in terms of the manpower committed and the men killed, the territory gained was limited, a point driven home when the French, in late 1916, regained many of their losses at Verdun, while in 1918 the Germans advanced across the Somme battlefield. The limited gains help ensure that the history of that year has come to be symbolic of the bloody havoc of war and of the futility of that war.

Both points are discussed elsewhere, but, as far as 1916 was concerned, the campaigns in Eastern Europe indicated that operations could deliver significant results. Benefiting from the increase in shell production and army numbers, the Russians under Brusilov attacked in southern Poland as part of the scheme for concerted pressure on the Central Powers. Their greatest success was won against the Austrians who were weakened by the movement of troops to the Italian front and by the effectiveness of Brusilov's methods. On 4 June, he achieved surprise across a broad front despite the skilful Austrian code-breakers providing prior warning of the attack, and the breadth of his advance meant that it was unclear where to deploy the Austrian reserves. After a short four-hour bombardment, the Russians bypassed Austrian strong points and achieved an advance in depth that wrecked the cohesion of the defenders. The defence was also poor and the Austrians did not know how to respond.[18]

In June, Brusilov made major advances and captured 380,000 prisoners as well as leaving 370,000 Austrian troops killed and wounded. Yet this offensive was pushed on beyond where it should have stopped in order to consolidate the gains. This persistence reflected the political need for success; a need felt keenly both in Russia and by its allies, who hoped that further advances would help on their fronts. In the heat of summer, the advance proved gruelling, while Russian logistics could not cope and Alexei Evert, the Commander of the West Front, refused to launch the planned supporting attack. Evert, a poor commander close to Nicholas II, claimed that his forces lacked sufficient shells. Meanwhile, the Austrians and Germans moved reinforcements by rail to counter Brusilov and seal that front, the Germans taking command of Austrian forces.

At least this response tested the Germans, whereas the belated frontal attacks launched by the Russians in July towards Vilnius against the Germans, far from reducing the pressure on Brusilov, were not a serious test and repeatedly failed. So also did those launched further south towards Kovel by the 'Special Army', a reserve force, mostly of the Imperial Guard, under elderly generals. Heavy losses were incurred without any benefit. In these attacks, the Russians did not use the methods developed by Brusilov, methods, instead, that contributed to the tactics the Germans were to employ successfully from late 1917.

The Russian army proved inadequate to the challenge, in part because its command culture remained anachronistic. Although the Russian General Staff graduates were a meritocratic group, exposed to a scientific approach to war,[19] they were also a small one. In general, the Russian army was characterized by an emphasis on lineage, connections and character, which did not guarantee an informed response to the problems posed by machine-guns and entrenched defenders.[20] This failure of response to these problems owed much to the continued conviction of the role of will in victory and therefore that the defence could be overcome.

The recapture of Brusilov's gains by the Austrians and Germans, Tarnopol falling on 25 July, did not reflect an impasse comparable to that seen on the Western Front where tactical factors played a bigger role in the difficulties of mounting a successful offensive. In contrast, on the far longer Eastern Front, force/space ratios were different, and the trench systems lacked comparable sophistication. Lower force/space ratios ensured that the defence was weaker, both at the front and in terms of reserves, but it was still possible if troops could be massed, to mount offensives successfully. As the fate of the Brusilov offensive showed, it was also possible to counter-attack successfully.

Moreover, the Germans were helped in this counter-attack and more generally by a consistent superiority in the use of Intelligence. Not only did they benefit from the interception of Russian signals;

they also proved adept at using Intelligence, notably of Russian dispositions and movements, to operational effect. This capability was linked to command superiority. Yet there is the problem of teleology when writing about the war on the Eastern Front. The conflict was to lead to the Russian Revolution, but in 1916 the Russian military effort had still not collapsed (indeed shell production rose) and, at the end of the year, German gains did not match those achieved by the spring of 1918, let alone in 1941.

The capability of the offensive was also demonstrated in the Balkans. At the outset of 1916, and as a consequence of the successful offensive against Serbia, its ally and neighbour, Montenegro was occupied by Austrian forces in January, as King Nicholas and his government fled. A more dramatic offensive was to be launched against Romania. Its government sought Transylvania (in which there was a substantial Romanian population) from Austria; and was encouraged to enter the war by Brusilov's success and by the promise of support from the Allies in Salonica. By going to war, the Romanians also hoped to benefit in what might be an imminent peace by winning an opportunity, as one of the victors, to make territorial gains, specifically Transylvania and Bukovinia from Austria. On 27 August, Romania declared war on Austria, Germany declaring war on Romania the next day, and Turkey and Bulgaria following.

Taking the initiative against the heavily outnumbered Austrians, the Romanians occupied the city of Brasov on 30 August and secured the major passes in the Carpathians between Romania and Transylvania by 2 September; but the advance was slow and, combined with the vulnerability of Romania's situation, this resulted in a shift in tempo. Bulgarian pressure from the south in the contested Dobrudja region, which the Romanians had seized from Bulgaria in 1913, led the Romanians to halt the offensive on 8 September.

Prefiguring the Polish crisis in 1939, the Romanian General Staff not only could not direct the tempo of the conflict, but had failed to prepare a comprehensive plan of operations enabling them to co-ordinate activity over the range of potential fronts.[21] In contrast, as earlier against Serbia in 1915, Austrian, German and Bulgarian forces showed an impressive ability to deliver a verdict. As against Serbia then and against Poland in 1939, the defeated state was attacked from a number of directions. A Bulgarian army – supported by German and Turkish units, under a German Field Marshal, von Mackensen, a veteran of the Franco-Prussian War, invaded south-eastern Romania rapidly, bombarding the frontier fortresses into submission; while a German and Austrian army, under Falkenhayn, who was keen to re-establish his reputation, defeated the invading Romanians at Sibiu on 30 September and then, in November, invaded Romania from Transylvania, advancing across the Carpathians. In mid-November, the two attacking armies joined forces and, on 6 December, they entered the capital, Bucharest.

Because German field marshals commanded the conquest of Romania as of Serbia, these victories, especially the first, usually appear in the literature as 'German' victories, much to the chagrin of Austrian and Bulgarian military historians. Romanian forces were driven back into Moldavia, near to the Russian frontier, and the Germans gained control of Romania's oil and wheat, although the British took steps to sabotage oil facilities at Ploesti, again anticipating attempts during the Second World War to use sabotage to block the movements of Romanian oil. The new front stabilized on 10 January 1917 after the Romanians had suffered 250,000 casualties out of their 833,000 strong army.[22]

This success was a valuable consolidation of Germany's position in South-Eastern Europe, one that put additional pressure on Russia by denying it the advantage of a regional ally, as well as an important strengthening of the German-run continental economy in opposition to the British-directed oceanic one. This strengthening helped counter the British blockade, and Romanian oil powered Germany's planes and submarines. The collapse of Romania also looked toward far greater German opportunities at the expense of Russia whose front, in addition, was now extended.

Further south, Bulgarian forces advanced in eastern Macedonia in late 1916, taking the Greek cities of Drama and Seres and the port of Kavala on the Aegean Sea. There was no comparable movement on the Italian Front in 1916, although there was much fighting. Both Austria and Italy launched offensives, reflecting the importance they attached to the lands in contest. To the Austrians, these lands were more significant than those being contested with Russia. Had Austria succeeded in knocking Italy out of the war, then there would have been a strategic purpose to its offensive, but that was a task too great for the Austrians alone. Instead, the attack launched, against German advice, from the Trentino on 15 May made significant gains and inflicted heavy casualties before the Italians were able to hold it by bringing up reserves. The Austrians suffered from having to deploy across mountains whereas the Italians backed onto the Venetian plain, and its superior communications served them well: troops were brought up by Fiat lorries, replicating the rapid move of reserves to block advances on the Western Front. These Italian troops could not therefore be used to support the costly Italian offensives to the east on the Isonzo river, whereas the Austrian troops would otherwise have been able to resist Brusilov on the Eastern Front.

The failure of both sides to break through in Italy in 1916 reflected in part the standard difficulties with offensive warfare, notably the problem of supporting success given the inability to disrupt the enemy rear areas through which they could deploy their reserves more successfully. There was also the issue of indifferent command on both sides. Conrad, the Austrian Chief of the General Staff, lacked strategic ability, as well as skills in operational execution and good personal relations, and he was dismissed in November by the new Emperor, Karl, the nephew of the Archduke assassinated at Sarajevo in 1914 and the grand-nephew of Emperor Franz-Josef who had died on 21 November at the age of 86. His death weakened the Habsburg empire and, even more, its polyglot army, as he was a key symbol for loyalty.

Luigi Cadorna, the Chief of the Italian General Staff, deserves some credit for thwarting the Austrian Trentino campaign in June, and went on, in August, to capture the town of Gorizia, in yet another Isonzo offensive, but his unimaginative emphasis on successive attacks there represented one of the least impressive instances of the failure to rethink goals and methods. The brutal Cadorna also treated his troops harshly, which contributed to the poor morale that was to be seen when they were attacked by the Austrians and Germans in

1917. In June 1916, the Italian government lost a vote of confidence in Parliament and resigned, a victim to a lack of victory and to disagreements over control of the war effort. Paolo Boselli replaced Antonia Salandia as Prime Minister.

The commanders on the Italian front could not have lost the war in an afternoon, as was famously remarked of Admiral Sir John Jellicoe, the commander of the British Grand Fleet at the Battle of Jutland of 31 May–1 June. The German plan remained that of falling upon part of the Grand Fleet with their entire High Seas Fleet. It had been tried in three other sorties earlier in 1916 that did not result in a battle, and was tried again in the Jutland operation. The British did not fall for this plan, but, despite having the larger fleet at Jutland, failed to achieve the Trafalgar or, as it was then seen, sweeping victory hoped for by naval planners. Instead, in the battle, the British suffered from problems with fire control, inadequate armour protection, notably on their battlecruisers, the unsafe handling of powder, poor signalling and inadequate training, for example in destroyer torpedo attacks. German gunnery at Jutland was superior to that of the Royal Navy, partly because of better optics and better fusing of the shells.

Command decisions were important. Jellicoe's caution possibly denied the British the victory they might have obtained had the bolder Admiral Sir David Beatty, commander of the battlecruiser squadron, been in overall command, although Jellicoe only needed to avoid losing. Beatty was regarded as more dynamic, Kitchener observing in late 1915: 'In the solution of the Dardanelles much I fear depends on the navy. If we only had Beatty out there I should feel very much happier.'[23]

The British lost more ships and men at Jutland than the Germans: 14 ships, including three battlecruisers, and 6097 men compared with 11 ships, including one battlecruiser, and 2551 men. Wilhelm II announced at the naval base of Wilhelmshaven on 5 June 'The English were beaten. The spell of Trafalgar has been broken'. Nevertheless, the German fleet had been badly damaged in the big-gun exchange.[24] Moreover, their confidence had been hit hard: 'more important was the spectre of irresistible coercive power which mere glimpses of the Grand Fleet had left in the minds and memories of German officers'.

Thereafter in the war, the High Seas Fleet sailed beyond the defensive minefields of the Heligoland Bight on only three occasions, the first on 18 August 1916, and, on each occasion, it took care to avoid conflict with the Grand Fleet.[25]

In turn, the High Seas Fleet posed a threat as a fleet-in-being, and this threat acted as a restraint on British naval operations. Their losses at Jutland made both Jellicoe and the Admiralty more cautious. British plans for bold large-scale operations, notably for sorties into the Baltic to help Russia, were not brought to fruition. Yet, the British employed their fleet by deterring the Germans from acting and thus challenging the British blockade or use of the sea. This deterrence thwarted the German option of combining surface sorties with submarine ambushes in order to reduce the British advantage in warship numbers. This advantage was supplemented by British superiority in the Intelligence war, notably the use of Signals Intelligence organized by Room 40. This usage was important to Britain's security as the location of German warships was generally known.[26]

On 4 July, recognizing that Jutland had left the British still dominant in the North Sea, the German commander there, Vice-Admiral Reinhard Scheer, suggested to Wilhelm II that Germany could only win at sea by means of using submarines. After Jutland, British leaders became more concerned about this threat, although it did not exhaust the German challenge. In particular, German destroyers and cruisers were to inflict serious damage on two Scandinavian convoys in October and December 1917. Further afield, German surface raiders were no longer a serious problem, although the potential for damage was revealed by SMS *Seeadler*, which sunk American cargo ships in the Pacific in 1917 before being shipwrecked near Tahiti, and SMS *Wolf*, a 5,809-ton armed freighter despatched from Kiel in November 1916 which, in an epic journey, returned home in February 1918 having sunk or mined 29 Allied ships off South Africa, India, Sri Lanka, Australia and New Zealand and having created widespread alarm.[27]

In October 1916, Jellicoe observed that the greater size and range of submarines and their increased use of the torpedo, so that they did not need to come to the surface and sink their target by gun-fire, meant that the submarine menace was getting worse.[28] The following month, Balfour wrote, 'the submarine has already profoundly modified naval tactics ... it was a very evil day for this country when this engine of naval warfare was discovered'.[29] The greater emphasis on submarines altered the nature of the war at sea, as submarine warfare did not offer the prospect of a decisive victory in a climactic engagement. Instead, the submarine conflict ensured that war at sea became attritional, indeed more so than that on land.

Combined with the British blockade of Germany,[30] the submarine conflict ensured that the war was more clearly one between societies, with an attempt to break the resolve of peoples by challenging not only economic strength but also social stability and indeed demographic health. This challenge necessarily directed attention to the ability of governments to safeguard the Home Front, and this ability became more important as the war continued without any end in sight. The absence of any diplomatic or military breakthrough suggested that it would continue for a long time, and, indeed, British hopes from the blockade were focused on victory in the early 1920s.

The Home Front had many facets, and government concerns stemmed from different drives and arose in contrasting as well as overlapping contexts. Increasingly, the need to support an arduous struggle took on a political dimension in which continued stability was a key goal and means for, and of, success. There was a major shift in attitudes towards the use of state power. The outbreak of war led in Britain to an initial period when the government proclaimed 'business as usual', but also, in August 1914, to the passage of the Defence of the Realm Act, which brought both government controls and the habit of control. The latter proved more insistent and lasting than had been intended. During the war, restrictions on state power across Europe declined and were not pressed.

Even in the early stages of the war, governments felt it necessary to abandon pre-war practices in order to mobilize resources. The regulation of financial transactions was an important initial step, as were measures to raise the sums necessary to fight the war. The Germans passed war finance laws on 4 August 1914. As it became clear that the war would not finish in 1914, so it also was apparent that it would be necessary to sustain a lengthy struggle and military requirements led to major shifts in economies, notably with an expansion of heavy industry. The demands of war drove the expansion of governmental control, as did the length of the conflict. Thus, in 1916, the German Supreme Command responded to the Somme offensive by trying to increase greatly the production of munitions.

The ability to mobilize resources, both men and munitions, was crucial. Thirty-seven million shells were fired by the French and Germans in their ten-month contest for Verdun in 1916. Such a use of artillery ensured that the cost of offensives soared, while, in 1915, the availability of shells became a political issue in Britain which lacked an adequate munitions industry, and a serious problem in France (which had such an industry) and Russia. The need for shells for heavy, rather than field, artillery exacerbated the issue. To deal with these and related problems, large sections of economies were placed under governmental control and regulated in a fashion held to characterize military organization.

For example, the Ministry of Munitions, created in Britain in 1915, was as much part of the military organization, and as vital, as the artillery it served. David Lloyd George left the Treasury, a key ministry, to become the first Minister of Munitions and made his name as a wartime leader in this role. Responding to the need to produce more artillery shells, Lloyd George bypassed established procedures by enlisting entrepreneurs in the cause of production. Moreover, a political purpose was served as Lloyd George used his ministry to demonstrate his belief that capital and labour could combine to patriotic purpose.[31] So also with the French ministry of munitions under, first Albert Thomas and, from September 1917, Louis Loucheur, key figures in the Allied war effort. Across Europe, many sections of society were not brought under the direction to which munitions production was subject, but can still be seen as part of the informal organization of militarized states, with governments extending their regulatory powers in order to ensure that resources were devoted to war and to increase economic effectiveness.

The major German industries were taken under government control: although not publicly owned, the German economy was publicly controlled. In practice, this control entailed an alliance between big business and the military. Rationing was widespread. Looking towards a policy that was followed far more systematically by the Germans in the Second World War, 60,000 Belgian workers (out of the 120,000 seized) were, in 1916–17, compelled to work in Germany, in order to compensate for the impact of conscription on the German workforce. In a harsh policy, brutally inflicted, that was driven by the military authorities and the industrialists to whom they were linked, 2,500 of the 120,000 died during their detention and many others soon after. Large numbers of prisoners of war were also set to work in Germany, while hundreds of thousands of civilians were conscripted for forced labour in occupied territories. The forced deportation of Belgians led to condemnation in Germany (by Catholics and Socialists in the *Reichstag* as well as by civilian officials) and America. Deportation, moreover, proved more troublesome than the use, from 1917, of wage manipulation in order to encourage the movement of about 120,000 Belgian workers to work in Germany.[32]

As in the Second World War, and anticipating the racist inflections of German policy then, harsher occupation policies were followed in Eastern Europe and the Balkans than in Belgium. In the Baltic provinces of Russia occupied by the Germans, forced labour was organized by the military by means of Civilians Workers' Battalions, whereas deportation from occupied Poland, an area under civilian administration, was shortlived. German economic exploitation was a factor in both Romania and Serbia, although, as also in the Second World War, this activity was in part in competition with that of Germany's allies; Austria and Bulgaria in the Great War.[33]

In an attempt to draw the sting of Serbian nationalism, Austria sought to integrate Serbia fully into its empire, although there were serious tensions between military authorities and civilian bureaucrats. Austrian occupation was less exploitative than that of Germany in Eastern Europe and the Austrians did not face popular opposition in Serbia comparable to that mounted by the Bosnian Muslims against occupation in 1878; and the brutal Austrian reprisals seen then, including the large-scale slaughter of men, women and children,[34] were not repeated. Nevertheless, when Romania attacked Austria in 1916, many of Transylvania's Romanian population were interned. As also in the Second World War, the Allies were more successful than their opponents in sharing the burden of the war effort.

The Russian economy, in contrast to that of Germany, was poorly managed and wasteful, with industrial production and transport both in grave difficulties by 1915. A serious munitions crisis affected Russia that year, and the Russians depended in part on French supplies. The War Industries Committees that had been set up were found wanting and, in 1916, state monopolies took over coal and oil production.[35]

In France, the government controlled bread prices, and state-supervised consortia directed the allocation of supplies in crucial industries, although the production of munitions was left to entrepreneurs. A government-directed shoe industry was created, as was a chemical industry. State control was widely extended, but, unlike in Germany, there was an appropriate level of care for civilian needs and, thus, morale.[36]

The French war economy benefited from the supply of coal, iron and steel by Britain (shipped in British ships), which in part, compensated for the loss of French production capability to German occupation. This was an important instance of an Allied co-operation seen, also, in 1916, with the establishment of the Inter-Allied Bureaux of Munitions and Statistics, which were designed to help co-ordinate and plan munitions provision, including purchase in America. These bodies led at the start of 1918 to the Inter-Allied Munitions Council,[37] although, despite the Inter-Allied Tank Committee, tank production proved an example of limited co-operation in large part due to a British lack of necessary willingness to do so.[38]

For all combatants, the mass management of resources, manufacturing and society became vital. The price of total war was vigilance as well as mobilization. In Germany, the military was given, under the Prussian Law of Siege, powers of arrest, search, censorship, opening mail, forbidding the sale of particular goods and closing businesses.[39] As an aspect of the transformation of society, the war led to a more hostile attitude to aliens, with anti-Germanism increasing markedly in Britain so that George V changed the family name from Saxe-Coburg-Gotha to Windsor. In 1914, Hankey was concerned about aliens in London, writing: 'They could do a tremendous lot of damage in an emergency by incendiarism (using petrol), destroying railways and telegraphs, and knocking on the head simultaneously most of the Cabinet ministers and principal government officials to say nothing of destroying power stations by short circuits, gas works, etc.'[40] Bad news was frequently interpreted in terms of treasonable activity and rumours were rife. Thus, in Russia, the Tsarina was suspected of being pro-German. In Australia in September 1917, the sinking of ships by a German raider, the *Wolf*, was to be publicly blamed by William Hughes, the Prime Minister, on terroristic bomb plotters and the press called for the internment of the entire German community.

Governments acted against those they suspected and to quieten public anxieties in Canada, the War Measures Act gave the government power over 'enemy aliens' and radicals. Britain interned 32,440 non-combatants, France about 60,000, and Germany 111,879.[41] Internment often involved expropriation and, in many cases, repatriation. Intelligence and surveillance agencies and activities dramatically increased in scale. In Britain, the Intelligence agencies MI5 and MI6 were created in January 1916 and grew rapidly, so that, by 1919, MI5 employed thousands. Surveillance was also greatly enhanced in the empire. Concern about Pan-Islamicism encouraged the Defence of India Act, passed in March 1915, which permitted more repressive responses to suspected agitation.

War therefore gave the states power and enabled them to circumvent many of the constraints and exigencies of pre-war politics. As such, the war was a catalyst for modernization, and this was certainly the case in industrialization, in the treatment of women and in financial terms. The needs of war work meant that women were recruited to industrial production, notably for munitions, as, for example, in Britain and Italy, freeing men for military service. The massive expansion of nursing was also significant and included the socially prominent such as Elizabeth Bowes-Lyon, later wife of George VI, who himself, as Duke of York, served at Jutland.

Governments were now able to tax and borrow as much as they thought necessary. Income tax in Britain doubled in the first year of the war, while in New Zealand it increased greatly from 1916. In 1917, personal income tax was introduced in Canada, as were taxes on profits in trade. A series of compulsory war loans in Austria hit support for the war, although as part of a brew including food shortages, inflation and defeat.

At the same time as governmental impositions, state power rested on a degree of social support. Pre-war, there had been a left-wing anti-militaristic tradition across Europe,[42] but it was always affected by the counter-effect of patriotism, and, in 1914, trade unions rallied to the state. In Germany, on 2 August 1914, unions signed an industrial truce that was designed to last for the entire war. Across Europe, many men wanted to fight. The initial rush in August 1914 to enlist in Britain, a country that had no tradition of conscription, admittedly when the expectation was that the war would be 'over by Christmas', was indicative of this. A sense of adventure was important, as was a presentation of the war as a struggle against evil.[43]

Nevertheless, many who were given the choice to volunteer in Britain did not do so, while in Germany large-scale enthusiasm for the war at its outset, especially among the male, Protestant urban middle-class, was qualified by the number opposed to the war, particularly among the workers. Once war had begun, the dominant theme in Germany was fatalistic acceptance, not enthusiasm. The middle class was more keen than the bulk of the population, and their voice was disproportionately strong, while propaganda played a major role in moulding the popular response and how it was perceived.[44]

In Italy, there had been pre-war left-wing pacifist activity against the war in Libya that began with the Italian invasion of 1911, notably in 'red week' of June 1914, and such views were voiced anew once the Great War broke out. The Socialist Angelo Tasca declared in August 'Between France and Germany, we choose the International'. Indeed, Italy's move towards war in May 1915 led to large-scale demonstrations and strikes that month, notably in the major industrial city of Turin, but, having opposed the war, the Socialist Party rallied to the flag. Moreover, the Romanian Social Democratic Party, which was very much opposed to entering the war, nevertheless agreed to support mobilization in order to defend Romania from attack. War brought a lessening of constitutional opposition to existing political arrangements elsewhere, as in Britain where the National Union of Women's Suffrage Societies decided to suspend their cause for the duration of the war, while a more radical section which also endorsed pacifism resigned and supported the Peace Conference at The Hague in April 1915.[45]

The creation and deployment of a mass volunteer army in Britain in 1914–15 was a testimony to the patriotic nature of public culture, as well as being a formidable administrative achievement. Furthermore, despite the strains of the war, as well as disturbances, including a mutiny at Etaples in September 1917,[46] there was to be no level of radicalism in the British army comparable to the French and Russian armies in 1917, and no collapse comparable to that of much of the Italian army that year. In 1916, Robert Blatchford, a patriotic ex-serviceman, attacked summary punishments in the army in articles in the *Sunday Chronicle* and the *Illustrated Sunday Herald*, but there was no widespread resonance within the armed forces. German interrogations of British soldiers captured on the Somme in 1916 revealed that many were optimistic. Later that year, missing home and wanting peace, Alan Thomson went into every gun-pit in his unit to wish his men a Happy Christmas: 'They were all plastered with mud but cheery as sky larks.'[47]

Concern about military morale, nevertheless, played a greater role for British as well as non-British commanders in 1917–18. Much of this concern involved a determination to improve conditions, in so far as was possible, but there was also an emphasis on ideology. This emphasis was helped by the extent to which in Britain and America the war was presented as a conflict between two contrasting value systems. Political instruction for soldiers was a theme in the British army in 1917–18, while, in 1917, Ludendorff instituted political instruction to explain what the Germans were fighting for. Doubtless exhausted, many of the soldiers slept. In America, the Committee on Education and Special Training of the War Department in 1918 pressed for educational institutions to play a role, specifically by setting up Special Army Training Camps to prepare recruits. In July 1918, an obligatory course was established on 'Issues of the War'.[48]

Among all the combatants, the war effort was underpinned at home by government- directed or supported propaganda, which became more important in 1916 as war-weariness and demoralization increased and opposition to the conflict became more frequently voiced. In Britain, where, despite the heavy sacrifices of the war, civilian support for it remained high,[49] a Department of Information was founded under John Buchan, the basis of what, in 1918, became the Ministry of Information under Lord Beaverbrook, who had earlier been Chairman of the War Office Cinematograph Committee. Aside from printed propaganda,[50] there were efforts to use new media. Thus, in Bulgaria, film as well as newspaper articles were used to promote closer ties with Germany. Pressure to provide military facilities for film propaganda could lead, however, to a hostile response from military authorities.[51]

Propaganda sought not only to encourage support but also to meet public interest. Buchan, who served in Intelligence, published a spy-thriller about a German threat to the British fleet, *The Thirty-Nine Steps* (1915), as well as the 24-volume *Nelson's History of the War* (1915–19). Publishers found that there was a massive market for maps of the war as readers sought to follow and understand operations. This interest was satisfied by newspapers and book publishers with works such as the *Atlas of the European Conflict* (Chicago, 1914), the *Daily Telegraph Pocket Atlas of the War* (London, 1917), *Géographie de la Guerre* (Paris, 1917), *From the Western Front at a Glance* (London, 1917), *Petit Atlas de la Guerre et de la Paix* (Paris, 1918) and *Bretano's Record Atlas* (New York, 1918).

Popular mobilization and concern about morale owed much to the extent to which the war was far more labour-intensive than conflict involving advanced industrial powers at the present day; not only were more men expected to serve, but the industrial and transport support systems required far more labour. Millions of men were needed both for the military and for its support system. Over 13 million men alone served in the German armed forces during the war, which was a formidable organizational problem for the military and one that also posed major problems of adjustment for civilian society, the economy and cultural assumptions. Women replaced many of those who served.

Very large percentages of the adult male population were called up and millions of men served without deserting or in any other way resisting control, although there were to be a number of declared conscientious objectors by the end of the war: 16,500 in Britain. Despite being far distant from the areas of combat, 40 per cent of all New Zealand men of military age (between 19 and 45), served overseas. Out of this 120,000, over 50,000 were injured and 18,000 died. On the Somme in 1916, the New Zealanders suffered 40 per cent casualties in just 23 days' operations. More generally, alongside often-enthusiastic support for state and cause, habits of mass mobilization acquired prior to the war, thanks to industrial labour, trade unions and the organization of democratic politics, contributed to this widespread willingness to accept military discipline and activity at the behest of the state, as also did passive acceptance of the social order. Alan Thomson's trusting attitude is notable. In October 1915, he wrote to Edith, 'I think the Germans are already feeling the pinch and that Lord Kitchener's public statement to the effect that they had, in his opinion, almost shot their bolt, has probably a great deal of truth in it. He surely would not have made it unless he really believed it to be true'.[52]

Yet, alongside a stress on enthusiasm, comradeship and consent, it is necessary to note the extent to which coercion, and the threat of coercion, were employed to ensure military service. The shooting of deserters after summary judgements was a potent threat, and the nature of the campaigning, especially on the Western Front, made desertion difficult. Moreover, the introduction and expansion of conscription was not universally welcome. Exclusions from conscription indicated limitations of state power that, in part, reflected restrictions on consent: conscription was not introduced in Ireland or in all Maori areas in New Zealand, and was opposed and widely ignored in French-speaking areas of Canada. Conscription was rejected by Australia in two divisive referenda.

In Britain, conscription was seen as opposed to the Liberal tradition of civil liberty, as well as opposed by much of the labour movement, and there was considerable opposition to it from within the Liberal Party, including by the Chancellor of the Exchequer, Reginald McKenna. Nevertheless, Lloyd George, the dynamic Liberal Minister of Munitions, who wished to mobilize all the country's resources for war, and the Conservatives, were determined to see conscription through in order to provide sufficient men for the trenches on the Western Front, not least due to the heavy and unexpected casualties of the first year of the war. A fudge, Edward, 17th Earl of Derby's semi-voluntary scheme, introduced in October 1915, failed to produce sufficient recruits, and political pressure, especially Lloyd George's threat to resign, led to the Military Service Act of January 1916, which introduced conscription for single men. In response to a sudden surge in weddings, married conscription followed in April.

Conscription helped to push the size of the British armed forces up to 4.5 million men in 1917–18, one in three of the male labour force. Claims for exemption were allowed and were considered by local tribunals which were civilian, not military, bodies. Many of these did not reflect an unwillingness to serve. In Stratford-on-Avon, nearly half the cases heard were claims by employers to exempt their employees, and while only 4.2 per cent of cases gained full exemption, most received conditional or temporary exemption.[53] In New Zealand, where conscription was introduced on 1 August 1916, the Labour Party split over the issue.

The extension of conscription helped lead to the major outbreak of opposition in Russia prior to the revolutions in 1917, the Muslim revolt in 1916. This widespread revolt against the introduction of conscription, specifically for labour battalions in the army, was defeated, with great brutality and heavy casualties. In Kazakhstan, organized rebel forces reached a peak strength of about 50,000 men. The conflict as a whole threw light on the possibilities of counter-insurgency operations: the mobile and experienced government forces benefited from their opponents' lack of organization, training and arms.[54]

On a far smaller scale, a nationalist uprising in Ireland, was also suppressed in 1916. Over 270,000 Irish men, both Protestant and Catholic, served in the armed forces, all as volunteers, for conscription was not introduced in Ireland. These men included some of the Protestant and Catholic volunteers who had organized in 1913–14 as sectarian politics came to the fore over the issue of Home Rule and Ulster. Moreover, the majority of the Irish population loyally supported the war effort against Germany. In contrast, the 1916 rising was very different in scale to the volunteer war effort. Planned by the military council of the Irish Republican Brotherhood, a general rising was intended, but it was largely restricted to Dublin: there was supporting action in parts of Ireland, but nothing of note. This ensured that the rising would fail militarily and, instead, it became a bold gesture. About 1,200 men rose in Dublin on Easter Monday, 24 April, seized a number of sites and proclaimed an independent Irish Republic, but the rebels suffered from bad planning, poor tactics and the strength of the British response, which included an uncompromising use of artillery to shell targets in Dublin. Under heavy pressure, the insurgents unconditionally surrendered on 29 April.

Although overcome, the Easter Rising, like that in Muslim Central Asia and the Austro-German declaration of Polish independence from Russia on 5 November 1916, indicated the pressure being brought to bear on the empires involved in the war. At the same time, as was common, empire was formed simultaneously as it weakened. Thus, in 1916, the British overran the sultanate of Darfur in West Sudan, whose Sultan, Ali Dinar, had heeded Turkish calls for pan-Islamicist action. Aircraft and light lorries were used by the British to provide speedy firepower and mobility. West Sudan was far distant from the killing fields of Flanders and the Somme, but it indicated the extent to which the war had more than worldwide impact: it was also waged in far-flung areas. Indeed, in August 1916, the British authorities in India intercepted letters revealing the 'Silk Letters' conspiracy, spearheaded by the Islamic 'Army of God' and allegedly including the rulers of Turkey, Afghanistan, Persia and the Hejaz (in Arabia),[55] where, in fact, there was a rising against Turkish control.

The war thus interacted with a range of disputes and tensions. In Ethiopia, it served as part of the attempt to assert national sovereignty and independence from European colonial control that had been so important from the 1890s. Italy's entry into the war on the Allied side in 1915 focused the issue, as Lij Iyasu, Regent of Ethiopia from 1911 for his grandfather Menilek II, who had had a very bad stroke, sought to push Italy out of neighbouring Eritrea and Italian Somaliland and thus prevent Italy from resuming its earlier attempt to subjugate Ethiopia. To that end he looked to the Central Powers, as Allied defeat appeared the way to secure Ethiopian independence. Iyasu also sought an alliance with Sayyid Muhammad 'Abdille Hassan, who was opposing the British in neighbouring British Somaliland. Alliances, however, are always precarious, as Sayyid Muhammad contested Ethiopian power in the vast Ogaden region, so that Iyasu's approach to him led to criticism in Ethiopia as did efforts to show favour to Muslims in Ethiopia's government.

International and domestic opposition came to the fore in Ethiopia in September 1916. On 12 September, the Allies sent a note to the Foreign Ministry seeking an explanation for Iyasu's policy and declaring an arms embargo, and, on 27 September, a meeting of aristocrats deposed Iyasu. However, on 8 October, he escaped into the Ogaden, launching a civil war. Initially, the auspices seemed good for Iyasu, but the regional potentates in southern and western Ethiopia deployed their strength to support the new government and on 27 October, at Segele about 40 miles north of the capital, Addis Ababa, Iyasu was defeated. This was a major battle that was very different to that then being waged on the Somme. The side with more troops and better arms won, but the key element was that the major clash in Ethiopia was over rapidly. The result benefited the Allies and represented yet another stage in the process by which opportunities for the Central Powers around the world were closed down.

However, the bulk of the fighting in 1916 was in Europe and the Middle East where, after Gallipoli, British pressure on the Turks was focused on Mesopotamia and Palestine. There was no attempt to repeat a naval or amphibious assault on the centre of Turkish power. Instead, the commitment to the defence of the Suez Canal was translated from defensive preparations to a forward defence in which the British moved into Sinai. However, there was no significant pressure on the Turks in Palestine until the following spring. As with

Kitchener's advance in Sudan in 1895–98, the background was a major attempt to create the necessary transport and logistical infrastructure.

In Mesopotamia, a British attempt to seize Baghdad with inadequate forces was checked at Ctesiphon on 22 November 1915, and the British force then fell back on Kut-al-Amara where it was besieged. Relief attempts failed with heavy losses, in part because of frontal attacks on Turkish positions, and, on 26 April 1916, the 10,000 strong force at Kut, short of food and hit by disease, surrendered. Subsequently, 70 per cent of the other ranks died in an often-harsh captivity; the officers fared better. The British were not to resume the offensive up the Tigris River until December 1916 and failure at Kut contributed to a sense that the war was being mishandled, as was indeed the case. Poor command focused on a serious underestimation of Turkish effectiveness alongside inadequate logistical and administrative management.[56] The Sykes-Picot Agreement of May 1916 designating British and French areas of post-war control and influence in the Turkish empire appeared highly premature.[57]

The Russians in the Caucasus, now commanded by Grand Duke Nicholas, were more effective than the British in Mesopotamia. The capture of Erzerum (13–16 February 1916) and Trebizond (18 April 1916) was impressive, not least because a major Turkish counteroffensive was defeated that summer at Erzingan west of Erzerum. Nevertheless, further south-east, Russian forces that had advanced to Bitlis and Mush to the west of Lake Van were pushed back in early August by Mustafa Kemal, later Atatürk, the 'father' of Turkish independence.

Pressure on border areas did not yet amount to a fatal crisis for the Turks. However, the combination of rule by the Committee of Union and Progress who were committed to a racial construction of the Ottoman, but to them Turkish, empire, and their concern about Armenian nationalism linked to the Allies, had already led to a murderous treatment of the Armenians in 1915. The circumstances and details remain contentious but large numbers of Armenians were killed while many, driven into an arid region, died as refugees.[58] This genocidal slaughter, in which over a million died in 1915–16, should not be forgotten in the focus on strategic, operational and tactical questions. The many Greeks living in the Turkish empire were also suspected of being fifth columnists and were poorly treated, although a concern to prevent Greece's entry into the war ensured that this treatment lacked the genocidal consequences of that visited on the Armenians.[59] Nevertheless, the Allies' Gallipoli offensive led to the deportation of Christians from the nearby region by the Turks.

Dissatisfaction with the conduct of the war played a role among all the combatants by 1916. In July, in Hungary a new party, the 'Independence and '48 Party' was established by Mihály Károlyi, in order to oppose the war, to press for a separate peace without territorial gains and to call for universal suffrage, goals supported from November by the new Emperor, Karl, who in Hungary was King Charles IV.[60] In Russia, there was growing criticism of the Tsar, Nicholas II, while in Germany Falkenhayn was replaced in August as Chief of the General Staff by Hindenburg, with Ludendorff as his deputy. With the army now the directing pivot of the German state and economy, the two men had in effect gained power from the Kaiser, Wilhelm II, and from the *Reichstag*, neither of which was in a position to exercise it. Civilian control, however, still operated in France, where Joffre was relieved of command on 13 December by the government of the Socialist Aristide Briand, with the sop of being called Marshal of France following on 26 December.

Problems resulted in ministerial changes. Romania's defeat led, on 24 December, to the formation of a government of national unity, now based at Iasi in Moldavia. In Britain, there was widespread political dissatisfaction with the conduct of the war and particular pressure from backbench Conservative opinion. Differences between Conservatives and Liberals prevented coalition cohesion and contributed to a sense of malaise. With Prime Minister Asquith, a vacillator, the management of the war seemed inadequate. This situation led to pressure in November 1916 for a small War Committee to direct the war effort. Asquith, whose son Raymond had died in an attack on the Somme on 15 September, saw this call as aimed against his premiership, but his effort to preserve his position collapsed in the face of the growing alignment of Lloyd George, the active Secretary of State for War from July 1916, with the Conservatives. Having lost three general elections before the war (in 1906 and two in 1910), and then drifting to the Right (and further from electoral popularity), not least by supporting Ulster's opposition to Irish Home Rule, the Conservatives had been offered by the wartime coalition an unexpected way back to the centre of politics from where they were able to benefit with their skills in flag-waving and the degree to which the war provided plenty of opportunities for them to do so. Lloyd George was happy to sound and be resolute, pressing for both a 'knock-out blow' and 'a fight to the finish', as in *The Times* of 29 November. Similarly, William Massey, the New Zealand Prime Minister, declared that there should be no negotiations until the Germans were driven beyond the Rhine.[61]

Such sentiments captured the strength of public determination and reflected opinion held at the front as well as at home. In September, Alan Thomson wrote from France to Edith: 'the Hun ... must be having a rotten time of it but I have no sympathy for him. I wish on the contrary that we could make life still more unpleasant to the loathsome boche', adding, in November, after HMS *Britannia* was sunk: 'It was probably a torpedo though the Huns will of course deny it. They really are the most loathsome race and there is only one thing to do and that is to go on and on and on until we are in a position to square our account with them properly'.[62] In April 1917, Tom Gurney, another officer, referred to the Germans as 'the fiends'.[63]

The sense of total war that nationalist ideology gave rise to was compounded by the length and bitterness of the struggle, the degree of mobilization to which this led[64] and, in particular, by the many casualties, the determined response to the loss of whom paved a route away from compromise. For example, Anglophobia played a major and increasing role in Germany,[65] becoming more potent than hostility to autocratic Russia as the weakness of the latter was increasingly more obvious.

In December 1916, Lloyd George took control of the British war effort. Less politically skilful than in the past, the overconfident Asquith was displaced, resigning on 5 December, and the government was recast. Lloyd George became Prime Minister, and both Conservatives and Labour continued to offer support. Stubborn as well as weak, Asquith, however, refused to hold office in the new government and was supported in this by most of the Liberal ministers who thereby lost their posts. Lloyd George, therefore, had divided the Liberals and, as a result of this division, Conservative support for the Government was much more important than when Asquith had been Prime Minister.

Lloyd George also brought new vitality to the government, not least with the formation of a War Cabinet of five members meeting every other day. This body was then given a secretariat and was made responsible for creating and co-ordinating policy, corresponding directly with government departments. However, there had already been relevant improvements in cabinet government in 1915 under Asquith, while Lloyd George's War Cabinet did not, in practice, take all-important decisions, instead becoming more supervisory with time. Instead, Lloyd George gave a degree of unity to government by controlling the executive authority of the War Cabinet. In 1940, Churchill was to revive Lloyd George's position with a similar War Cabinet.

On the other side of the Atlantic, Woodrow Wilson, the Democratic candidate, won re-election as President. He and his country were to play an important role in the remaining years of the war, but, although providing the Allies with key economic support (for which, as in the Second World War, they were well paid), the Americans were still resolutely neutral, most preferring, as in 1939–40, to treat the war as a matter in which America should not get involved.[66]

CHAPTER 5

1917

When one considers the millions under arms 30 or
40 thousand prisoners seems nothing very colossal.
Arthur Child-Villiers on the British
offensive at Arras.[1]

The unexpected and the failure of planning were both much in
evidence in 1917. The collapse of Tsarist rule in Russia, the subsequent breakdown of the Russian war effort and the Bolshevik
(Communist) coup in Petrograd (St Petersburg), led to a transformation of the war. There had been much talk of the need to help
Russia in order to prevent its collapse, but, when the latter occurred,
its scale and speed took most by surprise. Surprise was less the case
with American entry into the war, as that was an obvious consequence of the German decision to resume unrestricted submarine
warfare. However, the consequences of the latter were not as anticipated by the Germans.

If these developments provided key parameters for the events of
the year, demonstrating anew the close links between politics and war,
they scarcely exhausted the list of the unexpected, nor of failed plans.
Nor did they provide the sole themes for the year. Three others were
offered by the increasing pressure of the conflict on the combatants,
the related sense that the cataclysmic struggle being waged was a
total measure of peoples, and, conversely, significant improvements
in fighting technique and weaponry.

Moreover, the narrative of the war, always complex, became increasingly fractured as the toll on political stability increased, and this also ensured that there was fighting that in no way matched that on the front lines. In February, a Liberal rebellion against the rigged Cuban election of 1916 was firmly repressed by Marco Menocel, the Conservative president. In December 1917, the government of Portugal, which, under British pressure had entered the war on the Allied side that year, was overthrown by a Revolutionary Committee under Major Sidonio Paes. The confused nature of the confrontation in Lisbon was captured by Major-General Nathaniel Barnardiston, the Chief of the British Military Mission: 'the fleet got to work ... and the field pieces replied but were almost all short. I only saw one go over and none apparently anywhere near ... There was intermittent rifle fire all night as rioters were looting shops etc'.[2]

In Spain, neutrality did not prevent an increasingly disturbed situation in which pressure to intervene on the Allied side fed into political instability. The army suppressed a General Strike called by the Socialists on 13 August, while, in October, an army ultimatum forced a change in government.[3] The inflation and spread of trade unionism seen in Spain had an impact more generally. In Greece in 1917, King Constantine I was deposed with Allied support in June and the country, under his rival the pro-Allied Prime Minister Eleutherios Venizelos, declared war on Germany. The British and French attack on Athens is little known.

Developments in Portugal and Spain reflected a sense of chaos and uncertainty that owed much to the Russian Revolution. Russia was dealt a knock-out blow by the combination of defeat at German hands and the failure of its state to respond adequately, but the Germans, ironically instead, planned a knock-out blow against Britain by means of unrestricted submarine warfare. Having failed to drive France from the war at Verdun, and experienced the lengthy and damaging British attack in the Somme offensive, the Germans sought to force Britain from the war by resuming attempts to destroy its supply system. There was a parallel with the invasion of France via Belgium in 1914, in that the strong risk that a major power would enter the war as a result, Britain in 1914 and America in 1917, was disregarded on the grounds that success could be obtained as a result of the German attack. In 1917, however, the Germans, unlike in 1914, had had plentiful warnings as a result of their earlier use of unrestricted submarine warfare. There was also a failure of planning as anticipated outcomes from the submarine assault did not arise, and the timetables of success miscarried.

Yet, this account assumes a rationalist balance of risks and opportunities which ignores the extent to which the decision to turn to unrestricted submarine warfare reflected an ideology of total war and a powerful Anglophobia based on nationalist right-wing circles, for example the Pan German League, that saw British liberalism and capitalism as a threat to German culture. These ideas were given political bite by the argument that the German government, notably the Chancellor, Bethmann-Hollweg, was defeatist and interested in a compromise peace, and that support for unrestricted warfare was a sign of, and security for, nationalist commitment. Indeed, Tirpitz, who had links with such circles, was allowed to resign in March 1916 because his support for unrestricted submarine warfare had led him to quarrel with the Chancellor and to challenge the position of the Kaiser.[4] The following month, an American protest led Wilhelm II to order the suspension of the permission given that February for the sinking without warning of armed freighters; but not of passenger ships.

On 31 January 1917, however, Germany announced, and on 2 February resumed, unconditional submarine warfare, which led to America breaking diplomatic links the next day and declaring war on Germany (but not its allies) on 6 April. Congress had approved the decision, although six senators and 50 congressmen opposed it. The German military leadership, increasingly politically influential, was unsympathetic to American moralizing, while, as in 1941, there was also the view that America was already helping the British and French war effort as much as it could commercially. Moreover, there was a conviction that Britain could be driven out of the war rapidly by heavy sinkings of merchantmen: a belief that the submarines could achieve much, and that this achievement would have an obvious consequence. It was claimed that the British would sue for peace on 1 August 1917. Furthermore, many German submarine enthusiasts assumed that their force would be able to impede the movement of American troops to Europe very seriously and, more generally, there was a failure to appreciate American strength. On 31 January 1917, Eduard von Capelle, the German Naval Minister, unwisely told the budget committee of the *Reichstag* that, from a military point of view, America was as nothing.

In 1914, there was active hostility in America to the idea of participation in the European war. It was seen as alien to American interests and antipathetic to her ideology, although the liberal credentials of American policy were rather tarnished by interventions in Mexico in 1914 and 1916, Haiti in 1915 and the Dominican Republic in 1916. These interventions reflected imperialist assumptions, but not a drive for territorial expansion. The unrestricted submarine warfare that sank American ships (and also violated international law) led to a major shift in attitudes in which Americans became persuaded of the dangerous consequences of German strength and ambitions, and did so in a highly moralized form that encouraged large-scale commitment. Thus, America constructed national interest in terms of the freedom of international trade from unrestricted submarine warfare.

Germany's crass wartime diplomacy exacerbated the situation, notably an apparent willingness to divert American strength by encouraging Mexican opposition, including *revanche* for the major losses suffered in the Mexican-American War of 1846–48. The Americans were made aware of this when the British intercepted a telegram to the German Ambassador in Mexico from Arthur Zimmermann, the Foreign Minister. The logic of this apparently bizarre move was pre-emptive: the Germans wished to distract American energies from war in Europe. American sensitivity about German links with unstable Mexico was acute: later that year, the *San Francisco Chronicle* claimed (incorrectly) that German submarines were being constructed at a secret base in Mexico.

America had given neutrality added legitimacy to other states.[5] In turn, after America broke off diplomatic relations with Germany in February, it invited all neutral countries to do the same, and this appeal had some success. Aside from Latin American states breaking off diplomatic relations with Germany, others followed America in declaring war, including Cuba and Panama, both American client states, on 7 August, and Brazil, which also suffered from the unrestricted submarine warfare, on 26 October 1917. However, the Brazilian contribution was more modest than in the Second World War when about 25,000 troops were sent to fight. In the Great War, in contrast, only a small Brazilian naval squadron was eventually dispatched, and it did not see active service. Nevertheless, the Brazilian declaration of war contributed to Allied commercial warfare against Germany, Guatemala, Nicaragua, Costa Rica, Honduras and Haiti followed in declaring war in 1918, while Bolivia, Ecuador, Peru and Uruguay broke off diplomatic relations with Germany in 1917.[6] America had declared war on 7 December 1917 on Austria, but did not follow suit against Bulgaria or Turkey.

Seeking an opportunity to enter the conflict, China broke off diplomatic relations with Germany on 14 March 1917 and declared war on Germany and Austria on 14 August: Siam (Thailand) had done so on 22 July. Encouraged by Foch, Chief of the French General Staff from May 1917, the French proved receptive to the Chinese idea of an expeditionary force, but, although labourers in the 'Chinese Labour Corps', active since 1916, were acceptable, the other Allies were opposed to the dispatch of Chinese troops, for political reasons and because of concerns about fighting quality and the transportation burden, and the plan failed.[7] Japan was determined to retain its political position in China and was unwilling to see the latter contribute to the war effort. The following year, Ethiopia offered to declare war on the Central Powers in return for a role in the peace talks and new weaponry, but this offer, which challenged Italian ambitions for control over the country, was rejected.

Other powers remained neutral in 1917, finding that the pressures of what was seen as the total clash of industrialized societies pressed hard on their trade, not least as a consequence of the Allied blockade of Germany and of German submarine warfare. The Netherlands and Denmark, both of which were maritime trading powers bordering Germany, and thus key challenges to the blockade, found themselves under contrary pressures, and their use of diplomacy had to be accompanied by careful consideration of the military situation, for example the possibility of German invasion, and also of economic interests.[8]

Ironically, America's entry into the war increased the importance of submarines to German capability as it further shaped the balance in surface warships against Germany. America had the third largest navy in the world after Britain and Germany, and the Navy Act of 1916 had increased the shipbuilding programme. In part due to the dominance of the army's needs, and certainly compared to the grip of the British Admiralty over wartime procurement, the Germans added fewer battlecruisers and battleships to their fleet during the war than the British. Thus, the Germans did not have the margin of success in a large-scale shipbuilding programme to fall back upon, nor, more seriously, did they have the prospect of support from the warships of new allies that the British gained with the alliance of Italy and America. Furthermore, in late 1916, in accordance with a British request, four Japanese warships were sent to the Mediterranean where, based in Malta, they added to escort capacity as well as strengthening the Allied position in the equation of naval power. These additions more than nullified the success of German submarines in sinking Allied warships: in 1917, the British lost this way only one pre-dreadnought battleship and one armoured cruiser.

Dreadnought battleships and battlecruisers entering service before and after 1 August 1941

Country	Before 1 August 1914		After 1 August 1914	
	Battleships	Battlecruisers	Battleships	Battlecruisers
Britain	21	9	14	5
Germany	15	4	4	3
America	10	6		
Japan	4	6		
France	4	3		
Russia	2	4		
Austria	4	0		

Source: W. E. McMahon, *Dreadnought Battleships and Battle Cruisers* (Washington, 1978).

The German failure in surface-ship warfare, and in the arithmetic of surface-ship strength, helped to accentuate the importance to them of submarines. The initial rate of Allied shipping losses was sufficiently high to threaten defeat. Serious losses were inflicted on Allied, particularly British, commerce, in large part due to British inexperience in confronting submarine attacks. The limited effectiveness of anti-submarine weaponry was also an issue: depth charges were effective only if they exploded close to the hull. In February to April 1917, 1,945,240 tons of British shipping were sunk, with only nine submarines lost, and, in the first four months of the unrestricted attack, the British lost an average of 630,000 tons of merchant shipping per month.

In the event, as later in the Second World War, Britain survived the onslaught thanks to both outfighting the submarines and to success on the Home Front. The introduction, from 10 May, of a system of escorted convoys cut shipping losses dramatically and helped lead to an increase in the sinking of submarines. Convoys, which were introduced first in February 1917 to protect ships carrying coal to France, in response to calls from the French government, and then in April for the Scandinavian trade, might appear such an obvious solution that it is surprising they were not adopted earlier, but there were counter-arguments, including the number of escorts required, the delays that would be forced on shipping, and the possibility that convoys would simply offer a bigger target. They were also resisted by some naval circles for a time as not sufficiently in touch with the bold 'Nelson touch', although the Admiralty, where the Naval Staff had created a dedicated anti-submarine section and itself became better organized in 1917, eventually took the necessary steps.[9]

Aside from convoying, there was a major effort to employ Intelligence, notably the use of radio, in defeating the submarines. Convoys alone would not suffice as it was also important to weaken the submarine force by sinking boats, killing crew and weakening morale. Thanks to the tracking of submarine movements, the British acquired an edge, but there was not yet any equivalent to the sonar used in the Second World War in order to provide a local tactical advantage, and thus relatively few submarines were sunk by searching destroyers. Instead, mine-laying was crucial.

Only 393 of the 95,000 ships that were to be convoyed across the Atlantic were sunk. Moreover, convoys facilitated the transport of over two million American troops to Europe aboard thousands of ships, with the loss of just three transports, one of which managed to limp to Brest after being torpedoed, and with only 68 soldiers drowned. This convoying was the priority for the American navy and convoying owed much to American support. More generally, convoying was an aspect of the direction on a global scale by the Allies of most of the world's shipping, trade and troop flows. The Allied Maritime Transport Council oversaw an impressive system of international co-operation at sea, allocating shipping resources so that they could be employed most efficiently, which was important economically and also in lessening targets for German submarines. The Wheat Executive provided another aspect of this planning.

Convoys reduced the targets for submarines and ensured that, when they found them, the submarines could be attacked by escorts.[10] In providing sufficient numbers of the latter, the British were helped by their wartime shipbuilding programme, which included 56 destroyers and 50 anti-submarine motor launches. In August, the monthly tonnage of British shipping lost fell below half a million.

The American contribution was also crucial. Although they lacked experience in anti-submarine warfare, the Americans deployed their fleet to help protect communication routes across the Atlantic, and, from May, American warships took part in anti-submarine patrols in European waters, initially with six destroyers based in Queenstown, Ireland. American escort vessels contributed to the effectiveness of convoying, the key help being in destroyers, fast enough to track submarines and to keep them submerged, which reduced their effectiveness. To assist convoying in the Mediterranean, American warships were based in Gibraltar and Japanese ones in Malta.[11]

Convoys also benefited from the 'shoal' factor: submarines, when they found one, only had time to sink a limited number of ships. In coastal waters, convoys were supported by aircraft and airships, and this support forced the submarines to remain submerged, where they were much slower. More generally, anti-submarine warfare displayed the complex relationships between technological advance, industrial capacity, organizational capability, operational experience and tactics. Mines provided a key instance of these processes, for, although convoys limited the potency of German attacks, mines sank more submarines than other weapons. Intelligence information was important in the planning of mine-laying. Mines have been under-rated in favour of more spectacular weapons, but mine barrages limited the options for submarines, as for surface vessels. The Allies laid massive barrages across the English Channel at Dover in late 1916; the far-greater distance of the North Sea between the Orkneys and Norway, from March 1918 with the Americans playing a major role; and across the Straits of Otranto, at the entrance to the Adriatic, in order to limit the operational range of German and Austrian forces.

These massive mine barrages, the one across the North Sea containing 75,000 mines, reflected industrial capacity and organizational capability. In Britain, the industrial production of mines benefited from group manufacture techniques first used to make Stokes mortars. There were also important improvements in mine technology during the war, although these are apt to be overlooked. By the end of the war, magnetic mines had been developed and were being laid by the British.

Command and control was another area of naval operations that benefited from technological improvement. As on land and in the air, developments with radio made it easier to retain detailed operational control. Directional wireless equipment aided location and navigation, and was employed to hunt German submarines by triangulation, while radio transmissions changed from a spark method to a continuous-wave system.

Yet, alongside a focus on dramatically new technology and doctrine at sea, including submarines, radio, aircraft, airships and anti-submarine warfare, it is necessary to note the role of traditional practices, such as blockade, as well as of incremental improvement, less spectacular technology, and manufacturing capacity. For example, one of the advantages of aircraft (and airships) in dealing with submarines is that viewing submerged objects is far easier from above than from sea level. However, aircraft were not yet able to make a fundamental contribution to anti-submarine operations because key specifications they had by the Second World War were lacking during the Great War, while the anti-submarine weapons dropped by aircraft were fairly unsophisticated compared to those of the Second. Internal strategy was also crucial in anti-submarine warfare.

As in the Second World War, a major attempt was made to manufacture imported goods at home (product substitution) and to increase farm production. As more generally in the Great War, activity focused on government and led to an increase in its authority, power and impact, notably with the introduction of rationing. With the Corn Production Act of 1917, the British government created a Food Production Department and imposed a policy of increasing the amount of land that was ploughed, rather than under grass, because it was more efficient to feed people directly with cereals (the price of which was guaranteed), from the land, rather than indirectly via meat and milk. For example, in Wales, the percentage of tillage rose by over 40 per cent. As a result of this policy, production of meat and milk in Britain fell and butter was replaced by margarine, but County and District War Agricultural Committees oversaw a 30 per cent rise in national cereal production. Overall statistics, however, can be misleading, as the rise in food production in 1917–18 was a recovery after a major fall in 1916. Despite the attempts of the Board of Agriculture to claim the credit, the recovery owed much to better weather. Regulation was a key theme, with the committees visiting every farm, scheduling land for ploughing, allocating labour, fertilizers and farm machinery and removing unsatisfactory farmers,[12] again a policy followed in the Second World War.

The Germans also launched an air assault on Britain in 1917 because they believed, possibly due to reports by Dutch intelligence, that the British were on the edge of rebellion, which was very much not the case. As a result of this belief, the attacks were intended not so much to serve attritional goals, but rather to be a decisive war-winning tool. The use of bombers – the Gotha – from 25 May reflected the rapid improvement of capability during the war, as science and technology were applied in the light of experience. Zeppelins had been revealed as vulnerable to aircraft interception, as well as to the weather, whereas the Gotha Mk IV could fly for six hours, had an effective range of 520 miles, could carry 1,100 pounds (or 500 kg) of bombs and could fly at an altitude of 21,000 feet (four miles or 6,400 metres), which made interception difficult. Furthermore, the crews were supplied with oxygen and with electric power to heat their flying suits. The first (and deadliest) raid on London, a daylight one on 13 June, led to a public outcry in Britain. Fourteen aircraft, approaching at 16,500 feet and each carrying six 110 lb bombs, killed 162 people and injured 432, not least as a result of a direct hit on the North Street School in Poplar that killed 16 children.

In the rapid action-reaction cycle that characterized advances during the war, the raids resulted in the speedy development of a defensive system involving high-altitude fighters based on airfields linked by telephone to observers, which led to heavy losses among the Gothas and to the abandonment of daylight raids. By 1918, Britain's early detection and response system was effective, and it provided the model for that used in 1940.

More seriously, as so often with German war-making in the twentieth century, the rationale of the campaign was misplaced because, as with attacks on France, far from hitting British morale, the bombing led to a hostile popular response. This remained the case even in the winter of 1917–18, when the Germans unleashed four-engine Zeppelin-Staaken R-series bombers, able to fly for ten hours and to drop 4,400 pounds (or 2,000 kg) of bombs. They required, however, a major logistical support system and failed to inflict sustained serious damage.[13] As earlier with the Zeppelins, troops at the front were concerned about the fate of loved ones at home.[14]

Returning to naval warfare, the most significant amphibious operation in Europe was mounted by the Germans. It was the most successful amphibious operation of the war in European waters, and the sole German one. They conquered Russia's Baltic islands, a success helped by the disruptive impact of the March (February by the Russian, religious, calendar) Revolution on Russian forces.[15]

This revolution reflected the wartime strain on Russian society, strain that was accentuated by the pressures of the winter. The organizational weakness of the Russian state was particularly clear in transport and food allocation, and the resulting pressures were concentrated in the cities as the demand for food was greatest there, a demand driven up by the large number of refugees from the war zone. Thus, Russia's failure to protect its territory from invasion contributed directly to the socio-economic crisis. Food shortages became more serious in the context of a paranoia that drew on a lack of national unity and on related political and social tensions, with 'speculators' supposedly holding the populace in thrall while 'Germans', including the Tsarina, betrayed them. In practice, the 'betrayal' linked to the Germans was that obtained by the latter's skilful use of subversion, notably arranging the transportation of the Bolshevik leader Lenin to Russia. Alongside popular discontent, there was significant disillusionment among the elite focused not only on Nicholas II but also on Tsarism.[16]

A popular demonstration in Petrograd against the price of bread on 8 March 1917 focused tension, but the police failed to control it and the government turned to the army. Disaffected, the troops on 12 March refused to fire on the crowds and, instead, went on strike. The following day, the troops and the factories elected representatives for a soviet or council. In the face of mounting chaos, some politicians and generals thought it necessary to act, and did so by determining to get rid of Nicholas II. He abdicated on 15 March, and the *Duma* (Parliament) established a provisional government under the reformer Prince Georgy Yevgenyevich Lvov. Soldiers had played a major role in the overthrow of Nicholas II, not so much that some units demonstrated for change, but rather that there was also a lack of willingness to fight for the tsar, in part because of divisions within the officer corps.[17]

The establishment of the provisional government unleashed political debate, but did not solve the problems of a state that could not wage war effectively nor of a society under tremendous pressure. Inflation continued to bite, while the transport system remained ineffective. The war, moreover, went on, though without success. Indeed, the eventual fall of the new government in November owed much to its failure to win success on the battlefield; or, alternatively, to pull out of the war altogether.

The Western Allies hoped that the change in government would make Russia a more liberal state and acceptable ally, and would revitalize the Russian war effort, and the Russian General Staff pressed for an offensive in order to help France and Britain on the Western Front.[18] On 1 July, Brusilov, now the commander in chief, launched an offensive into eastern Galicia, winning a breakthrough success at the expense of the Austrians, but limited resources and motivation hindered the advance, and a rapid German counter-attack on 19 July led to Russian defeat, heavy losses, retreat and the collapse of the Russian army. Much of it anyway did not wish to fight. Brusilov was replaced on 1 August.

This failure contributed greatly to the weakness of the government, which had been headed from July by Alexander Kerensky, a Socialist who had played a leading role in the March Revolution. This weakness provided the Bolsheviks with an opportunity to seize power, after the army's new commander-in-chief, General Lavr Kornilov, had failed to overthrow Kerensky in an attempted coup, a confusing episode that led to an increase in the influence of the radical Bolsheviks as Kerensky cast around for support. Lenin, the Bolshevik leader, had been returned to Russia from Switzerland in April, helped by the Germans in an attempt to sow disaffection, while, en route to St Petersburg, Leon Trotsky was arrested and detained by British naval authorities at Halifax for a month because they believed he was a German agent.[19] Lenin, who was against the war and confident that it would pull down the Provisional Government, more than fulfilled German hopes and justified the tens of millions of marks provided to further his activity.

The Provisional Government tried to hit back in August, but failed to crush the Bolsheviks. The sense of crisis increased when, after an intensive but short bombardment, a German offensive across the River Dvina above Riga, the largest city in Latvia, launched on 1 September, broke through the Russian positions and led the Russians to abandon Riga. The Bolshevik influence in the St Petersburg Soviet increased, and, on 7 November, a coup led to the overthrow of the government with little resistance. The government was unable to rely on the military because the governmental willingness to fight on against the Germans compromised military co-operation. Alongside disaffection among the soldiers, some of the senior commanders were unwilling to fight for the government.[20]

The Germans had far less success against Romania in 1917, in part because the army of the latter had been greatly improved by a military mission under General Henri Berthelot that had arrived in October 1916. Aside from providing much training, the French also transferred artillery and machine guns as well as installing telegraph lines for communications. In August, in one of the campaigns that is neglected in most accounts of the war, Mackensen attacked near Mărăşeţsi in an attempt to knock Romania out and open a way to the Russian Black Sea port of Odessa, a crucial centre of grain movement from Ukraine. In the event, the Germans suffered 60,000 casualties pushing forward six or seven kilometres along a 30-kilometre front, while the Romanians only suffered 27,000 casualties and held the line.

The offensive was stopped on 3 September so that the Germans could transfer troops to Italy. The Germans tried there to repeat their success against Russia, seeking to link political purpose to military effectiveness. In particular, what were later called *blitzkrieg* tactics were employed. The so-called, although not by the Germans, Hutier tactics built on Brusilov's 1916 offensive and on a captured French manual. Reginald Benson, a British liaison officer with the French, wrote a memorandum in July 1917 about German attacks near the Chemin des Dames: 'surprise attacks usually at day-break or dusk: assaulting infantry keep up with the [creeping barrage] ... Stosstrupps [stormtroopers] ... They consist of bombers, pioneers carrying flame-projectors, wire-cutters, and artillery liaison officers'. Benson reported that such units had been utilized ably since the beginning of the year, but that they drained the best men from the German infantry.[21] The Germans had used stormtroopers and infiltration tactics from the spring of 1916.

The tactics were used by the Germans on a large scale and in a major offensive on the Eastern Front at Riga in September 1917 with General Oskar von Hutier, the commander of the Eighth Army, combining stormtroopers with a heavy neutralization artillery bombardment. Then, these tactics were employed that October and November by the Austrians and Germans on the Italian Front at Caparetto. The emphasis was on surprise and speed, not attrition. Benefiting from the cover of fog, the Austrians and Germans moved rapidly with machine guns and light artillery on lorries, avoiding Italian strongpoints as they advanced, and destroyed the coherence and communications of the Italian defence. Poor command contributed greatly to the Italian collapse, but this collapse also indicated the potential effectiveness of the offensive using the new tactical approach.

Italy was nearly knocked out of the war. Its forces were pushed back 80 miles and lost possibly as many as 700,000 men, especially if deserters are included, as well as nearly 5,000 pieces of artillery. This military disaster was linked to a slower-moving political and social crisis in Italy, one that led to concern that it would collapse, rather as Russia had and as France was to do in 1940. In August 1917, there had been demonstrations against the war in the major industrial city of Turin, with crowds calling for peace and bread. Moreover, Caporetto focused a fear that much of the peasantry did not want to fight for the state, and raised questions about Italy's regional cohesion, as there was concern, in particular, about Southern support for the war, revisiting a fear raised when Italy last attacked Austria, in 1866. Indeed, there were demonstrations in the South in 1917–18, with calls for peace and bread focusing on the men absent at the front and thus unable to bring in the crops. Catholic criticism of the war was linked to this peasant opposition. Yet, large-scale desertion from the army also affected troops from central and northern Italy.

In the event, a new government, under Vittorio Orlando, was formed, with Orlando making the dismissal by the king of Luigi Cadorna, the Chief of General Staff, a condition of taking office.[22] Pacifism was repressed on the Italian home front and, in November, a new front line on the Piave River was shored up with major Allied contingents, despite the opposition of Western Front generals, most notably Haig, to this transfer. Thus, the Austrians and Germans had failed to knock Italy out, but had succeeded in increasing the pressure on the Allies on the Western Front. Caporetto also led the Allies to establish a Supreme War Council in November in order to provide a forum for co-ordination for Britain, France and Italy, and to help increase civilian control over the military: each country sent the Prime Minister, another government minister and a permanent military representative.

1917 was also a year of failure for the Allies on the Western Front. Indeed, given the pressure on the Alliance in Russia, Italy and at sea, the failure to do better on the front in which it was easiest to apply force was particularly serious. Moreover, this failure still left the Germans in control of their 1914 gains: most of Belgium and part of France. When combined with ever-greater German territorial success in Eastern Europe, it was scarcely surprising that the situation did not lead the military who dominated Germany to seek a change of policy. Indeed, their position was both demonstrated and strengthened when the Chancellor, Bethmann-Hollweg, was removed. There was no intention of restoring Belgium. Its coal and iron were regarded as key industrial reserves, while, strategically, it was seen as a threat to France and as a challenge to Britain's naval position.

These political pressures helped explain why it was necessary for the British and French to renew their attacks on the Western Front. The psychology of their commanders contributed greatly to this. Joffre's replacement, the vainglorious Robert Nivelle, was convinced that he could break through the German lines, and he won the confidence of the French and British civilian leaders. Haig was also confident of his own success. At the same time, there was a sense that the resources available had to be employed to put pressure on the Germans, and, in particular, that the guns and shells that had been supplied provided an opportunity for victory. The British used 2,879 guns – one for every nine yards of front – for their attack near Arras in April 1917, and the guns were 'like a continual roar of thunder in the distance'.[23]

Artillery tactics, moreover, had become more sophisticated, not least as a result of improved aerial reconnaissance. Opposing lines were accurately mapped, while Allied guns were capable of throwing down a creeping barrage as well as providing accurate counter-battery fire against the Germans. The need to co-ordinate artillery and infantry was well understood. The commander of the British 169th Infantry Brigade observed on 16 February, 'The importance of moving close behind our barrage cannot be exaggerated.[24] However, the task was not an easy one.

The Germans, nevertheless, pre-empted the Allies, notably the plan for a resumed Somme offensive, by using the winter months of early 1917 to pull back from the large salient between Arras and the Aisne, a surprise move, replacing a front-line that simply reflected the fighting that had taken place, with a new shorter one that was designed to offer a more effective defence. This Siegfried Line, known to the Allies as the Hindenburg Line, shortened the front by 25 miles. Moreover, German defensive tactics had improved as a result of the repeated Allied bludgeoning on the Somme in 1916. In place of deep dugouts and continuous trench lines packed with infantry, came mutually supporting concrete bunkers, surrounded by obstacle belts, able to provide a flexible defence in depth. With its three defence lines, the 'Line' was up to 15 miles deep. Reverse slope positions (troops dug in on the back of the slope facing the enemy) were used to reduce vulnerability to artillery.[25] Reducing the stress of the defence, this withdrawal also freed up German troops, adding 13 divisions to the reserves, and left the Allies, as the basis for their new position, with land that had been deliberately wasted by the retreating Germans in Operation Alberich. Wells were poisoned, trees cut down, the Oise Valley flooded, villages destroyed and booby traps scattered. Moreover, the German withdrawal affected British preparations for a new offensive. The destructiveness of the Germans as they moved back to the Hindenburg Line helped to justify the French demand for heavy post-war reparations (compensatory payments).

The Germans also benefited from a major attempt to improve the training of their troops. In place of training as an activity that happened at home before troops were deployed, there was an emphasis on training in the front line, which was seen as permitting an accurate response to the developing nature of war. A training system had been established for storm troops in 1915, and, subsequently, concerned by the nature of conflict, Ludendorff, Deputy Chief of Staff from August 1916, made advanced training universal for the German army, seeing it as a way to restore and nurture morale.

He recognized the need to rebuild the army for defensive warfare, and appreciated that morale was more important in trench warfare, rather than its mobile counterpart.

On the Allied side, there was no repetition of the joint, Anglo-French, battle seen at the Somme, but, instead, a series of separate battles. In April 1917, the British attacked at Arras and the French across the Aisne against the Chemin des Dames. The British, using Third Army under Edmund Allenby, attacked first on 9 April, in order to make the Germans commit their reserves, which was intended to aid the French offensive. The initial phase of the British operation succeeded, with the Canadians capturing Vimy Ridge, the first battle where the four Canadian divisions served together and under a Canadian commander, Arthur Currie. To do so, they deployed 1,130 guns, an artillery concentration more than double the density employed the previous year at the Somme. An effective creeping barrage helped the highly impressive Canadians capture the German positions, and, with them, 4,000 prisoners.[26]

The initial response to the success at Vimy was optimistic. Den Fortescue wrote to his father on 15 April:

> it really has been a wonderful show and it must make the Germans scratch their heads about what will happen when the summer comes and other people have a dart too: the cavalry put up a jolly fine show the other day but were rather thrown away.

Two days later, he added:

> the papers really give a very fair idea of the show apart from the fuss that is made of the Canadians: their share of it was really very small though they did very well: they pulled the fat out of the fire remarkably well the other day when the Bosche broke through', [the Canadians launching an excellent counter-attack] 'the bosche was in the end running up and down his

own [barbed] wire looking for gaps with machine guns on him from every direction.[27]

Fortescue's remark was less than fair to the major contribution made by the Canadians, a contribution of which they are justifiably still very proud.

It was hoped that the war would soon be over.[28] Tom Gurney, a major in the Life Guards, claimed:

> I think we shall have them back on the line of the Meuse by August, but they will go back in their own time – and they are fighting against time on account of the submarines. I do not think there will ever be a chance of giving them a real hurting – there are too many machine guns. Their infantry is finished, and it is only a matter of crumps [artillery] and machine guns now with them entirely. There is no doubt they [the Germans] are getting a hellish time of it now …. They [Allied troops] got the Vimy Ridge easily really – all our bombardments. All the German batteries were shelled with phosphorus shells. Then after some hours the bombardment was lifted. The Germans thinking the attack was coming manned their trenches and then we trench mortared them, and afterwards resumed the bombardment! All the Germans I saw were literally smashed to pieces.[29]

In poor weather, however, it proved impossible for the Allies to sustain the offensive successfully, in large part due to German defences in depth that also benefited from the ability to deploy reserves by train. The principal phase of the Allied operation ended on 14 April.

The problem at Arras, as with other battles in 1917, was the inability of the British to break into the full depth of the German defences, to consolidate and to press home any advantage that arose, so that break-in could be converted to break-through. The standard message form on maps used by British field units included

'Am held up by a) M.G. [Machine Gun] b) wire at …'.[30] Moreover, German counter-attacks had to be neutralized, but artillery and trench mortar tactics had yet to become sufficiently developed at interdiction, although Arras, in its turn, helped provide the lessons from which better tactics developed. The inability to exploit success was as much a problem of communication and control as it was one of planning, stamina and reinforcement. Planning, however, was defective as in the failed hope of using cavalry in exploitation. Gurney noted:

> They got us through the gap, but we couldn't get on, as we were put through before the infantry … you want an awfully wide front for cavalry to operate on successfully. However, the thing has been tried now, and the casualties have been suffered and let's hope the 'Gap' scheme is now dead. As it ought to have been some time ago.[31]

Arras became an attritional offensive, with heavy losses in the air as well as on the ground, and Allenby came in for criticism, first for wanting too short a preliminary bombardment and, later, for not ending his assault when it had clearly ground to a halt and become attritional. Whether the latter was due to his lack of awareness of the true situation because of poor communications, his stubbornness or a genuine belief that he could achieve his objective if he kept pushing, is not clear. Allenby had an aversion to heeding what he thought was bad advice, but his failure to show the necessary flexibility in command, led to complaints from three divisional commanders. In the face of such complaints, he could no longer remain in command in France and was sent to Egypt. The weaknesses of British offensives there had been shown in March and April when attacks on the Turkish Gaza positions were repulsed. Child-Villiers remarked in June 'I trust that there will be no more Somme and Arras battles and that we shall be content to have big attacks without continuing the battle for weeks as hitherto – we cannot help winning if we do not fritter away men as hitherto.'[32]

Launched on 16 April 1917, the French offensive to the north of the Aisne east of Soissons was a disaster. Security was poor, and the Germans knew what was coming, which greatly lessened the impact of the bombardment on which Nivelle had counted heavily. Basing himself on the tactics he had used at Verdun, Nivelle had promised 'Laon in twenty-four hours', but that town proved as elusive as the other targets, with attacking French forces, hindered by the sleet, shot down in large numbers from the well-prepared German defences. Minimal advances, to the Chemin des Dames on the heights dominating the Ailette Valley, were won at the cost of 130,000 men, the majority on the first day. German losses were far lower. Further east, the French Fourth Army launched a supporting attack east of Reims on 17 April, but, in the Battle of Moronvilliers, also made scant progress for heavy casualties. The commander of the French Sixth Army, Charles Mangin, acquired the nicknames 'The Eater of Men' and 'The Butcher', and was sacked by his patron, Nivelle, but the latter's attempt to find a scapegoat led to his being relieved on 15 May.

Politics played a major role. Briand had backed Nivelle, but he fell in 1917 and his successors were far less enthusiastic. Moreover, Nivelle's relations with Haig were poor and whereas Lloyd George, a critic of Haig, had been happy to place the general under Nivelle's command, he backed away from Nivelle when the latter failed. Part of the French army passively mutinied in response to the losses suffered in the failed offensive.[33] Units refused to obey orders and return to the front. Yet, this was no collapse. Only about 40,000 troops were involved directly, which meant that most of the army, including the front-line troops, did not listen, and, far from being a determined mutiny, those troops returned to duty when treated with due care. The dismissal of Nivelle helped, as did the cautious nature of his replacement, Pétain. Action was taken against the ringleaders and 49 men were executed, but Pétain deliberately saw the activity as disobedience and poor discipline, not mutiny. In order to overcome the crisis and improve the situation, he set out to address the grievances, which he understood as a result of visiting front-line units. The leave system was improved, with a better rotation of units, as was the disciplinary system and the provision of food. These measures addressed key grievances.

Similarly, Armando Diaz, who replaced Luigi Cadorna as the Italian Chief of Staff after Caporetto, relied on material improvements for troops in the field as well as on the repression of pacifism both at the front and on the Home Front.

Pétain's preference for the defensive was also significant. For the remainder of 1917 and in early 1918, there were no large-scale French offensives. Instead, Pétain repeated the policy he had followed earlier, that of small-scale, competently mounted, attacks designed to achieve specific objectives. Well-prepared and successful, these operations helped restore the morale and reputation of the French army. Although important, however, such an improvement was not the means to victory, and notably so in a strategic environment in which the prospect of American troops was overshadowed by the likelihood that German troops would be transferred from the Eastern Front.

The best form of defence appeared to be attack on terrain of Allied choosing and where they could accumulate troops, guns and *matériel*. Moreover, it seemed necessary for the British to lessen pressure on the French, while an attack on the Western Front might well bolster Russia and thus make it harder for the Germans to transfer troops. The front chosen was that in Flanders, and for a number of reasons that reflected the accumulative nature of strategy. The costly vulnerability of the Allied position in the Ypres salient required improvement, the Germans lacked many commanding defensive, surveillance and artillery positions in the low terrain, other than the Messines ridge, and the German submarine facilities at Bruges, Ostend and Zeebrugge provided a worthwhile objective, one that had strategic point given the significance of the submarine war.

The initial British attack, on the Messines ridge on 7 June, was preceded by a heavy bombardment, the successful mining of the German positions, and the simultaneous explosion of one million pounds (454,000 kg) of explosives, which devastated them. A well-prepared artillery victory, and a credit to careful generalship, in this case that of General Sir Herbert Plumer, this attack, however, was not exploited by further follow-up attacks.[34] Instead, after considerable vacillation on the part of Haig, the main attack in the Third Battle of

Ypres, generally called Passchendaele after a ridge that became a key target, was launched on 31 July.

This campaign came to symbolize the horrors of the Western Front, and the word Passchendaele frequently serves to represent its futility. The very heavy preliminary British bombardment both surrendered surprise and churned up the battlefield, a problem exacerbated by the combination of heavy rain and a high water-table. Mud became a key problem for the troops, both for attacks and for supplies, and also prevented the effective use of tanks. The poorly prepared initial advance suffered from the failure to destroy many of the German strong points and supporting guns (and thus establish clear artillery supremacy). In part, this was due to the mud, which absorbed explosive force (as at Waterloo in 1815), but also to the inability of the guns to destroy concrete structures. A similar problem was experienced on D-Day in 1944 when few German bunkers were destroyed by the Allied firepower, which included the use of heavy bombers and 14- and 15-inch battleship guns. Attacking St Malo, later in 1944, the Americans took to using artillery and tanks to fire point-blank at embrasures.

In addition, the creeping barrage did not live up to expectations when the Third Battle of Ypres was launched. Losses were heavy, but there was no repetition of the first day of the Somme. Some ground was taken near the Ypres area, but Haig wanted more. His desire for a breakthrough was not sensible in any case, but the incessant rain in August made such hopes even more implausible and hit morale hard. The waterlogged terrain and heavy mud proved both ghastly living and fighting conditions and accentuated the frequent problem on the Western Front in which tactics swallowed operations. Unduly heavy rainfall ensured that the artillery lacked firm ground from which to fire and on which to move, while low cloud limited aerial observation for the guns. Although the location of the Ypres salient promised much if a breakthrough could be achieved, it was the wrong place to launch an offensive because of the terrain, and, as soon as it became clear that the battle was a slogging match, it should have been abandoned.

The initial operations were conducted by Hubert Gough, the

commander of the Fifth Army, but failure led to a shift to Plumer who proved a more adroit, and luckier, commander, albeit one who is praised largely because the comparisons were so maladroit. An advocate of the 'bite and hold' principle, rather the attempted breakthrough, Plumer did not want advances beyond the range of supporting artillery nor the exposure of exhausted troops to the risk of counter-attacks by fresh German reservists. Plumer also benefited from more reinforcements than Gough had obtained, as well as from better weather, which helped the ground to harden to a degree. Creeping barrages before limited advances brought successes in September, but the rate of losses remained high not least as the Germans used mustard gas for the first time, and the advances covered only limited territory, notably failing to reach the German gun-line. More was needed if the war was to be won, as 'bite and hold' could not bring victory, and Haig ordered the continuation of the attacks which he hoped would destroy German morale. Plumer took as many losses as Gough when the later attacks in September 1917 were carried out without sufficient preparation.

The battle certainly showed that a learning curve was in evidence for the troops. Some would agree that this learning curve was stimulated by the Canadians or Australians, and Currie's Canadian Corps took on useful lessons from French practice in advance of Vimy. However, the British formations were as likely to improve as those of the Australians and Canadians, although, as the Passchendaele campaign showed, the process was uneven.

Allied attacks, in October and early November, ending with a final assault launched on 6 November, were hindered by the resumption of the rain and a return to the mud which came to characterize the campaign and helped make it seem futile. The campaign came to concentrate on Passchendaele. Thus, the Second Anzac Corps attacked toward the village on 12 October in wet and cold conditions with insufficient preparation and a lack of sufficient artillery support. The two New Zealand brigades lost over 600 men killed and 2,000 wounded, many falling victim to machine gunners while held up by mud and intact barbed wire. This remains the worst day in the country's military history.

The village of Passchendaele was captured on 6 November, although it was readily apparent, not least to Haig, that the British gains were vulnerable to counter-attack. Indeed, all the gains were re-taken by the Germans in the Lys offensive of April 1918. The British lost at least 240,000 troops in the Passchendaele campaign, 70,000 of them dead, the Germans 200,000. Although the British losses were lower than those at the Somme, they were still extremely high. Moreover, they were largely of conscripts, and thus seemed a second half to the loss of the volunteers at the Somme.

The casualty figures, the reality of attritional warfare, provided the basis for a long-lasting debate about the merits of Haig's generalship. Alongside the heavy British casualties, there was the pressure on German reserves and resources caused by the frequent heavy British attacks. A defence of Haig claims: 'had he decided to halt the Flanders offensive after 4 October 1917, historians would undoubtedly have had a field day in blaming Haig for throwing away the opportunity to capitalize on the crisis in the German Army created by Plumer's offensives'.[35]

While a reasonable point, Haig's performance in command was patchy, and only pretty good on occasion. Confidence was important to success, as the German East Prussian campaign of 1914 demonstrated, but confidence had to be matched to an adroit understanding of the situation. Given military limitations and political constraints, it is not surprising that many commanders, such as Haig and Nivelle, emphasized willpower as well as artillery, but this emphasis proved a poor substitute.

At best Haig's victory was pyrrhic. He bears much of the responsibility for failure not only for choosing the zone for attack and for the commitment to success through breakthrough, but also because he failed in the management of his forces. Haig did not provide consistent support for his generals and failed to ensure that they co-operated. Instead, his determination to reap plaudits and avoid blame interacted with his practice of keeping decisions focused on himself and playing off others to that end.[36] The case that the development of British fighting methods in 1917 proved very important to victory a year later has been ably made,[37] but the long-term seemed increasingly precarious in late 1917 as Russia slipped away.

The British operations of late 1917 certainly drew attention not only to serious flaws in generalship but also in the conduct of the war, both by the military and by the government. Intelligence estimates of German weakness were shown to be flawed, but so, more seriously, was that of oversight by the Prime Minister and the War Cabinet. In part, however, Lloyd George's room for manoeuvre was limited by his earlier, misplaced, support for Nivelle, to whom he had attempted to subordinate Haig in February. Lloyd George was also affected by the extent to which Haig was backed by both King George V, with whom he had a close correspondence, and the Conservatives. The generals, moreover, were wary of civilian oversight. Haig remained in command, whereas Jellicoe, who had become First Lord of the Admiralty in November 1916, was replaced in December 1917: he proved more vulnerable to criticism than Haig. In turn, Passchendaele and the German counter-attack at Cambrai in November increased doubts within the military about Haig, lessened political support for him, and made it possible for Lloyd George to take more control of strategy in 1918.

Meanwhile, the British army was changing. Artillery was certainly more plentiful, and was not simply a matter of heavy guns, nor of a marked improvement in logistics.[38] In addition, deliveries of trench mortars from Britain rose, from 12 in the last quarter of 1914 to 2,145 in the last quarter of 1917. There were also important qualitative as well as quantitative improvements in the production of munitions as a result of involving the trade and introducing co-operative group manufacture, whereby each manufacturer within the group made some of the components of the munition. This allowed inspection to be carried out at one location, the premises where the components were put together, instead of at the premises of each manufacturer, thereby speeding up production. The increased skill of the trade reduced rejections, and the inspectors from the Outside Engineering Branch of the Ministry of Munitions ensured that production increased to meet demand. In 1916–17, various unnecessary components in British shells were eliminated, which also speeded up production. One of the problems faced by the British in 1915–16 was the poor quality of the shells. So great was the improvement brought about by better working practices, greater experience, and the inspectors, that prematures fell to 0.0004 per cent, one in 250,000, the best rate in the Allied armies, and a formidable achievement of industrial application.[39]

Infantry weaponry also continued to improve. By mid-1917, the Stokes light infantry mortar had become a reliable infantry support weapon that could be quickly used to engage German strongpoints, mortars and machine guns. Such weaponry ensured that the infantry benefited from the support of integrated firepower. Tactics for the use of rifle grenades also became more effective during 1917, and Lewis guns were employed against German advances,[40] while the British employed the Vickers machine gun to suppress enemy troop movements behind the front by indirect fire into map references over the heads of friendly troops. A report on the operations of 56th Division in the Fauquissart section, noted of the resistance, from 14 January 1917, to German counter-attacks after a section of the German front line had been occupied, that the British infantry made extensive use of Stokes mortars, Lewis guns and rifle grenades, and that the supporting artillery opened fire very rapidly.[41] The quantity of weaponry available to the British rose greatly in the last quarter of 1917. The French also made greater use of grenadiers and trench mortars, with a section of grenadiers formed in every company of an infantry battalion in order to throw grenades.

In the air, the Germans had gained the advantage in the winter of 1916–17, thanks in part to their Albatross D-1. The advantage was apparent to troops on the ground, the report on the operations of the British 56th Division noting for 21 January, 'The hostile bombardment was very accurate, evidently as a result of aerial reconnaissance carried out the previous day'.[42] However, the Germans lost their aerial advantage from mid-1917 as more and better Allied planes arrived. As a result, the British were able to use ground-support in a more sophisticated fashion than hitherto at Passchendaele. Despite this, the Germans did not lose in the air as they were to do in the Second World War, a contrast that indicated the more limited capability of earlier aerial conflict.

New weaponry provided opportunities, but also posed tactical issues, notably how best to use and maintain this weaponry, and how to integrate it with other arms. Training and doctrine were both at issue. In late 1917, these issues became readily apparent in the case of tanks. Their use had been considered from the start of the war. In December 1914, Hankey wrote a memorandum noting that 'such deadlocks are not a feature peculiar to the present war .... Either a special material has been provided ... or an attack has been delivered elsewhere ... can modern science do nothing more?' He suggested:

> Numbers of large heavy rollers, themselves bullet proof, propelled from behind by motor engines, geared very low, the driving wheels fitted with 'caterpillar' driving gear to grip the ground, the driver's seat armoured, and with a Maxim gun fitted. The object of this device would be to roll down the barbed wire by sheer weight, to give some cover to men creeping up behind, and to support the advance with machine gun fire.[43]

Tanks were first used by the British at the Somme on 15 September 1916,[44] and by the French the following April. The Germans did not have their own design, the A7V, until 1918, and thus used captured and repaired Allied tanks. The tank seemed a fitting means to, and symbol of, the overcoming of the impasse of trench warfare. Tanks could be hit by rifle bullets and machine guns without suffering damage, and they could also smash through barbed wire and cross trenches. The tank, however, had its disadvantages. Many tanks broke down, even before reaching the assault point and, in battle, tanks rapidly became unfit for service, understandably so given their technical problems. It was also unclear how best to integrate tanks into Allied tactics and operations. The number of tanks was too small to make much of a difference: for example, initially only one with the 169th Infantry Brigade, the order for which noted 'The tank is to be considered purely as an accessory to the attack, and the attack must on no account be allowed to check if the tank should fail to carry out its programme'. At this point, Child-Villiers was uncertain of their value.[45]

The British use of 348 tanks en masse at Cambrai on 20 November 1917 was certainly a shock to the Germans. The impressive commander of Third Army, General Julian Byng, organized an effective combination of infantry, tanks, artillery and aircraft, and drove the Germans back four miles, breaking through their line and capturing a considerable number of prisoners. However, celebrations and hopes in Britain proved premature, and effective German command led to the rapid movement of troops who sealed the attack. The British tanks also took heavy losses: on 20 November, thanks to German artillery fire, 179 were destroyed while, on 21 November, when the attack resumed, more tanks were lost as a result of inadequate infantry support. The tanks had played a significant role in the initial British success, but a heavy, well-planned, artillery bombardment, reflecting recent developments in British artillery tactics, was also important in combining surprise and success.

After sealing the Cambrai attack on 21–22 November and blocking further British assaults on 23–28 November, the Germans successfully counter-attacked on 30 November, employing the infiltration tactics used at Caporetto, notably 'storm troopers'. After a short artillery barrage, the British were driven back, in part due to the success of these tactics and in part due to the lack of British reserves, a consequence of the losses suffered earlier at Passchendaele. The German advance was supported by aircraft. The front line was stabilized on 6 December after further German attacks and limited British counter-attacks. Haig's failure to exploit and sustain the initial success at Cambrai further compromised his reputation with Lloyd George, while he could also be criticized for trying to persist in the attack after the possibilities of major results had been exhausted.[46] More generally, the British army had lost heavily at Passchendaele, the auspices were not good for 1918, and yet the French, in October 1917, were insisting that the British take more of the burden in the shape of a larger section of the front line.

Alongside both British and German tactics at Cambrai, Allenby's career after Arras indicated the variety of methods that could lead to success in conflict, and thus the room for disagreement over best practice. Allenby regarded his dispatch to replace Sir Archibald Murray, the dismissed commander of the Egyptian Expeditionary Force, over which he assumed command on 28 June, as a mark of disfavour; but he transformed the situation in Palestine. His diligent oversight of his new command exuded vigour and raised morale. Moving his headquarters closer to the Gaza front was important both in practical terms and as a morale-boosting move. Allenby, however, faced the serious problem of coping with very different expectations from his superiors. The hyperactive Lloyd George wanted bold offensive thrusts and the capture of Jerusalem to help morale; while Sir William Robertson, the Chief of the Imperial General Staff, favoured a more cautious approach. Defeats at Gallipoli and Kut served as stark warnings of the dangers of boldness at the expense of the Turks.

Allenby's Boer War experience of working with Australian troops served him in particularly good stead as his new command was very much that over an army of the British empire. Having revived the army, which he strengthened with troops, heavy artillery and aircraft, Allenby decided to implement the plan for a new offensive that had been already prepared by his new staff. The resulting Third Battle of Gaza led to a shift in the axis of attack, away from Gaza and the Mediterranean coast (the axis in the costly and unsuccessful first two battles in the spring of 1917), towards the eastern end of the Turkish positions near Beersheba 30 miles inland. The town was captured by the Australians on 31 October after a long advance across terrain with very little water, an advance that required Intelligence, reconnaissance and engineering work. This was a surprise attack launched without a prior bombardment, and the Turks were unable to destroy Beersheba's valuable water wells as expected. Cavalry helped provide the British with the necessary mobility, but flexibility of mind was required to vary the direction of attack. Near Gaza, moreover, where the attack began on 27 October, Allenby's forces used tactical lessons from the conflict on the Western Front to help break through the Turkish positions.

Victory was exploited with the capture of undefended Jerusalem on 9 December. Earlier, there had been tough fighting in the hills of Judea as the Turkish lines were broken through on 8 December. The British suffered 18,000 casualties but the outnumbered Turks took heavier losses. The fall of Jerusalem helped to catapult Allenby into prominence. On 11 December 1917, he publicly entered the city in a carefully scripted display. Rather than riding in, as Kaiser Wilhelm II had arrogantly done in 1898, Allenby dismounted and entered on foot. He read a proclamation of martial law and left again. Back home, he was lauded as a latter-day Richard the Lionheart, Richard I, the commander of the Third Crusade. In a season without good news for the British public, Allenby's success was very welcome to the government and press, which therefore devoted considerable attention to it.

The Turks, however, who had not been crushed, regrouped on a new defensive line to the north of Jerusalem. Their ability to do so has been ascribed by some critics to overly cautious generalship on the part of Allenby, but this caution was in keeping with his preference for methodical warfare, a preference towards which strong logistical pressures powerfully contributed. There was not enough water for the cavalry, the prospects for campaigning were affected by the winter rains (the climate was not only a factor in European campaigning), and the strength of the opposing rearguard was also a factor. The British Cabinet wanted Allenby to press on for Damascus, but, like Kitchener advancing on Khartoum in 1895–98, he urged the need to wait until the necessary infrastructure, including a double-tracked railway, was ready.

The importance of adroit generalship and methodical campaigning was also on display in Mesopotamia where the British position had been greatly compromised by the Kut debacle in 1916. Stanley Maude, appointed commander in September 1916, carefully prepared his reinforced forces and renewed the offensive in December. Influenced towards caution by the Mesopotamia Commission established to allocate blame for failure at Kut,[47] he based his advance on a methodical, logistical campaign articulated by improved communications; again on the pattern of Kitchener's advance on Khartoum rather than campaigning on the Western Front. Maude benefited from the strength of the Indian army and his forces outnumbered the Turks. The latter's positions at Kut were enveloped in February, obliging them to retreat, and Maude pressed on to capture Baghdad on 11 March 1917. After the summer heat and concern about a possible Turkish-German offensive had led to a pause, the British advanced up both the Euphrates and the Tigris, capturing Tikrit on 2 November, but Maude died that month from cholera.

The campaigning of 1917 thus indicated that, alongside offensives and campaigns that miserably failed to achieve their goals, notably the Arras, Champagne and Flanders attacks on the Western Front, and fronts that remained immobile, such as the Macedonian front near Salonica, it was still possible to achieve significant outcomes through taking the initiative. Moreover, although not in the case of the war with Turkey, the political consequences of some of the campaigning were striking. The Bolsheviks were willing to negotiate separately, and a Russo-German armistice was arranged in December. Furthermore, with Russia knocked out of the war, Romanian resistance crumbled.

The military consequences appeared clear. Germany would be able to redeploy much of the army to the Western Front where the Allied campaigning had had an attritional impact not only on the German defenders but also on the Allied forces. In a race to apply manpower, there was the countervailing prospect of large numbers of American troops, but, to the great disappointment of Britain and France, the Americans, who had lacked realistic pre-war contingency planning,[48] had only 194,000 men in France by the end of 1917, and there was great concern about shortages of American *matériel*. The focus in 1918 would therefore clearly be the Western Front, although it appeared highly unlikely that the war would end there. France had seemed vulnerable after Nivelle's failure, but Pétain had steadied the army, and the consequences of Caporetto had shown that it was more difficult to overthrow one of the Allies in Western Europe, where resources could be readily redeployed to its assistance, than in Eastern Europe.

Nevertheless the pressure on France in 1917 had acted, rather like the Verdun offensive in 1916, in throwing greater weight onto the British war effort. There was no doubt of the resolve of the British government, but troop numbers had been hit hard in 1917, notably, but not only, at Passchendaele. Yet, the challenge of unrestricted submarine warfare had been overcome, while there had also been marked improvements in the potential of British offensive operations. Moreover, the British empire was standing firm. There was no repetition of the Easter Rising and domestic opposition to the war was limited.

Negotiations with Germany were proposed by Arthur Henderson, the Labour member of the War Cabinet and leader of the parliamentary Labour party, and he resigned when they were rejected, but Labour remained in the Coalition and the pacifist stance of many members of the Independent Labour Party, including Ramsay MacDonald, and of the Union of Democratic Control, which included a number of left-wing intellectuals, such as Bertrand Russell, did not become that of the Labour Party. Yet, the traditional language of radical patriotism already seemed less convincing to many on the left before it was challenged by the example of the Russian Revolution.[49] Henderson's attitude was a response to the possibility that Russia would leave the war and a product of concern about inadequate consultation and personal pique. His stance was also an echo of the trade unions' and the Labour Party's disquiet about consequences of the conflict, including food shortages and rising prices. There was also an increase in workers' grievances and strikes including by the coal miners in South Wales that autumn. These grievances were directed both against aspects of the war, such as wage controls, labour direction and profiteering, and also against facets of social difference that appeared less acceptable in a period of total war.[50]

Britain, however, had not faced a collapse comparable to Romania, where the major defeat of late 1916 led to an attempt to rally support in order to sustain the war effort. On 5 April 1917, as anti-war sentiment rose in Romania, Ferdinand I issued a proclamation to his troops promising land and the right to vote as soon as the war ended; and an expropriation of land to enable an increase in peasant holdings was agreed in July.

In France, there was also a slow-moving crisis, albeit with the remedy of national unity still advanced as the defence of an endangered people. As part of the crisis of legitimation that the costly intractability of the war was causing, there was a series of strikes in France in early 1917 and growing opposition in the Socialist Party to participation in the government which had been based since 1914 on the *Union Sacrée* (Sacred Union) of all the parties behind the war. The strains of the war were important in the fall of the ministries of Aristide Briand, Alexandre Ribot and Paul Painlevé in March, September and November 1917 respectively, successive falls that created an impression of military weakness.

There was also interest among French politicians in peace talks with Germany, interest that the Germans instigated and encouraged in order to divide and weaken their opponents, and thus help ensure peace on German terms[51]: war and peace were both part of the same process for Germany. The Germans unsuccessfully tried to buy French newspapers, and also approached senior politicians, notably Joseph Caillaux and Briand, former Prime Ministers, and Jean Malvy, the Minister of the Interior. They responded cautiously and were certainly not German agents, but reflected a constituency for negotiating peace. Dictating peace was scarcely an option for France with the Germans in control of so much of Belgium, Romania, Russia and France.

As part of the process of socio-political mobilization that the severity of the struggle created for all the combatants, these attitudes were countered in France by politicians and journalists ready to search for treason as the cause of the failure of the Nivelle offensive in April, a failure that had hit civilian morale hard, part of the two-way link between morale on the front and at home. In July, Georges Clemenceau, a Radical politician and former Prime Minister, who was President of the Senate committees for War and Foreign Affairs, and the editor of the newspaper *L'Homme Libre*, attacked Malvy, another Radical, for being unpatriotic, and the fall of the latter in August led to that of the ministry of Alexandre Ribot the following month.

That did not end the crisis. Talk of treasonable support for peace among senior politicians continued, with Clemenceau attacking Briand, and there was also the challenge posed that autumn by Pope Benedict XV's call for a peace based on pre-war boundaries, a call with which Emperor Karl of Austria sympathized: he was anxious about the future of the Habsburg state and aware of its weaknesses and growing unpopularity. The Pope, who in his Peace Note of August 1917 criticized the 'useless slaughter' of the war, was concerned about both pan-Catholicism and his flock, for Catholics made up much of the population of Austria, France and Italy, and he worried that the conflict would lead to the rise of Communism, an atheistical and actively anti-clerical movement. In contrast to the Pope, however, most clerics spoke to the nationalist drumbeat.[52]

Earlier in the year, Karl had made a secret peace approach to France via his brother-in-law, Prince Sixtus of Bourbon-Parma, an officer in the Belgian army. In letters of 24 March and 9 May, he proposed a peace based not only on the restoration of Belgium and Serbia, but also on the return of Alsace-Lorraine to France, which Austria was in no position to deliver. However, this approach failed as France insisted that Austria also give its territories with an Italian ethnic majority to Italy.[53] The French leaked news of Austria's approach in order to weaken the latter and sow dissension among the Central Powers. A furious Wilhelm II forced Karl to accept subordination to Germany, which ended the prospect of further negotiations. As a result, exploratory peace-talks in the winter of 1917–18 in Geneva between Jan Smuts, a member of the British War Cabinet, and Count Mensdorff of Austria proved fruitless as Austria was tied so closely to Germany.[54] As an instance of the range of negotiations during the war, there were soundings in 1918 between the Turkish Governor of Syria and Emir Feisal, the leader of the Arab Revolt.[55]

The German government was not interested in a peace that did not bring territorial gains that could justify both the war and the position of the military. German nationalists also pressed strongly for gains and reparations, and their unrealistic claims played a disproportion- ately large role in public debate. In contrast, the opposition Social Democrats called for a 'peace without annexations or indemnities' and the *Reichstag* passed a Peace Resolution on 19 July 1917, but this pressure had no traction for a government in occupation of most of Belgium and much of France and expecting to benefit greatly from the collapse of Russia. These assumptions were not only held by the High Command, for, alongside a sense of endurance and fortitude, many German soldiers gained purpose from military service and some found enjoyment in fighting and/or as occupiers.[56] September 1917 saw the launching of the German Fatherland Party, which was committed to victory and annexations and opposed to the support of the Social Democrats and others for a peace without annexations. This party rapidly became a mass organization with a membership of about 1.2 million and its propaganda fostered the expectation of victory.[57]

As yet, there was no challenge to the control exercised by the German government. In October, Sir John Simon, the former Liberal Home Secretary, who had resigned from the British government in opposition to the introduction of conscription and then enlisted in the army, wrote to his father:

> The schemes of German conquest, which most undoubtedly inspired the German government, are being knocked on the head, and all that remains is that the German people should realise that they have been worshipping the wrong god. When that happens ... the war must be ended of course by negotiations. All the blather about unconditional surrender ... is nonsensical.[58]

As yet, however, his confidence that these schemes of conquest were failing was greatly misplaced.

In France, the weak ministry of the Socialist Paul Painlevé (who was also War Minister as he had been under Ribot) was finally replaced on 16 November 1917 with one under Clemenceau, who also became War Minister. He declared 'No more pacifist campaigns …. Nothing but the war', and pressed for '*la guerre intégrale*', a focus on mobilization of national resources to ensure that war was total. Clemenceau, later seen as the 'father of victory', added a powerful strand of authoritarianism to the French war economy and this helped focus industrial production on the war effort.

Action, sometimes brutal, was taken against those who sought peace. In January 1918, Caillaux was arrested in France as a prominent target in the drive against defeatism. On 29 November 1917, Henry, 5th

Marquis of Lansdowne, a former British Foreign Secretary and leader of the Unionist (mostly Conservative) peers, published a letter in the *Daily Telegraph* advocating a compromise peace, but this call, which *The Times* had refused to publish, was ignored by the government. In Italy, pacifists were put on trial and those accused of defeatism were roughed up by interventionist activists without the police or judiciary doing anything to support of the rule of law; instead the latter was subordinated to the cause of the Fatherland.

Opposition to the war was also suppressed in America, with an Espionage Act in 1917 and a Sedition Act in 1918. Eugene Debs, who had stood as Socialist candidate for the presidency, and had opposed the war as an imperialist conflict run for the benefit of big business, was arrested for an anti-war, anti-conscription speech in Ohio on 15 June 1918. Sentenced to ten years in prison, he was pardoned on Christmas Day 1921. However, Debs was only a minor nuisance to Wilson and there was little sustained opposition to the war in America, although Irish nationalists were hostile to alliance with Britain. In New Zealand, where conscription was introduced in 1916, politicians who denounced it were jailed for sedition.

During the war, the American Protective League acted with government support, to intimidate opposition. Political practice was also changed in order to deal with opposition. A filibuster in the Senate against Wilson's move to war led to the adoption of Rule XXII by which if two-thirds of the senators present voted in support, it was possible to move to cloture: to end a filibuster and force a vote. Hostility to the disruption and regulation stemming from the war, combined with the call for its more energetic prosecution, helped lead to the Republican gain of both houses of Congress in the mid-term congressional elections on 5 November 1918, but these were the first elections Wilson had to face after declaring war.

In Austria, the *Reichsrat* (Parliament), which had been suspended since before the start of the war, was reconvened in May 1917, only to meet with separatist demands from the various nationalities within the Habsburg empire, especially the Poles. The following month, the Social Democrats turned down an approach for participation in a coalition government. That November, the Social Democrats organized demonstrations in favour of peace on the basis of pre-war boundaries. A more serious challenge for the government was posed by the drought of the summer of 1917, which led to a poor harvest and hit the availability of bread. Food shortages destroyed the cohesion of Viennese society, wrecking morale and encouraging ethnic tension. As such, the food queues that became a ubiquitous characteristic of the war in Vienna undermined the cosmopolitanism of the Habsburg state: these queues were an appropriate symbol of the new insecurity of civilian life.[59]

There were also food shortages in Bulgaria, which sapped support there for the war. In April 1917, the General Staff took over control of supplies, and thus of the Bulgarian economy. Tension was far higher in the occupied zone in Serbia, although the Toplica Rising there in 1917 was suppressed. Collaboration with the occupying authorities, however, was limited and guerrilla activity continued.

In Britain, the government sought to respond to public concerns and, the strains of the war, with more controls. In 1917, control was taken over the coal mines and essential food prices were fixed. Coal and food were rationed from that year, while, in America, food and fuel supplies were brought under federal control and monitoring. Intervention was more successful in Britain, where civilian life expectancy rose, and in France, than in Germany, where living standards fell, leading to a rise in death rates. This was in part due to the Allied blockade, but was also a consequence of less effective German social administration in the fields of supplies, social welfare and medical services, although it is difficult to assess the balance between these two causes. The blockade had significant consequences, and contrasted greatly with the ability of Britain and France to draw for resources both on the New World and on their empires, but the failure of German food administration and agriculture when compared to those of Britain was also important.[60] Moreover, the German government focused the war economy on the military to the exclusion of civil society. As with other combatants, notably Bulgaria and Italy, Germany was also affected by the impact of conscription on the labour force available for agriculture. Increased hardship in Germany led to rising social tension between town and countryside including a growth in anti-Semitism, as well as to tensions over food supplies and prices.[61] There were disturbances over food supplies in Berlin and Leipzig from April 1917 and serious strikes in major cities in January 1918, strikes that were rapidly stopped by the army, which put many of the strikers into uniform.

Lenin's hope that revolution in Russia would be followed in Germany still seemed a distant prospect, although for the Austrian leadership there was an increased fear that the empire would not survive the war.[62] The rival alliances were under great pressure by the end of 1917, at the same time that, through new military methods and as a result of changes in the participants, the option of military success seemed clearer than a year earlier. It was scarcely surprising that the war went on.

CHAPTER 6

1918

Zero was a magnificent sight as my headquarters was on high ground in rear of the batteries and I could see the flashes from guns and the shrapnel bursts from Valenciennes in the north stretching as far as one could see southwards ... the gradual decrease of the Huns' shell fire told us that our lads were getting on all right.

Colonel Alan Thomson to wife Edith about the attack of the British 4th Division on the Western Front on 1 November 1918.[1]

There is a certain symmetry to the Second World War that is lacking for the Great War. In the Second, Axis success rose to a peak and then receded, providing a basic narrative for the war, and thus a clear structure for, and prompt to, analysis. Of the major Axis offensives in the latter half of the war, all bar one were, like Kursk in 1943, Leyte Gulf in 1944 and the Bulge in 1944, counter-attacks, and unsuccessful ones at that; the exception, Operation Ichigo, brought much of southern China, a substantial area, under Japanese control in 1944–45, and is invariably underplayed in general histories of the war.

In the Great War, there is no similar pattern. Central Power attacks were very important not only in the initial year of the war, but also in 1915, 1916 and 1917. And so also for 1918. Indeed, in so far as there is the peak referred to above, it occurred in July 1918, with the end of the German attacks on the Western Front, and, in so far as there was a symmetry, it was in 1918 with Central Power strength still apparent in the first half of the year and increasing in Eastern Europe, but subsequently brought low, and to a far greater extent than the earlier successes of the Central Powers.

At the beginning of the year, the strategic situation was propitious for the Germans as a result of the Russian Revolution, but it was unclear how rapidly the Revolution would lead to an end of the war in the East and how quickly the Germans would be able to redirect their military effort elsewhere. There was scant comparable interest in the redeployment of Austrian forces which, indeed, on average, lacked the fighting quality of the Germans and certainly the *matériel*. In January 1918, Balfour, then British Foreign Secretary, suggested that the Allies help anti-Bolshevik movements in Russia that

> might do something to prevent Russia from falling immediately and completely under the control of Germany ... while the war continues, a Germanized Russia would provide a source of supply which would go far to neutralize the effects of the Allied blockade. When the war is over, a Germanized Russia would be a peril to the World.[2]

Lenin wanted the spread of Communism, not the Germanization of Russia, but, in Allied eyes, his desire for peace amounted to, and led towards, the latter. He had hoped that the spread of revolution would affect Germany and make negotiations unnecessary, but, instead, the Germans drove the pace of negotiation. When the Bolsheviks refused to accept the terms offered, the Germans rejected their policy of 'neither peace nor war' and, on 18 February 1918, resumed the offensive. Their rapid success forced the Bolsheviks to accept even harsher terms in the Treaty of Brest-Litovsk, signed on 3/16 March. The Bolsheviks agreed to cede sovereignty over much of western Russia – Russian Poland, Lithuania, Ukraine, Courland (modern western Latvia) and Finland. These lands, which had been inhabited by about 30 per cent of the pre-war population of Russia, included territory that had been Russian since the seventeenth century.

The situation in these areas remained unclear, and the Germans moved forward in order to seize control. In April 1918, they overthrew the democratic government that had gained power in Ukraine and installed a puppet regime, although its protection then led to a commitment of many German troops. German pressure in the former Russian empire meanwhile continued, much of it motivated by the economic requirements of the war effort, requirements that also led to a determination to retain the labour of Russian prisoners of war. Georgia, Armenia and Azerbaijan declared independence from Russia in May, following Finland, Estonia, Latvia and Lithuania. Germany and its opponents saw opportunities from these new states and manoeuvred for advantage.[3] In addition to their own efforts on the ground, the Germans sought to manage the situation by agreement with the new Bolshevik regime, prefiguring the situation during the Nazi-Soviet Pact of 1939–41. On 27 August 1918, Lenin accepted trade terms with Germany providing grain and other economic concessions. The Bolsheviks also conditionally abandoned sovereignty over Estonia, Livonia and Georgia. Subject to a referendum, moreover, the Russians were to return to the Turks the lands they had gained in 1878.

The benefits the Germans appeared likely to derive from the changing situation in Eastern Europe led the British and French to support plans for overthrowing the Bolsheviks. Furthermore, a British force under Major-General Dunsterville was sent from Baghdad in January 1918 in an attempt to seize the key oilfields at Baku in Azerbaijan, to block Turkish-German advances across the Caucasus, and to protect north-west Persia (Iran), and, thus, the approaches to India and the wider Indian-based strategic situation; prefiguring the British decision to send troops into Persia in 1941. However, the British force, which was operating beyond the bounds of effective logistical and military support, was defeated at Baku on 14 September 1918: as earlier, political aspirations, notably those of the Eastern Committee of the War Cabinet chaired by the presumptuous George, Earl Curzon, exceeded military practicalities. With better logistical support and in far greater numbers, the Japanese, in contrast, successfully moved into the Russian Far East.

Romania, which had driven the Bolsheviks out of Bessarabia (now Moldova) in late January 1918, also moved from armistice to peace. Exposed by the change in Russian policy, Romania accepted preliminary terms from Germany with the Peace of Buftea signed on 5 March. Berthelot, the head of the French military mission, then left. The Peace was followed by the Treaty of Bucharest of 7 May. Under this, Romania agreed to accept both occupation and German control of its oil and wheat, the oil being necessary for German aircraft and submarines. The terms included a German monopoly over the oil industry for 90 years, German control of navigation on the River Danube, the demobilization of most of the Romanian army and the loss of territory on the Transylvanian frontier, especially the mountain passes, thus ensuring continued vulnerability. Much of the country, including that occupied by 72 per cent of the pre-war population, remained under the occupation of the Central Powers. The harshness of these terms helped explain why other powers felt it important to fight on against Germany rather than to negotiate. As with Russia, however, the Germans failed to gain the full benefit they sought. The Romanians refused to heed German demands to join the war against Britain and France, which might have provided more troops for the Salonica and Italian fronts, while transport problems helped ensure that Germany's benefit from Romanian wheat was limited.

Strategy was not only considered by politicians and generals, Arthur Child-Villiers linked the state of affairs at the front both to domestic politics and to the weakness of Britain's allies bar France and America:

> The Germans will be such a menace if the war stopped now that it seems bound to continue for a long time yet unless the German people do throw over their government and elect their Snowdens [Philip Snowden was National Chairman of the Independent Labour Party]. This is not likely unless they attack and fail. It is this fact which makes me

think that they may not attack but just sit tight and exploit Russian territory.[4]

Benefiting from their successes over Russia and Romania, the Germans transferred troops, especially front-rank troops, from the Eastern Front, and 62 divisions from there were employed in their offensives on the Western Front in 1918, comprising close to a quarter of the divisions used in them. However, aside from numerous desertions by troops who did not want to be moved to the Western Front and who benefited from being transited across Germany, more troops could have been transferred, and the German High Command can be faulted for failing to contain the new military commitments in the East. This failure reflected the continued German determination to derive territorial benefit from the war.

In part, German policy reflected the opportunities that appeared to open up, but there was also a contempt for the local peoples that encouraged a reliance on a military response to the issues of control. German successes, especially in 1915, had led to the development of new categories of viewing Eastern Europe, and to the attempt to create a new-model society under military direction. A disparaging sense of the people overrun, not least seeing them as weak, dirty and diseased, became commonplace, in part in response not only to those who were conquered but also to the challenge posed by the vast areas that now had to be psychologically understood and overcome.[5] There was a prejudiced attempt to categorize the population. For example, Jews were prominent in the Russian borderlands that were overrun, and were presented as a target for forced sanitation against lice and typhus, both of which worried the occupying authorities.[6] Moreover, the German military administration became interested in 1917 in clearing away the local population and in bringing in soldier-farmers who would realize the agricultural potential of the land.

The nature of the occupation of much of Russia has been seen as important to the development of a hostile and violent response to conquered peoples as a central aspect of German war policies, although it is possible that, in part, this view represents a retrospective perspective, owing something to knowledge of what was to happen in the Second World War. Indeed, a less critical view of the German army in the Great War has also been advanced,[7] and the Nazi dimension was, of course, absent then. Moreover, German policies can also be linked back to the harsh response to native revolts in South West and East Africa in the 1900s. At the same time, the Great War was more generally important for the perpetuation, sharpening and creation of racial stereotypes. For example, in a highly critical racist fashion, German propaganda identified the French with the African soldiers they deployed, and similar complaints were made about the British. Whereas American black soldiers were poorly treated by their commanders, the French army proved more accommodating.

The prospect of transfers of large numbers of German troops to the Western Front encouraged Haig to press for far more British troops, but he received significantly fewer troops than requested, in part because Lloyd George was dubious about the value of placing such a large percentage of Britain's forces under his command. This failure to send more troops, however, affected the availability of reserves for dealing with German attacks, and thus increased British reliance on the French on the Western Front.

Numbers were not the sole issue. The Germans were to gain major swathes of territory in their 1918 offensives on the Western Front, in part as a result of the effectiveness of their tactics, although their success at deception was also important in securing surprise. German stormtroops advanced in dispersed units under cover of artillery barrages and broke into Allied trenches, bypassing strongpoints. Their firepower was increased by their carrying lightweight arms, including hand grenades, flame-throwers, trench mortars and submachine guns. Instead of lengthy preliminary bombardments, that gave ample warning of attack, there were short bombardments, with a pre-registration of the artillery, so that it could be aimed successfully, and the use of a mixture of shells delivered in massive quantity, for example the 'iron hurricane ... the avalanche of missiles' that launched the Aisne offensive in May 1918.[8] The rise in German shell production in the summer of 1917 was important in providing the material for such hurricanes, which were planned by General Georg

Bruchmüller, Ludendorff's artillery specialist. Moreover, the output of gunpowder rose considerably in 1917–18.

German training was also significant. In the winter of 1917–18, German units were taken out of the front line and trained with an emphasis on what soldiers do as individuals. Training as a psychological process was thus embedded in the German army. Moreover, prior to the Spring Offensives, troops were trained in infiltration tactics using Hermann Geyer's manual *The Attack in Position Warfare* and were extensively prepared on mock-ups of opposing trench positions, a practice used by the British and French since 1916 for both large-scale and small-scale operations including raids.

The German offensives emphasized penetration, surprise, tempo and tactical flexibility with, for example, not only a short, but intensive, preparatory artillery bombardment designed to suppress the Allies' artillery, but also a non-linear infantry advance benefiting from a rolling barrage. The Germans aimed for breakthrough, not as an end result of heavy fighting, as in German and Allied offensives on the Western Front in 1915–17, but as the immediate goal.[9] The army commanders on the Western Front in 1918 included Otto von Below, the victor of Caporetto, and Oskar von Hutier, who had seized Riga in 1917.

The series of German offensives in 1918 began with Michael, the Somme offensive, from 21 March to 5 April; followed by Georgette, the Lys offensive, from 9 to 30 April; Blücher-Yorck, the Aisne offensive, from 27 May to 4 June; Gneisenau, the Matz offensive, from 9 to 12 June, and *Friedensturm* (peace assault), the Champagne-Marne offensive, from 15 to 17 July. Superiority in particular directions was achieved and the initial offensive proved particularly devastating for Gough's Fifth Army on the Somme. In the area of Michael, the British were outnumbered by 52 to 26 divisions, while, although the British were in the process of developing deep defences with mutually supporting zones, there was, as yet, a lack of defence in depth as well as a shortage of reserves. Haig was also foolishly confident that Passchendaele had exhausted the Germans. The Germans benefited from contingent factors, notably heavy mist and the weaknesses of the Fifth Army's defensive preparations, but also from being able to take the initiative in a situation of tactical strength having gained the element of surprise through the careful use of disinformation.

Private Stanley Green of the 17th London Regiment, recorded that the Germans attacked on 21 March 'with a preliminary bombardment of gas which covered the ground in mist and swamped our clothes ... in overwhelming force ... as the shelling increased, the phone lines naturally were broken'. His unit retreated 'in indescribable confusion', and Green was struck by the pace of the German attack: 'the mobile artillery that kept up with Jerry's front line ... by means of motor tractors ... those pincers of storm troops ... hitting every time with uncanny skill those parts of our line most thinly held and creeping round in enfilading and enflanking movements that we could not stop'.[10]

Although the supporting German attack on the night of 20–21 March by destroyers and torpedo boats on Allied coastal communications failed, it was a peripheral effort and the British on land suffered heavily in men and guns and were pushed back nearly 40 miles. Hugh, Viscount Ebrington, noted on 10 May, 'I am where I was in March and April 1915 – little did we think we should be here now'.[11] British morale, in the bitter spring weather, was fragile, Thomas Gurney, now a colonel, welcoming the idea of getting wounded in order to go home and see his family.[12] Child-Villiers was concerned that 'the resistance has not been what it might have been'.[13] On the first day, 21,000 British troops were captured.

The crisis tested the Anglo-French alliance. There was a danger that Britain and France would follow their own path, and literally so in retreating in separate directions, the British towards the Channel Ports losing touch with the French retreating on Paris, and both being defeated separately, rather as Napoleon had planned in 1815 to drive the British and Prussians back in Belgium on divergent axes of retreat. In 1918, British plans for a threatening future included the wrecking, without French support, of every French harbour on the Channel as far west as Cherbourg, in order to pre-empt the risk of German invasion of England.

A new command system played a crucial role in steadying the situation. At Doullens on 26 March, an emergency Allied conference presided over by President Poincaré decided, on the recommendation of Alfred, Viscount Milner, that Ferdinand Foch (who had replaced Pétain as Chief of the General Staff when the latter replaced Nivelle as Commander-in-Chief) should be appointed as Allied overall military commander in the West to co-ordinate the defence. Haig had been critical of the Supreme War Council established in November 1917 as it might limit his role as British commander: 'From the earliest days, history shows that Aulic Councils, Councils of War, and Committees had invariably failed in discharging the executive duties of command. What is required in war, and especially during the course of a battle, is quick decision', which, he argued, was not possible from a committee.[14]

In the event, Haig, whose command was criticized at the meeting of the British Cabinet on 4 April, and the British government both now accepted that a supreme commander was necessary. Foch had had valuable experience of working with the British in 1914–16, notably as commander of the Northern Army Group in 1915–16. The appointment, in succession to Sir William Robertson, of the franco-phile General Sir Henry Wilson as Chief of the Imperial General Staff in February 1918 was also important, not least because he was a friend of Foch.

Meanwhile, the Germans had failed to destroy their opponents' fighting ability or break their line. While German tactics frequently proved successful, these infiltration methods faced problems when against a continuous good defence, while gaps through which the Germans could advance could also be fire zones used by their opponents. More generally, the greater tactical effectiveness shown by the Germans in their Spring Offensives was not matched opera-tionally: advancing troops were affected by logistical problems and by the failure of artillery and machine guns to maintain the same rate of advance and they also suffered from a focus on the line of least Allied resistance.[15] There was also the problem that, in local battles, the British sometimes fought the German attackers to a standstill, by not falling back and by counter-attacking, so that the advantages of infiltration were lost. The German army failed to adapt to such situa-tions because the highly trained stormtroopers had moved on, leaving the lesser trained follow-up troops to deal with resistance.

Furthermore, the Germans outran their supplies and were eventually stopped by Allied reinforcements. Replacing earlier confusion, Foch allocated reserves in an effective fashion and British and French divisions were used to seal the advance with a new front line before Amiens. The Second Battle of the Somme ended with Amiens successfully retained, the Australians counter-attacking outside the city on 4 April. The Allies had been able to deploy sufficient reserves to stop the German tactical success and operational impetus being translated into strategic victory.

Michael drove the British back, but left the Germans with a large salient, anticipating the situation created by the German counter-offensive of December 1944, the Battle of the Bulge, which also had an initial operational success but became a strategic irrelevance and, indeed, failure. Being able to bombard Paris, 75 miles away from 23 March 1918, was not a means to victory.

In part, German failure in the successive offensives reflected the resilience of the Allies, but German deficiencies were also significant. Although much territory was gained by the Germans, they failed to sustain their Spring Offensives in any particular area, instead launching successive attacks in different directions. In a repetition, at the operational level, of the failure in 1914–17 to focus their principal effort on one opponent for longer than one campaigning season, German strategy was poor in 1918. Instead of maintaining their initial advantage by keeping their opponents off-balance, the successive German attacks were disjointed. Ludendorff altered his plans in the midst of the offensive, only for the attacks to stutter to a halt each time. Moreover, the Germans failed to achieve their original goals: separating the British and French forces, pushing the former back to the English Channel, and driving on Paris.

The German attacks also exhausted their forces and were very costly, and persisting in them exacerbated these problems. The cumulative impact of very heavy casualties hit German combat effectiveness and morale, both of which were further sapped in June by a powerful epidemic of Spanish influenza.

Launched on 9 April, the Lys offensive benefited from the movement of most of the British and French reserves to deal with Michael. The

Germans broke through at the weakest point, the line held by the poorly prepared Portuguese Corps, who played a role comparable to that of the Romanians in the face of the Soviet counter-offensive at Stalingrad in 1942. The Germans went on to take the high ground in the Ypres area, including the Messines ridge, on 10 April 1918. A rattled Haig next day issued a dramatic Order of the Day: 'With our backs to the wall, and believing in the justice of our cause, each one must fight on till the end. The safety of our homes and the freedom of mankind alike depend upon the conduct of each one of us at this critical moment'. Arriving from the Piave River front in Italy with the first battalion of the Devonshire Regiment, Lieutenant-Colonel Percy Worrall thought the situation near the Lys Canal:

> desperate. [Before the action] I found Brigadier-General Rees ... I asked him what units were in front of me and who was in charge of the sector in front of me, and he said he did not know where anyone was, or who was in charge along the front or at the back [on the river] and said that he was going.

Worrall showed far more grip and this helped steady the situation. Repeated attacks on Worrall's unit were made from 13 April, only to be

> mowed down by our controlled fire .... A good system of observing was established, communication maintained, and the artillery and machine gun corps did excellent work in close-cooperation ... it was seldom longer than 2 minutes after I gave 'X-2 minutes intense' when one gunner responded with a crash on the right spot and I cannot speak too highly of our artillery support.

He also commented on the benefit from 'well concealed Lewis Gun positions'.[16]

Reserve French divisions, deployed by bus and rail, which Foch, concerned about the French sector of the front, had initially refused to provide, eventually helped the British hold the line. Fresh German attacks from 24 to 29 April made additional gains near Ypres, especially at Mt Kemmell to its south-west, but without breaking through. On 29 April, the Germans, unable to drive in the British positions, let alone break through to the Channel Ports, and now operating across broken ground against firm resistance, stopped having suffered 110,000 casualties. The Allies had lost about 117,000, but the exhaustion of the German Fourth and Sixth Armies was an important blow to German effectiveness. Indeed, in May the Germans pressed the Austrians to provide troops for the Western Front.

Blücher-Yorck, the German Aisne offensive, launched on 27 May, was preceded by a heavy bombardment of two million shells from 6,000 guns in four and a half hours. The outnumbered defenders (16 divisions to 40 German ones), foolishly, had been concentrated in the poorly fortified front line and were devastated by this bombardment. Having overcome them, the Germans captured the town of Soissons and broke through to the Marne from which they could bombard Paris. However, 30 French reserve divisions brought up by rail, supported by Americans, sealed the line, the American First Division fighting at Cantigny on 28 May, and two more at Château-Thierry in early June. American divisions were larger in size than their British and French counterparts. A Franco-American counter-attack on 2 June ensured that the Marne could be held. Ludendorff halted the offensive. Until these American successes, there was great uncertainty on both sides about the strategic significance of the growing American presence. Cantigny was a shot in the arm to the Allies' morale, one that was powerfully amplified when the Marne battles confirmed the first impression.

The Matz offensive, launched between Montdidier and Noyon further north on 9 June, failed to gain much territory and showed that the German methods were no longer working. Aerial reconnaissance and deserters had provided advanced warning, and the French had organized a defence in depth. The offensive came to an end by 12 June, in part due to a Franco-American counter-attack on 11 June in which the French used 144 tanks as well as plentiful mustard gas.

On 2 July, however, a meeting of the German Supreme Army

Command at its headquarters at Spa was still confident in pushing for bold war aims, an aspect of a serious lack of strategic reality. Ludendorff then mounted what was seen as a key offensive, the *Friedensturm*, which was intended to threaten Paris, fixing French forces and reserves, as a preparation for another offensive, *Hagen*, designed to capture the Channel Ports and lead the British to evacuate France. Launched on 15 July, 52 divisions took part, but the French, thanks to deserters, prisoners and aerial reconnaissance, were expecting the attack and used effective counter-battery fire and defence in depth to blunt the German attacks. The successful development of 'anti-tactics' was such that the heavy German bombardment fell only on lightly manned forward defences; and the second French line proved more resilient when the Germans advanced.

Stopped on 17 July, in part by the American Third Division, these advances were then countered by a successful French-led Allied surprise offensive that included the effective use of tanks and aircraft and that reflected the effectiveness of French logistics. Artillery was also important. On 18 July, the French counter-offensive was supported by a creeping barrage, with one heavy shell per 1.27 yards of front and three field artillery shells per yard. In face of this pressure, large numbers of German troops surrendered or reported as too ill to fight. This counter-offensive, which included 45 French divisions, nine American, four British and two Italian, was a key turning-point in the war, and indicated the contribution of the French not only to the Allied defence in 1918 but also to the subsequent attacks.[17] The Germans were pushed back across the Marne, bringing the Second Marne battle to a close.

The Germans had been left by their offensives in the disadvantageous situation that had preceded their withdrawal to the Hindenburg Line in 1917, with an extended front (up from 390 to 510 kilometres) much of which was difficult to defend and with 900,000 fewer men with which to do so. Lower morale, notably a sense of failure, was more significant as a problem for the Germans, and helped ensure that the Allied defensive victory of 1918, which was very much a French as well as a British effort, was more important in leading to German defeat than the attrition battles of 1916–17. The latter did not dictate the strategic options for 1918, but the German assumption that they could use shock to force an Allied collapse had proved misplaced, and the divisions transferred from the Eastern Front in the winter of 1917–18 had been used up, although most of the fighting was carried out by troops already on the Western Front. Furthermore, there were no realizable political goals to accompany the offensive, not least because the Army leadership remained opposed to a compromise peace and insisted, instead, on a territorial settlement providing plentiful gains and focused on strategic factors, namely ending German weakness in the face of a renewed two-front war.

The Allies were not going to accept this. Political support for the war was sustained during the crises of the German attacks. In Britain, Lloyd George's war leadership was challenged by Asquith in a debate over the availability of troops for the Western Front and whether, as in fact was the case, reserves had been withheld from Haig, an issue on which Lloyd George had given the House of Commons misleading information. Major General Frederick Barton Maurice had resigned after publicly criticizing Lloyd George for his claims. Lying to Parliament, Lloyd George, however, survived the parliamentary attack in May, in large part thanks to Conservative support, although the Liberals were now very bitterly divided. Meanwhile, Clemenceau continued to press hard for the movement of troops from Britain to France in order to confront the crisis caused by the German attacks. Concerned about preserving British forces, Lloyd George, however, was determined to prevent Haig from launching another Passchendaele. In April, Lloyd George also removed the War Minister, Edward 17th Earl of Derby (a Conservative peer with links to George V), whom he thought overly inclined to take the side of his generals. Milner replaced him on 20 April.[18]

In France Clemenceau had revived the government and dominated both the Cabinet and the Chamber of Deputies. The division in the latter in the debate of 4 June after the German advance in Champagne was 377 to 110. The Socialists had launched a strong attack on Clemenceau in March, and the *Union Sacrée* had been formally abandoned, but, despite British concern about the possibility of France and Italy collapsing, French political and public support for the war was strong and grew as the chance of defeat re-emerged.[19] A large-scale strike in Paris in May came to an end as trade union officials, fearing national defeat and revolution, moved back from the brink. Thus, instead of provoking division, if not collapse, the Germans were now in a situation of waiting to be attacked, a position shared by their allies.

Moreover, the economic damage they had inflicted had not wrecked the French war economy, while it was also unable to inflict damage on those of its allies. French coal production and industry were threatened by the German advance, and great strain was placed on French railways, but the German offensives were insufficient to lead to their overthrow.

The failure of the German submarine offensive contributed greatly to the weak German position. By 1918, the rate of Allied tonnage sunk per German submarine lost had fallen and the strategic irrelevance of the submarine threat had been demonstrated. Nevertheless, the Germans continued to inflict considerable damage, with at least 268,000 tons of British shipping sunk each month from January to August. Although the tonnage lost was lower than in 1917, there were heavy concentrations of losses in the Western Approaches and the Irish Sea. The hard work of convoying under continual threat of submarine attack continued until the end of the war, and the threat from submarines led to a bold and partly successful attack on 22–23 April on the Zeebrugge entrance to the canal to Bruges from which German submarines sortied. German surface ships made far less of an impact other than in diverting Allied resources, although in January 1918 the *Goeben* and *Breslau* sortied from the Black Sea into the Aegean, sinking Allied shipping until the *Breslau* hit a mine and the *Goeben* returned to the Black Sea. British planes and submarines had failed to sink it.

The arrival of American troops and *matériel* made the strategic irrelevance of the German navy in 1918 abundantly clear, although, despite Wilson's remark, 'At Château-Thierry we saved the world', a reference to the defensive role of the Second Division at the start of June,[20] the American role has to be put in context. The Americans were indeed instrumental, but so were the British and the French and

Foch and control of the Atlantic sea lanes and American industrial power. What was to bring the Germans in the West to defeat was the combined weight of the whole Allied effort, including the concert of action Foch achieved, the pressure of the British offensives, the continuing French role, and the presence of an American field army aimed directly at critical communications.

The continuing ability of the war to raise partisan hackles is reflected in the case of the American contribution,[21] which was greatest in the shape of industrial capacity and credit, and was crucial in that respect to the Allies from the outset; while the Americans also fed the Allies. In 1915–16, shells from America and Canada were necessary for the British, while French munitions production, which was more effective than that of Britain, was dependent, in part, on American steel.[22] By 1917, British production of munitions had greatly increased as an effective war economy had been developed, but inter-Allied economic assistance continued to be essential. For example, American and British technicians and locomotives helped to sustain the French rail network. Ironically, by the time America sent its army to France, American production was so committed to producing munitions for the Allies that American industry was unable to supply the American army. Thus, the French and British had to equip the Americans with French and British artillery and other munitions: the Americans were particularly dependent on the French for artillery and machine-guns, and on the French and British for tanks and training in their use.[23] The Americans had their own design of hand grenade, but used the British Brodie helmet, not one of their own design. The American infantry were saddled with the inadequate Chauchat light machine gun, but, more helpfully, the Americans also had the French 75-mm gun and the VB rifle grenade. Most of the artillery, tanks and aircraft used in the Meuse-Argonne offensive were provided by the French, who produced more munitions than Britain in 1918. As a result, the French were able to fire formidable numbers of shells, both in opposing the German offensives and, subsequently, in support of their own attacks.

American entry into the war made any idea of a decisive German naval sortie less credible. Five American dreadnoughts, the Sixth

Battle Squadron, joined the British Grand Fleet in December 1917, four of them sailing with it on 24 April 1918 when it failed to intercept an ultimately unsuccessful German sortie into the North Sea aimed at a Scandinavian convoy. In the face of the clear Allied superiority, the German surface fleet thereafter languished while its men became seriously discontented, leading to their mutiny at the close of the war.[24]

The American war effort was very wasteful, the equipment was often second-rate, the training haphazard and there was much controversy about profiteering. Yet, although the American military machine had many deficiencies, it had moved on from some of the unpreparedness and administrative shortcomings revealed by the Spanish-American War of 1898. This was partly because, by 1917, despite Wilson's reluctance, the Americans had had several years to prepare for conflict, and their industry was already geared up to supplying the Western Allies. On land, however, the Americans, despite legislation of 1916, were limited by the small size of their pre-war army, which was seventeenth by size in the world in 1914, by its lack of training for trench warfare, and by the problems, already faced by Britain in 1914, of a state without a background of conscription, suddenly developing a mass army. Wilson wished to fight the war as a naval conflict and without introducing conscription, but Britain and France were unwilling to accept this.

American support was qualified by Wilson's determination to pursue national exceptionalism in the sense not only of particular interests but also a view of how international relations should be pursued. America entered the war not as an ally of Britain, France and their allies, but as an Associated Power, because Wilson wished to dissociate America from their supposed imperial self-interest. The American insistence that their forces fight as a separate army on its own section of the Western Front, rather than being fed in as smaller units to support the British and French armies, also lessened their value by hindering their training and delaying their deployment. However, integrating these troops into Allied formations was probably not feasible politically and, had they been so amalgamated, it is unlikely that the British and French armies so reinforced would have conducted an offensive that threatened the Germans at every point along the front, which was crucial to their defeat.

Command faults were significant in the case of the Americans. John J. Pershing, the commander of the American Expeditionary Force, was convinced that American methods were superior to those of the European powers and also clashed frequently with Foch over the latter's attempts to direct American operations.[25] Born in 1860, Pershing had served in campaigns against Native Americans, as well as in the invasion of Cuba in 1898, and in counter-insurgency operations in the Philippines in 1899–1903 and 1909–14. An observer in the Russo-Japanese War, he commanded a force sent into Mexico in 1916–17 against Pancho Villa. This varied career did not equip him for the Western Front. Pershing insisted that his men train for 'open', instead of trench, warfare, and he put an emphasis on rifle marksmanship which he felt, mistakenly, could prevail against machine guns. There was an overconfident failure to appreciate the nature of the conflict and the characteristics of trench warfare, and to learn from Allies; although the Americans reproduced British and French manuals about, among other things, grenades and mortars, and their tactical use. American troops tended to repeat the British and French mistakes of 1915 and 1916 before they took heed of the lessons and applied the newer tactical methods to the battlefield. Moreover, although the large American regiments and divisions provided plentiful manpower, they proved difficult to use effectively in the confusion of conflict. Yet, to be fair to Pershing, much of the 1918 fighting was indeed open, not static. Furthermore, by taking up large sectors of the front, the Americans contributed not only their own efforts but also freed up French units to fight elsewhere. Two American divisions, moreover, fought as part of the Australian Corps, taking heavy losses as they attacked the Hindenburg Line.[26]

Overconfidence and lack of experience helped lead to heavy American casualties in 1918 when up against determined opposition in the Meuse-Argonne offensive launched on 26 September.[27] Though the American First Army supported by French divisions had earlier cleared the St Mihiel salient south of Verdun, in an offensive launched with overwhelming force on 12 September, that offensive had been against German troops that were already withdrawing and also showed the Americans the problems of commanding and re-supplying their forces. Commanders prominent in the Second World War, notably Douglas MacArthur and George C. Patton, acquired experience, Patton being wounded by machine-gun fire while leading his tank unit on foot.

From July, the Americans came to play a significant part in Allied operations, but they alone were not decisive. It cannot be said that their attacks inflicted key defeats on the Germans, and the Germans were sceptical of their tactical skill.[28] Yet, the Americans fought bravely, advanced successfully and inflicted, as well as suffering, heavy casualties. Moreover, because the Germans were threatened every-where, they could not produce any reserves. Indeed, each piece of the Allied counter-offensive was instrumental. Segregated Black units were among those who fought well in the American army, although they were not treated fairly, receiving less training and equipment.

Quantity as well as quality was an issue. The Americans trans-formed the numbers of war, benefiting from measures put in place from 1916, notably the National Defense Act of 1916 that prepared the way for conscription and provided for federal first call on all state guards and militias. In April 1917, the Americans had about 128,000 regulars under arms, as well as 80,000 National Guardsmen, but conscription helped lead to a major increase in the army.

In 1917, the American rail network, the key system for the movement of troops, was brought under government control, while the declaration of war was followed by the first of five Liberty Loan Acts. These permitted the sale of bonds to the American public, which helped finance the war effort and also permitted loans to Allied governments to finance war purchases, but only in America and in dollars. In April 1918, on the first anniversary of the declaration of war, Wilson told an audience in Baltimore that America would provide 'Force without stint or limit'.

America also sent tractors. American tractors and tractor ploughs arrived in numbers in Britain in 1918, and, although (as with tanks) their introduction involved problems, they helped deal with the manpower difficulties in agriculture caused by military recruitment and also by work in construction and munitions. Yet, as with the tanks, it is important not to push the technological interpretation too hard, as, aside from the limited use of tractors and tractor ploughs, greater benefit in raising British agricultural production was derived from the Women's Land Army, which had been established in 1917, and from prisoners of war as well as soldiers not then in service at the front.

Once America had entered the conflict, Wilson agreed to the French request to provide one million troops by July 1918, in which month indeed American divisions formed part of the effective French-commanded Marne counter-offensive. That July, he agreed to another request for 100 divisions by July 1919, although there were serious concerns about the shipping capacity required to support such a deployment.[29] In April-October 1918, over 1,600,000 American troops crossed the Atlantic, transforming a German superiority on the Western Front of 300,000 men in March 1918 to an Allied superiority of 200,000 men four months later. In response to the pressure of the German attacks, the numbers crossing rose from 93,000 in April to 280,000 in June. Drawing on the sophisticated Services of Supply system established by Pershing, there were about two million American troops in North-West Europe by the Armistice on 11 November 1918, and more American than British troops on and behind the Western Front, although the French troops were more numerous. This was the largest movement to date of troops across an ocean, and it was one accompanied by the deadly Spanish influenza (flu) which was to kill so many later in the year.

As with the movement of German troops from the Eastern Front, the arrival of Americans was important because of the state of the forces on the Western Front. The French, in particular, had lost much of their available manpower and their effective strength had fallen. The Americans, a very 'fine lot of men' to Arthur Child-Villiers[30], were fresh troops and well fed, and, had the war continued, they would have made a crucial difference, not least as they would have been better trained and many would have been blooded. Furthermore, the knowledge that they would be a factor both helped stiffen Allied resolve and influenced the German Supreme Army Command.

If the war had continued into 1919, the American military, with three armies at the front by December 1918, would have been the cutting edge. Pershing was planning for an American breakthrough in Lorraine near Metz, which he correctly saw as a key pivot of German rail communications.

As the war ended before American forces could play the role envisaged for the 1919 campaign, their potential was not yet clear to all contemporaries, although the Germans were well aware of the issue. Having failed to win a quick victory by unrestricted submarine warfare or by attacking in the West in the spring of 1918, Germany had lost. The example and its implications had not been adequately digested by Hitler and his circle when Germany declared war on America in December 1941.

The French and Americans each played a major role, but the key weight in the Allied defeat of Germany on the Western Front in 1918 was British, Britain understood as including imperial forces, most prominently Canadians and Australians, but also the New Zealand Division which, like the army as a whole, fought more successfully than in its previous offensive at Passchendaele.[31] The Dominion forces were effective, well motivated, fit and well-armed troops.

Before examining the victory on the Western Front, it is important to address the contrast between accounts of Allied victory that focus on the outfighting of the German army on the Western Front and these that emphasize, instead, the internal crisis created by the strains of the war, specifically the blockade. There are conceptual and methodological problems in comparing these rival interpretations, each of which has considerable merit, but there are also historiographical and cultural issues that attract attention, some of which can be paralleled in the case of the Second World War.[32]

The historiographical emphasis on the Home Front, seen in the dominant 'War and Society' approach, favours an account of 1918 in terms of domestic strains, especially those in Germany as a result of the Allied blockade. Moreover, the extent to which the Germans were in practice outfought was not one that was to attract adequate subsequent attention at the popular level including among the victors. The Germans, in particular, preferred the 'stab-in-the-back' legend, attributing defeat to left-wing disaffection at home, an argument that was to be employed by the Nazis, but not only by them. In fact, the German forces in 1918 were defeated and dramatically driven back on the Western Front, in the very theatre of operations where their strength was concentrated. There is a parallel for Germany's allies. Bulgaria, for example, suffered from rising food prices and increased popular discontent, which affected army morale,[33] but the failure at the Salonica front was the vital change in September 1918. Again, distracting attention from victory at the several fronts, post-war criticism among the Allies, particularly Britain, of the war, specifically its human cost and the peace settlement, tarnished the presentation of success. More recently, academic study of the war-making, specifically of improvements in British fighting techniques, has had scant impact on popular views. Instead, the emphasis is still on the first two or three years of the war and its apparent futility.

This problem by no means exhausts issues posed by the breakthrough campaign of 1918, as, focusing on the fighting, it is necessary to qualify, if not challenge, the explanation of victory in terms of new weaponry, specifically the tank, but also with an emphasis on aircraft. This explanation draws on powerful strands in military history, namely the stress on material culture and a related concern with explanations in terms of dramatic new developments. In a series of articles for the *Daily Mail* published in 1913, the novelist H. G. Wells predicted that science and engineering would be crucial in winning the next war, which would be more mechanized than any hitherto, putting a premium on 'the best brains'. The war indeed witnessed important advances in this sphere, although the problems of using innovations to effect in a conflict of this scale were considerable, particularly with the size of the forces deployed. These factors tended to lessen the impact of the change, and to ensure that it was easier to be effective where the number of units was more limited: at sea, the sphere in which machines were more significant compared to land, as man does not fight naturally on the sea.

Nevertheless, the war saw the first use of new weapons, notably the tank but also poison gas and mobile flame-throwers, the first large-scale military use of recently developed weapons, particularly aircraft, and also major changes in older but still relatively recent weapons, especially submarines. All of these weapons, however, faced serious limitations. For example, the flame-thrower was first used by the Germans who then introduced the weapon to their Austrian allies in 1914. It was used in significant numbers by the Germans at Verdun in 1916 and was also used by the British and French. However, the one-and-two man flame-throwers of this war, as well as the wheeled and static models, were not mobile in the fashion of backpack models of the 1930s and the 1940s, and they were also severely hampered by being capable of only short-range bursts. Flame-throwers were more effective in the Second World War thanks to the invention of thickening agents which allowed the fuel to be projected a reasonable distance without being consumed in the process. Thickened fuels, particularly napalm, also stuck to the target.

Some of the statements subsequently made on behalf of the wartime impact of the tank, as of aircraft, reflected the competing claims about weapons systems made by their protagonists in the 1920s and 1930s, rather than an informed critical assessment of the operations in the war. There was also to be a projecting back onto 1918 of the role of the tank in the Second World War and subsequently. Nevertheless, the tank opened up a clear difference between the Allies and the Germans. The latter deployed tanks in 1918, but did so in far smaller numbers and to less effect than the Allies: German tanks, of which about 170 were captured from the Allies, did not influence the outcome of the Spring Offensives. German industry was unable to manufacture their large A7V tanks in sufficient quantities: fewer than 60 were in service and there were far more tanks on the Allied side. The French had invented them independently of the British in 1915. French tanks contributed little to the Nivelle offensive in 1917, but, by 1918, they had 3,000 tanks, including the Schneider-Creusot, which carried a 75-mm gun, and the faster and lighter-gunned Renault; and, that November, they planned to deploy 600 to support an advance into Lorraine. One of the consequences of wartime experience with tanks, trucks and motorbikes was that many more men in the 1920s were familiar with industrial machinery, especially transport, and, if nothing else, knew how to drive.

The first tank battle was between several A7Vs and British Whippets and MkIVs in April 1918 at Villers Bretonneux, but Allied tanks focused not on conflict with the relatively few German tanks, but rather in support of infantry attacks. Tanks played a prominent role in operations after Foch, on 26 July, issued orders for a general advance on all fronts. No fewer than 430 British tanks broke through the German lines near Amiens on 8 August, a battle that Ludendorff described as 'the Black Day' of the German army. The British captured 12,000 prisoners and advanced seven miles that day, and the Germans were unable to reverse their loss. Although the meeting of the German Supreme Army Command at Spa on 13–14 August decided that a successful defence would thwart the Allies, ending their drive to fight, the Allied victory at Amiens has been seen as important both to the Allied victory that year and to the transformation of warfare in the early twentieth century.

Certainly, taking forward cavalry doctrine, tanks seemed to overcome one of the major problems with offensives against trenches: the separation of firepower from advancing troops and the consequent lack of flexibility. Edward Heron-Allen, a visiting civilian, was impressed by British tanks when he saw them crossing a road on 16 October 1918. His account, described the subordination of terrain by the new weapon:

> really a fearsome sight … the road was on a slope of the hill, and the tanks just crawled up the slope, up the right bank nose in air, down with a bump into the road and across it – almost perpendicularly up the left bank, and down with a bump behind it and so onward up the hill without a moment's pause or hesitation.[34]

By carrying guns or machine guns, tanks made it possible for advancing units to confront unsurpassed positions and counterattacks. They offered precise tactical fire to exploit the consequences of the massed operational bombardments that preceded attacks. The value of tanks and their likely future consequences attracted much attention from commentators. Commanders had to decide how best to employ tanks, and to combine them with infantry and artillery, an issue made dynamic by the variety of tank types and by developments in them. A memorandum of June 1918 from the British Tanks Corps Headquarters claimed:

> Trench warfare has given way to field and semi-open fighting... the more the mobility of tanks is increased, the greater must be the elasticity of the co-operation between them and the other arms. The chief power of the tank, both material and moral, lies in its mobility, i.e. its pace, circuit, handiness, and obstacle crossing power.

Now the tank commander had to make sure he was not too far in advance of the infantry:

> whilst formerly he merely led the infantry on to their objective protecting them, as best he could, now he must manoeuvre his tank in advance of them, zig-zagging from one position to another, over-running machine-guns, stampeding away and destroying the enemy's riflemen, and all the time never losing touch with the infantry he is protecting. The increased power of manoeuvre of the Mark V Tank demands an increased power of manoeuvre on the part of the infantry. By this is not meant a higher rate of advance, but skill in the use of ground and formations suitable to the ground and the tactical situation ... demands more and more initiative on the part of the infantry leaders ... Though the effect produced by tanks leading forward infantry may be compared to that of the artillery barrage, the infantry should not look upon it as such, but should regard the tanks as armoured fighting patrols or mechanical scouts thrown out in front of them, not to exonerate them from fighting.[35]

191

Tanks were indeed important but their value was lessened by their limitations, especially durability, but also firepower and speed. The British light infantry mortar in practice was more effective, reliable and capable of providing flexible infantry support, than the tank, which was consistently under-powered, under-gunned, under-armoured and unreliable. Moreover, it was difficult for the crew to communicate with each other, let alone anyone outside the tank, and this drawback made it harder to get a tank to engage a target of opportunity. The value of tanks was also affected by the difficulty of providing sufficient numbers of them, which reflected their late arrival in wartime resource allocation and production systems.

The ability to devise anti-tank tactics was also significant. German anti-tank measures were quite effective. Tanks were vulnerable to other tanks, as well as to mines, artillery pieces firing low-velocity shells and machine guns firing armour-piercing bullets. The M-98 Mauser anti-tank rifle fired armour-piercing bullets. Wherever tanks met real resistance, they did not do nearly as well as anticipated. The use of artillery against tanks was particularly important in this respect, and reflected the extent to which the incremental nature of improvements in artillery was a matter of tactics as well as technology and numbers. Percy Worrall wrote of the German attack on his positions on 14 April, 'When the armoured car attacked us – all the Lewis Gun team but two were killed or wounded, but two of my braves continued to fire at the aperture of the armoured car and actually drove it off .... A tree was later felled across the road to block any further attempt'.[36]

To operate most effectively, tanks needed to support, and to be supported by, advancing infantry and artillery, a lesson that had to be learned repeatedly during the century in the face of pressure from enthusiasts for tanks alone.[37] British successes at Cambrai and Amiens provide misleading examples of the usefulness of tanks because they did not meet organized resistance, and most of the tanks engaged in these battles subsequently broke down or were otherwise immobilized within a few days. Indeed, the Amiens offensive ceased on 11 August, with the Germans benefiting from the deployment of reserves and the delays created by the war-damaged terrain, while there were few British tanks still in operation. Thomas Blamey,

Chief of Staff to the Australian Corps, recorded that, on 9 August, tank support was 'with very reduced numbers owing to casualties suffered on the 8th .... Direct fire [on 9 August] was responsible for considerable casualties among the tanks supporting the 1st Australian Division'. The Allies' need to resort to artillery at Amiens emerged clearly. On 11 August, Blamey wrote, 'owing to the greatly increased enemy resistance in the Lihons Ridge and the fact that there were but few tanks available to support the advance, it was decided to employ a creeping artillery barrage'.[38] Arthur Child-Villiers wrote: 'The battle has proved a real success and is the most successful action fought by the British since the war begun. It is a pity that it would not have been on a scale sufficiently large to do something bigger'.[39]

As was only to be expected of a weapon that had not had a long process of peace-time development and preparation, there were major problems with the reliability of the tanks; these were exacerbated by the shell-damaged terrain across which they had to operate. Many tanks broke down even before reaching the assault point, and, in battle, tanks rapidly became unfit for service, understandably so given their technical problems. The British also suffered from a failure to produce sufficient spare parts. Tank numbers fell markedly in September and October. Moreover, tanks were appropriate for infantry support, but were not yet a fast-moving mechanized force. For these reasons, there was a reaction in British circles against the use of armour after August 1918.

A different use of motor vehicles was provided by lorries which provided mobility for both troops and supplies, and underlined the value of oil supplies. By 1918, the French army had nearly 90,000 motor vehicles, although the Germans had only 40,000.

Had tank production been at a greater level, then tanks might have made a greater contribution in 1918, but the idea that massed tanks would have made a significant difference to Allied capability had the war continued into 1919, as planned for by J. F. C. Fuller, is contentious. Assuming that, in order to produce the huge numbers required, the tank could have been mass produced, which was not the case hitherto, nevertheless the same basic problems of unreliability, slow speed, vulnerability to anti-tank measures and field guns, under-gunning, poor inter-communication capabilities and poor obstacle-crossing capability would have remained. There is little to suggest that the tanks would have performed well, while resupply with ammunition and fuel would have been a serious issue. If the British tanks of the 1920s are considered as an extension of the line of development from the Great War, it is difficult to see how they would have been decisive.

Furthermore, this approach ignores the anti-tank technologies that would have been developed by the Germans. Indeed, the chances are that anti-tank guns would have been superior to the tanks. These problems affect the extent to which there was really a choice at the operational and tactical levels of war between manoeuvre supported by firepower and firepower supported by manoeuvre, each of which had advantages. In practice, aside from the shortages and deficiencies of tanks and the less costly nature of the focus on artillery, for which the British were anyway well prepared, there were key capability strengths as far as artillery was concerned, both tactically and operationally.

It is also necessary to qualify assumptions about the role of air power, where, again, there was a subsequent tendency to read back in order to justify institutional and other assumptions. Leading air power advocates of the inter-war years had taken command positions in the war, including Guilio Douhet, author of *Il Dominio dell'Aria* (The Command of the Air) of 1921, who had been appointed head of the Italian Central Aeronautical Bureau in 1917, Billy Mitchell, the senior American air commander in the war, and Hugh Trenchard who commanded the British Royal Flying Corps in France during the war and was the first Chief of the Air Staff from 1918 to 1929.

Alongside bombing, there was a development in ground-attack, with the capability and range of ground-support operations expanding. In 1918, the Germans used ground-attack squadrons to support their offensives on the Western Front, while regular Allied air attacks on their supply links inhibited German advances. The British ground attacks on the Western Front in late August were affected by German airpower: 'During the whole of these operations enemy low flying aircraft were extraordinarily active, bombing and machine-gunning our troops'.[40] German aircraft destroyed moving French tanks in Champagne, and the British used air strikes in their advances in Palestine and in Macedonia.

By the close of the war, the extent and role of air power had been transformed. By 1918, the British had 22,000 aircraft, while the combined Franco-American-British force of 1,481 aircraft employed to support the American attack on the St Mihiel salient on 12 September was not only the largest deployment so far, but also gained air control, which was not usually possible during the war. Massed offensive tactics were also used by the Americans in support of the Meuse-Argonne offensive at the end of September, and by the French and the British.[41]

At the same time, anti-aircraft capability increased considerably, and, that year, the German Air Service's anti-aircraft guns shot down 748 Allied aircraft. Edward Mannock, the leading British ace, was shot down by ground fire on 26 July; he had brought down 73 planes. Aside from the guns, there were specialized spotting and communication troops, as well as relevant training, manuals and firing tables. In September 1918, Child-Villiers noted 'They [the British] seem to be getting more clever in bringing down the night-flying aeroplanes. Quite a number have been brought down close to where we are'.[42]

Air power also developed at sea, with Britain taking the lead in the use of aircraft for reconnaissance, patrols against submarines and attacks on shipping. In July, Britain conducted the first raid by planes flown off an improvised aircraft carrier. In the following month, British seaplanes eliminated an entire naval force: six German coastal motorboats. In September, HMS *Argus*, an aircraft carrier capable of carrying 20 planes with a flush deck unobstructed by superstructure and funnels – the first clear-deck carrier – was commissioned by the British, although she did not undergo sea trials until October 1918. At the end of the war, the Royal Naval Air service had 2,949 aircraft and was planning an attack on the German High Seas Fleet in harbour.

Yet the extension of air power to the sea made scant impact on the course of the war, while, on land, many of the hopes of air power were based on a misleading sense of operational and technological possibilities and, in practice, the prime value of air power remained aerial reconnaissance throughout the war. Nevertheless, the Royal Air Force was established as a separate force on 1 April, and this independence from the army was not only a testimony to the argument that such an organization would make it easier to pursue air control but also a reaction to the demand for retribution for the German raids on Britain. Air power was designed to surmount the deadlock of the trenches by permitting the destruction of the enemy where vulnerable.[43] The German cities of Frankfurt, Mannheim and Cologne were all attacked, but the purpose of degrading industrial and logistical capability proved difficult in practice. Moreover, there were civilian casualties, which underlined popular bitterness. At any rate, the British exaggerated what their bombers had achieved, and this greatly affected inter-war discussion of strategic bombing, leading to a misrepresentation of its potential.[44] The war ended before the British could use the large Handley Page V/500 bombers they had built to bomb Berlin.

Air superiority did not have the same effect that was to be seen in the Second World War. On 8 and 9 November, Alan Thomson benefited from information from a plane about the situation ahead and also telephoned back the news, while, on 9 November, near Malplaquet, a famous bloody battlefield from 1709, he watched British planes dropping ration boxes by parachute as the cratered roads had made it impossible to bring up supplies. Yet, he was bombed that night and, on the last night of the war, a German plane flew over.[45] The Fokker D7 fighter, which had entered service in April 1918, provided the Germans with a highly manoeuvrable and effective plane. Moreover, the effectiveness of air power remained dependent on the weather, so that, when the weather was 'wonderful for observing', the sky was 'full of aeroplanes'.[46]

Despite the limitations of both tanks and air power, the Germans, thanks to Allied improvements, had lost their superiority in weapons systems, while, in turn, the Allies had preserved, if not enhanced, their advantages. This was particularly the case with artillery. On the Allied side on land, in place of generalized firepower, there was systematic co-ordination, reflecting precise control of both infantry and massive artillery support and better communications between them.[47] The

British army had 440 heavy artillery batteries in November 1918, compared to six in 1914. British gunnery inflicted considerable damage on German defences. The use of the creeping barrage had developed appreciably, as had counter-battery doctrine, science and tactics, and the British benefited greatly when they captured the outer defences of the Hindenburg Line on 18 September and breached the Line itself on 27 September. The absence of comparable co-ordination hit the Americans hard when they attacked towards Soissons in 1918.[48]

Aside from artillery-infantry co-ordination, the British had successfully developed planned indirect (three-dimensional) firepower. In contrast to direct fire, the use of indirect fire depended on accurate intelligence including the extensive use of aerial photography as well as of sound ranging, surveying and meteorology. There was also a great expansion in the production of maps in order not only to record German positions but also to permit the dissemination of the information. When the BEF was sent to France in 1914, one officer and one clerk were responsible for mapping, and the maps were unreliable. By 1918, the survey organization of the BEF had risen to about 5,000 men and had been responsible for more than 35 million map sheets. No fewer than 400,000 impressions were produced in just ten days in August 1918, a key element of the use of geographical and cartographic talent for the war effort.[49]

This cartography was important in the development and use of fire plans, with accurate fire from artillery batteries the end-product in a large-scale process of Intelligence acquisition and application, a process in which rapid communications helped relate firepower to need and opportunity, and to do so in a rapidly reactive fashion. Thus, preparation, attack breakthrough and counter-attack all triggered planned artillery sequences with differing types of levels of direction.[50] The improvement in the availability and use of Intelligence seen with aerial spotting and mapping was matched by the development of other forms of Intelligence, such as sound-ranging signals Intelligence.[51] The use of artillery indirect fire has been seen as the birth of the 'modern style of warfare' in the advent of three-dimensional conflict, with what followed later in the century as 'no more than complementary and incremental improvements upon the conceptual model laid down in 1917–18'.[52]

Artillery certainly emerged as the key element in after-action reports in 1918. Thus, for the British in the Battle of the River Selle of 19–23 October on the Western Front:

> The 5th Battalion Machine Gun Corps and 5th Divisional Artillery put down a magnificent barrage – 4 minutes on railway – jump to road beyond and rest for 8 minutes – creep forward 10 yards in 4 minutes arriving at protective line … smoke shells were used to denote the beginning and end of each pause, and thermite shells to denote boundaries and to help guide advancing infantry…. Notwithstanding the heavy and accurate barrage of our artillery, the enemy stood his ground and the advance was held up. [new attack] a fine barrage … men … kept up well under the barrage …. The five minutes' bombardment demanded by the C.O. undoubtedly saved the battalion many lives and won for them an almost impregnable position.[53]

Field artillery complemented the heavy guns: Thomson recorded the 'close support' the guns of his Artillery Pursuit Group provided to the advancing British infantry on 5 November, adding, for 10 November, 'Advanced section went on and did splendid work, actually getting into action *beyond* the front wave of the infantry and killing Huns at 1000 yards rise over the open sights'. The Brigadier-General he was supporting added on 12 November that 'the Infantry always knew the guns were close behind and ready to help them when required … the keenness and push of the officers in charge of the forward sections allotted to my attacking battalions each day … my battalions are full of praise for the shooting of your gunners'.[54]

Artillery also became more important on the Italian Front, with the Italians firing more shells in 1918 than in 1915–17 in part due to a major increase in munitions production. The role of gas in the Allied victory on the Western Front is a matter of controversy. Particularly as used by the British, gas became highly effective as the Special Brigade Royal Engineers became very skilled in gas warfare. It has been argued that the British artillery made effective use of gas shells in order to silence German guns, which has been seen as an instance of the British success in responding to possibilities and problems.[55]

The scientific use of artillery was more significant and this use reflected a range of improvements including Intelligence, but also the guns and their equipment. For example, improved artillery capability owed much to better time and impact fuses. Tactics were linked to technology, and the tactical dimension was important: more and better guns alone did not suffice. This dimension reflected the long-term development of training, organization and equipment, one that began for the British in 1915 and gathered pace in 1916, as in the enhancement of both field artillery and infantry platoons through reorganization.

The rapid infantry advance tactics that the British, like the Germans, employed in the latter stages of the war were linked to the development of more portable weapons, which could be carried forward by the infantry while still providing considerable firepower. Grenades, both thrown by hand and fired from rifles, were important, as were lightweight machine guns and mortars and light artillery pieces. Thus, on 28 September 1918, a company of the Devonshire Regiment 'advanced under considerable machine gun fire by dribbling men across open spaces under covering fire from massed company Lewis Guns.'[56]

Much of the recent British literature on the Western Front has focused on the development of the appropriate artillery and infantry tactics, a development to which the ability to overcome shell shortages greatly contributed. The armies of 1914 had lacked suitable tactics to cope with firepower and stalemate, but the invention, in the form of grenades and trench mortars, of reliable trench warfare munitions, which did not exist before early 1915, allowed tactical changes which were not otherwise possible. Moreover, the development by the British of deep battle, in which targets beyond the front, including reinforcements and headquarters, were being bombarded, made use of the tactics of the Stokes 3-inch mortar. This development benefited greatly from aircraft, aerial reconnaissance and air-ground support made possible by advanced and reliable aircraft, which was not possible before 1917. Thus, the evolution of trench warfare into deep battle was a continuum in which the relationship between technology and tactics changed because technology was viewed differently from hitherto, with armies being more willing to appreciate new weaponry and its possibilities, as in the calibration of each gun each day according to the weather conditions.

Firepower and careful planning were combined to great effect in 1918. There were important advances, in particular by British, Australian and Canadian forces, in the last months of the war, and a series of attacks maintained the pressure on the Germans without exhausting the Allied forces. Thus, after the attack by the British Fourth Army at Amiens on 8–10 August, additional attacks included those at Arras on 17 August, at Bapaume on 21 August by Byng's Third Army (the Battle of Albert), and at St Quentin on 28 August.[57] German resistance, however, led to heavy casualties and posed serious problems, as for the first battalion of the Devonshire Regiment:

> [30 August] The advance was extremely difficult owing to the open nature of the country and the strength of the enemy resistance …. Small parties pushed on to Beugny, where they were met by intense rifle and machine-gun fire, both from their flanks and rear. This made it necessary to withdraw … [31 August] hostile machine-guns fired immediately on any movement.[58]

Although smaller than in 1914, improvements in the French army also enabled it, like the British, to move from the eventually successful defensive against the German Spring Offensives onto the attack. The French played a major role in the closing offensives, including the recapture of the territory lost in the German Aisne offensive. The French took heavy losses in these and later offensives which indicated the extent to which they still had plenty of fight in them,[59] and

British commentators noted this. The French First Army supported the British Fourth in the Amiens offensive and subsequently pushed forward, to Chimay in Belgium, while the Tenth Army captured Laon, and the Fourth advanced to Mezières on the Meuse. The French captured fewer prisoners and guns than the British, but far more than the Americans.

There was still considerable Allied pessimism in August that the war could be won that year.[60] However, on 2 September, Ludendorff ordered a retreat to the Hindenburg Line, which entailed both a surrender of the gains made earlier that year and an admission that the Germans could not successfully resist the Allies unless powerfully supported by major prepared positions.

Contemporary explanations of Allied success tended to discuss tanks as part of a more general improvement in capability. In his report on operations from 8 August 1918 to the end of the war, Thomas Blamey, Chief of Staff to Monash and the Australian Corps, noted that the campaign:

> differed from similar operations carried out in 1916 and 1917
>
> a) Every possible effort was made to obtain surprise both strategically and tactically. It was, therefore, determined that there should be no preliminary bombardment or attempt at destruction of enemy defence systems.
>
> b) Careful concealment of our intentions.
>
> c) Emplacement of a large proportion of artillery within 2,000 yards of the front-line which enabled the advance to be covered by an effective barrage to a depth of 4,000 yards into enemy country, and thus ensured that the advance of the infantry beyond the line of the enemy's field guns should be protected by a barrage.
>
> d) No registration of guns in new positions. This was made possible by the careful calibration of guns as new artillery came into the area.

e) The employment of a large proportion of smoke shell in the barrage with the object of enabling the infantry to appear suddenly before any enemy defences and rush them before the enemy was able to realize what was happening.

f) i) The employment of tanks …. All infantry engaged was given an opportunity of training with tanks prior to the operations. ii) The 17th Armoured Car Battalion, Tanks Corps, was placed at the disposal of the Australian Corps. It was given an independent mission to move direct against enemy centers of communication, headquarters etc. Its operations were brilliantly successful and its exploits read like a tale of the old days.

As a reminder, however, of the danger of selective quotations, the details provided on particular operations indicated the vulnerability of tanks to strong resistance, and the continued problems encountered from unsuppressed machine guns. The Germans still fought hard, and Allied casualties were very heavy, the British losing more men than in the Passchendaele offensive. Blamey recorded that near Peronne on 2 September the attack was 'met by hurricane machine gun fire', while, in the main attack on the Hindenburg Line,

on the 27th American Division front, trouble from hostile machine guns inside the barrage was experienced from the start. A number of the tanks supporting the 27th American Division were put out of action by enemy shell fire and by anti-tank mines, and with this support gone the infantry in this sector of the attack rapidly lost touch with the barrage. Enemy machine guns were thus free to harass the main weight of the attack with the result that only isolated parties were able to get forward.

On the front of the 3rd Australian Division, 'the tanks detailed to assist ... suffered considerably from hostile shell fire'.[61] The capture of the Hindenburg defences led to heavy casualties, as was more generally true of Allied operations in the last months of the war, not least because of their range and tempo, which prefigured the comparable situation in 1944–45. Switching to a war of movement also left troops exposed away from the relative safety of the trenches. The Canadians lost more men in the battles of Arras, the Canal du Nord and Cambrai, between 26 August and 9 October, than they did in other battles. The British war poet Wilfred Owen was killed on the Sambre Canal on 4 November.

Command factors were significant to Allied success. There were mistakes in planning and execution as with the attack on the Hindenburg Line mentioned above. Nevertheless, the Line was breached, suggesting that no German defensive position was invulnerable, while, by 1918, alongside improvements in the effectiveness of staff work at the General Headquarters and at corps headquarters, British commanders, at both senior and junior levels, had greater relevant operational experience than in 1916.[62] This was important because officers on, or close to, the battlefield had to be able to take appropriate command decisions in order to sustain the tempo of effective attack. Due to the complexity of operations and to problems with communications, supreme commanders and their staffs were not well placed to provide these decisions. In part, this situation represented the extent to which the strategic level was swallowed up by the operational and the operational by the tactical. Yet, command operated at multiple levels. On the Western Front, the adoption of unity of command under Foch greatly helped the Allies, while his methodical qualities were also important.

Political support for the war remained strong among the Allies, but the political situation was far less favourable for the Central Powers. Germany was affected both by the crises of its allies and by its grave domestic problems. The first ally to go was the weakest, and the last into the war, Bulgaria. With Romania and Serbia in the hands of the Central Powers, Bulgaria was not really greatly vulnerable to attack, but the Bulgarians were the key force containing the long-quiescent 200,000 strong multi-national Allied army at Salonica, while also ensuring that it was not diverted to fight the Germans on the Western Front.

At the same time, Bulgaria, never wealthy, was under great economic pressure as a result of the war, while its leaders were disillusioned by the little they had gained from the conflict. The character of Allied command proved crucial in Bulgaria's defeat. In June, General Guillaumat, who had not achieved much, was replaced by Louis Franchet d'Esperey, a bold, energetic leader, who had played a key role on the Marne in 1914. He focused the offensive, launched on 15 September, to the west of the River Varder, using his Serbian and French troops to attack in difficult terrain on only part of the front line, while Anglo-Greek attacks on the right fixed the Bulgarian reserves. Complete success was achieved by 16 September.[63] The Bulgarians were defeated and, harried by British air attacks, pushed back. The Allies, having taken Skopje on 29 September, advanced into the Kosovo region of Serbia. They were helped by the effectiveness of guerrilla opposition in the Bulgarian occupation zone.

There were no German or Austrian forces available to shore up the front in time, and, on 25 September, Bulgaria itself was invaded. There was already tension in the alliance because Germany had ended financial subsidies to Bulgaria in February, cut arms supplies in March and supported the Turks in pressing for the return of territory ceded to Bulgaria in 1915. German control of part of the Bulgarian economy also increased popular anger. Discontent among the army rose with defeat. With political chaos increasing, Bulgaria asked for an armistice, which was agreed at Salonica on 29 September. Hostilities were to cease the following day, and the Allies were to have the right to occupy and use Bulgarian space.

The Allied forces were able to press on in the Balkans in October and, by early November, to occupy Bulgaria, Serbia and Albania. Belgrade was liberated by Serbian and French troops on 1 November, Serbian territory was cleared of foreign troops on 3 November, and the Serbian forces then invaded Austria's South Slav territories.

Bulgaria's collapse, which was cemented with the abdication of King Ferdinand on 3 October in favour of his son Boris III, destroyed, moreover, the cohesion of the Central Powers. It showed how quickly an army could be defeated and a state give in, broke the links to Turkey, and threatened Austria with attack from the Balkans. D'Esperey planned to advance on Budapest.

Bulgaria's armistice also challenged the position of the Central Powers in Romania. On 10 November, Allied forces, advancing from Salonica, crossed the Danube into Romania, which, in pursuit of Transylvania and equipped by the French, re-entered the war on the Allied side. Allied and Romanian forces advanced into Dobruja, Wallachia and Transylvania, while the Germans began to withdraw on 10–11 November. On 1 December, King Ferdinand of Romania entered Bucharest at the head of his forces.

By the time of the Bulgarian armistice, the Turks, who had to cover a number of qualitatively different fronts, were already under serious pressure in Palestine. The campaign there had been affected by the state of operations on the Western Front, which was an aspect of the interdependence that was so important to the conflict. The Allies suffered in this interdependence from their exterior lines but their position was eased as a result of their control of the sea. Allenby had captured Jericho in February 1918, as part of an advance into the Jordan Valley which put pressure on the Turkish flank. However, he was then held back by the extent to which his army was used to provide reinforcements for the British forces in France that spring. Fifty-four battalions were transferred and troops were moved likewise from Mesopotamia. Their poorly trained Indian replacements took a while to adapt and Allenby was concerned about Turkish attempts to exploit Muslim sentiment in their ranks. Rather than exhausting it through a premature attack, the summer provided a welcome opportunity to develop the army, through the introduction of improved weaponry and the creation of a better logistical structure, while a Turkish attack at Abu Tulul was defeated in July.

On 20 September, Allenby launched his final offensive against the Turkish forces in Palestine, deploying 69,000 troops and 550 pieces of artillery against 34,000 and 400. This battle was called Megiddo as Allenby's forces advanced by this ancient mound, the supposed site of the final battle (Armageddon) mentioned in the Book of Revelation. As part of his superiority in Intelligence and its application,[64] Allenby kept the Turks guessing about the direction of attack: he began by raiding the eastern end of the Turkish line, creating the impression that he would repeat his 1917 attack; but, in the event, did the opposite, using effective artillery–infantry co-ordination near the Mediterranean coast, to break through the opposing lines. The artillery bombardment only lasted 15 minutes, showing that Allenby was able to master the equation of time and shock. The Turks were both under-strength and badly equipped. Crucially, Enver Pasha, the War Minister, was more interested in exploiting the Russian Revolution to regain past territorial losses and forward his longstanding and quixotic pan-Turkish plans for expansion into a Central Asian Turkish heartland.[65] He concentrated Turkish forces in the Caucasus, taking troops from the Palestine and Mesopotamia fronts.

Operations near the coast also enabled Allenby to benefit from naval support. This success provided an opportunity for the cavalry to exploit. They swung to the east, cutting the line of Turkish retreat, while other cavalry units advanced along the coast, capturing both Haifa and Acre on 23 September. Palestine allowed broad sweeping movements by mobile forces, and Allenby's men took many prisoners for only 5,666 casualties. The demoralized Turks, their coherence fractured by the rapid British advance, readily surrendered, although some units mounted rearguard actions. Megiddo is widely seen as the last great cavalry battle, the British cavalry charging as well as acting as mounted infantry. Moreover, armoured cars provided significant mobility. Allenby's use of air power was also highly effective. He was able to prevent the German air contingent supporting the Turks from flying reconnaissance sorties; whereas the British had an accurate picture of the Turkish position. Air supremacy also prevented interception of British bombers which were used to bomb rail junctions and telephone exchanges in order to disrupt communications and to destroy the Turkish forces when they retreated.

A rapid British advance on two axes then further exploited the situation. Along the coast, troops advanced to capture Tyre, Sidon and, on 2 October, Beirut. The previous day, Australian cavalry, that had advanced from the Sea of Galilee, joined Arab forces (advised by T. E. Lawrence) in taking Damascus. These Arab forces played an important role in attacking Turkish targets to the east of the River Jordan, and notably in cutting rail links. Syria was rapidly conquered, with Aleppo, which had become the front headquarters the previous month, falling on 25 October. The British also advanced in Mesopotamia, occupying Mosul on 3 November.

On 30 October, meanwhile, an armistice signed at Mudros ended the conflict. The Turkish wartime cabinet had already resigned on 13 October. Isolated from their allies, under heavy pressure, and attracted by the opportunities of gains from Russia, the Turks sought an end to war with the Allies. The armistice decreed demobilization, the expulsion of German forces, the opening of the Dardanelles and Bosporus to Allied shipping, and the Allied right to occupy any territory they judged appropriate.[66]

The Austrians meanwhile had found it impossible to repeat their success at Caporetto. An offensive launched against the Italians on 15 June, on the Piave River front towards Padua, with an attack further west to the south of Asiago towards Verona, was beaten back with heavy losses. Drawing on their experience, the British helped improve the effectiveness of the Italians in trench warfare, which was part of a process by which Italian war-making improved during the war alongside the many deficiencies on which it is easy to concentrate. The Austrians crossed the Piave but could not secure their position on the western bank. Instead, under pressure from the impact of air attacks and a rain-swollen river on their supply routes, and affected by the Italian ability to deploy reserves, the Austrians withdrew their troops. A supporting naval attack on the Otranto barrage was abandoned after a battleship was lost to an Italian torpedo boat.

As a result of bad harvests in 1917 and 1918, the Austrian forces in Italy were desperately short of food, and desertions were soon large scale as they also were among troops redeployed from the Eastern Front but not yet sent to another front. Failure in June encouraged a breakdown of the army in Italy. Moreover, the army as a whole was increasingly affected by nationalist separatism, as its constituent parts saw themselves in ethnic terms rather than as a separate force, an approach encouraged by Allied psychological warfare.[67] Defeat took the empire to the breaking point caused by the combination of nationalist separatism with a weak and exhausted imperial system, the counterpart to the poor generalship that had also done so much damage.

The collapse of the ethnic cohesion of the army was followed by that of the empire, with a National Council of Serbs, Croats and Slovenes established in Zagreb on 6 October and a Czech national committee in Prague.[68] A lack of any confidence in the purpose of the war had led Emperor Karl to appeal unsuccessfully to the French for negotiations in the spring and to press the Germans in August and September for immediate peace talks, again without success. On 16 September, Karl followed up by publicly appealing to President Wilson for peace, and on 16 October declared Austria (though not Hungary) a confederalist monarchy, as a way to link the dynasty with the mass of competing nationalities. Next day, István Tisza, the former Prime Minister of Hungary and a supporter of continuing the war, announced in Parliament that it was lost. On 20 October, the Hungarian Parliament voted for constitutional change: the end of ties with Austria bar for the common monarch. The Hungarian monarchy, however, itself disintegrated, with a Czechoslovak Republic being proclaimed in Prague on 28 October, and the Croatian parliament in Zagreb, next day, declaring Croatia independent within the new federation of South Slavs, later Yugoslavia.

Worried that they would miss the boat and that their territorial claims would be sidelined in a peace agreement accepting national self-determination, the Italian government, under great pressure from its allies to act, ordered Armando Diaz, the Italian commander, to do so. He did not wish to advance, and, instead, preferred to wait for the spring of 1919, but he was pushed into attacking on 24 October. The Italian attack on the Austrian positions near Mount Grappa was a dismal demonstration that warfighting did not necessarily improve during the war. Linear advances into Austrian firepower led to no gains and nearly 25,000 casualties, but, further east, with the British Tenth Army playing a key role which the post-war Italians were not keen to recall, and French forces from the Twelfth Army also taking a part, the River Piave was crossed from the night of 26 October.

The bridgehead was rapidly expanded in the face of weak resistance by demoralized troops. The Austrians began to withdraw from Italy, losing many prisoners to the pursuing Allied forces. Aircraft attack made the retreat more deadly.

On 26 October, Emperor Karl informed Kaiser Wilhelm that he needed an armistice and a separate peace, and on 3 November Karl agreed to the non-negotiable Allied terms for the armistice. Trieste and Trento were occupied by the Allies the same day. The Battle of Vittorio Veneto came to an end with hundreds of thousands of Austrian prisoners, the armistice taking effect at 3.00 p.m. on 4 November.

This collapse left Germany exposed. The armistice terms included not only a reduction of the Austrian army to 20 divisions and the provision that all German troops had to leave Austria within 15 days, but also that the Allies would have free use of all imperial transport networks, and thus be able to attack Germany. Karl had been very concerned by this provision, but he was prevailed upon to agree. The Austrian fleet had already been handed over on 31 October.

Germany was under multiple pressures. The exacerbation in 1918 of military, economic and domestic problems destroyed the will to fight. As in Austria, serious food shortages greatly hit civilian morale and reduced energy and resistance to disease. Manpower shortages affected not only the army, but also the economy, creating competition between the two. These shortages, which became more apparent from early 1916, led to calls for the use of prisoners of war: Germany held 2.4 million, mostly Russians, during the war. However, the pressure of military demands hit the German economy hard. Due to a lack of miners, coal production fell in 1917, and both this and the lack of workers affected the rail system which, from 1916, was also under great pressure due to the focus of steel production on armaments. The cumulative impact of such shortages was a run-down in the economy and its growing atomization, which hindered attempts to co-ordinate and direct production.

Germany had no equivalent to the support provided to Britain and France by the Americans, nor to the prospect of future help that it offered. Pressing the German domestic population harder only helped to undermine public backing for the war.[69] The strain that the attempt to mobilize the resources for total war imposed on German society was heightened by the failure of the 1918 Spring Offensives, which led to the loss of many of the best German troops and, more generally, to the exhaustion of the army. Army morale collapsed after the offensive did not bring the victory promised by Ludendorff, and this collapse led to a loss of fighting resilience and of unit cohesion, a situation exacerbated by the increasing superiority of Allied forces. Large numbers of troops surrendered as the Germans were pushed back onto the defensive, and German officers no longer felt they could rely on their units. For the first time in the war, significant numbers of German troops deserted, while many who did not became *Drückeberger* who avoided combat.[70]

Like its opponents, for example the American First Army in the Meuse-Argonne offensive, the German army was also badly affected by the epidemic of Spanish influenza then sweeping the world, an epidemic that by 1920 had killed more people worldwide than died on the battlefields of the Great War. This epidemic hit the German Spring Offensives and the subsequent German resistance, with the crisis in German food supplies ensuring that the situation at the front and in the rear was more serious than it was for the Allies. Moreover, the crisis at the German front interacted with that at home, each accentuating the other.

These factors helped ensure that the Allied expectation that the war would continue until 1919 was not fulfilled. Instead, an armistice came into force on 11 November. Success at Amiens had been followed by further pressure on the Germans, helped by the good weather,[71] and, on 3 September, by orders from Foch for an attack along the entire front. On 14 September, an Austrian request for talks with the Allies was rejected by the Germans. The successful Allied assault on the Hindenburg Line near Cambrai on 27 September, as well as the sense of crisis emanating from the impending collapse of Germany's alliance system, led Ludendorff, in a crucial step, to change his views next day and on 29 September to recommend an armistice in order to preserve the army and thus enable it to repress radicalism. He put the stress on Bulgaria's decision to seek an armistice, which threatened Turkey, Austria and the grain and oil obtained from Romania. The news of this decision reached Germany on 28 September. Allied successes against the Germans on the Western Front were probably more important, but it was preferable to blame the Bulgarians. On 2 October, however, the Supreme Army Command in a briefing to the leading politicians in the *Reichstag* emphasized the situation on the Western Front, notably the shift in troop numbers as a result of American reinforcements. Allied tanks were also mentioned.

Ludendorff saw an armistice as the basis for an honourable peace, and not for a dictated one. To that end, a new government was appointed on 3 October under the moderate Prince Max of Baden, a measure designed to appeal to Wilson and to meet domestic pressure for change. Propounded in a speech to Congress, Wilson's distinction between the German people and, on the other hand, the Hohenzollern dynasty of Wilhelm II and the High Command, opened a way to negotiations on the basis of political change in Germany. In contrast, Ludendorff saw an armistice and the subsequent peace as a way to discredit the Left.

On 4 October, Max approached Wilson for peace on the basis of the Fourteen Points that Wilson had outlined on 8 January 1918 as the basis for an eventual end to the war; but Wilson, who played a key role in the negotiations in late 1918, demanded, in a note of 14 October, that Germany be transformed into a constitutional state and that the armistice terms be such that Germany be unable to renew hostilities. Suspicious that Wilson was trying to act as an arbiter, Britain and France were particularly insistent on the latter point. Allied leaders and generals initially thought that the conditions offered to Germany would be judged unacceptable, and that they would have to use tanks and the Americans to win victory in 1919, but, on 17 October, the German War Cabinet decided to accept Wilson's terms. Ludendorff and Hindenburg, however, were unwilling to do so. On 24 October, Ludendorff denounced the proposed terms, and said that Germany would fight on. He was dismissed two days later.

Meanwhile, the continuation of the Allied advance indicated that this campaign was to be different from the others, prefiguring the marked improvement in Soviet operational capability in 1944. Not only had the Allies overcome the tactical problems of trench warfare, but they had also developed the mechanisms, notably greatly improved logistics, and deployed the resources, particularly large numbers of guns, necessary to sustain their advance and offensive in the face of continued resistance and across a broad front. The contrast with the German offensives in the spring was readily apparent.

A series of attacks along the front line were designed to wear out the Germans and crumble their defences, making it impossible for them to consolidate a new front. Thus, for example, on 26–29 September, there were a series of attacks, including by the Americans, Belgians and French, and by the British First, Second, Third and Fourth Armies, a series that helped lead Ludendorff to explore the option of an armistice. The crossing of the Canal du Nord by the Canadian Corps on 27 September proved particularly important.

German resistance, however, continued to be strong[72] and to cause heavy casualties, notably from machine guns. Blamey recorded that on 3 October, 'considerable opposition was met with along the Beaurevoir-Masnieres Line which was too wide on the front of the right brigade for the Whippet Tanks to cross. The heavy tanks encountered much anti-tank fire but a few reached the line of La Motte Farm and ably assisted the progress of the infantry'.[73] Alan Thomson wrote, 'We attacked on the 6th [November] but the Hun had a very strong position …. He had hundreds of machine guns in action. His shell fire was very heavy and we did not get on'.[74] Launched on 26 September, the American Meuse-Argonne offensive had taken heavy casualties as it fought its way through strong defences; and this costly progress remained the pattern when the reinforced offensive was resumed on 4 October, although the Germans were driven from the Argonne Forest. On 1 November, the last of the American offensives was launched as the Americans fought their way across the River Meuse.

Successive German defence lines were broken through. Thus, the line of the River Selle was crossed by the British Fourth Army on 17 October and by the British Third Army on 20 October. Despite strong resistance and logistical problems, both of which encouraged

Haig to be pessimistic, the correspondence of many Allied officers and soldiers reflected both confidence in their activities and also a sense that the situation had changed abruptly. On 3 November, Den Fortescue disabused his father of his notion that the German retreat reflected a decision to fall back: 'all his captured orders emphasize that fact that position after position must be held at all costs but so far he has not been able to – what has regulated our pace much more than the Bosche resistance is the difficulties of our own communications: however now the old system should be already joined up with the old Bosche system so it ought not to impede us so much for however much railways are blown up they can be easily repaired whereas building lines across 10 miles of trenches many of which are thoroughly strafed is a biggish job. The same with roads'.

Fortescue also noted that the Germans were heavily outgunned as many of their guns had been captured.[75] The force opposed to Thomson retreated on the night of 6–7 November and, on 8 November, he recorded a further advance as the Germans had again retreated in the night 'leaving a few machine-gun posts behind'. However, their destruction of roads and cratering of roads delayed the advance of Thomson's batteries on 8 and 9 November.[76]

The German submarine force, meanwhile, continued its attacks, but with less effectiveness. Only 288,000 tons of British shipping were sunk in September and October combined. The German navy recalled its submarines on 21 October and handed over 176 after the war.

The strains of war had gathered to a point of political crisis in Germany with the mutiny of the sailors in the High Seas Fleet on 27 October proving a key precipitant for rebellion across the country, as well as thwarting the German naval command's plan for a final sortie to begin on 29 October, leading to a fight to the finish with the Grand Fleet. Combined with Wilhelm II's decision on 29 October to leave Berlin for the military headquarters at Spa, this plan suggested that a counter-revolution was being planned, although, in fact, the plan was devised, without consulting Wilhelm, in order to provide the navy with an outcome that would justify post-war political support for its position. In the event the naval mutiny prevented the fleet from sortieing, and it was to sail forth only to surrender, nine battle-ships and five battlecruisers entering the Firth of Forth to do so on 21 November, escorted by the Grand Fleet in an impressive display of British naval power.

In practice, by late October, support for the war in Germany and confidence in victory had largely collapsed. The impetus was now very much from those demanding political change, notably with the establishment of radical Councils across Germany. The Social Democrats were able to use this development in order to press for a new political order, including the democratization of state govern-ments. Aside from developments within Germany, there was to be a new political order in its conquests: on 3 November, Wilhelm II established a civilian government in the east, bringing the military administration by the *Ober Ost* (High Command Eastern Front), established for Hindenburg and Ludendorff in 1914, to an end.

Ideas of a different German sphere in Europe fell victim to the crisis at home as the Allied advance robbed the army leadership of confidence and created a sense of inexorable failure. Under pressure from Wilhelm Groener, Ludendorff's replacement, Wilhelm II was forced to abdicate on 9 November in the face of incipient revolution. The new provisional republican government, estab-lished that day, was eager to end the conflict, not least in order to prevent a deterioration in the situation that might open the way to a more radical outcome, as in Russia in 1917. The Social Democrats who dominated the government found Wilson's Fourteen Points acceptable.[77]

Wilhelm fled to Doorn in the Netherlands, and a plot to capture him from there to face war crimes charges was unsuccessful. Living till 1941, Wilhelm hoped for the restoration of his family, moved toward the Nazis in 1928, became an even more clear-cut anti-Semite, and saw Hitler's victories as a vindication of his policies in the early 1910s.

In a sense, Russia in 1917–18 became Germany in 1918, although there was no comparable social collapse. Groener believed peace necessary, not least so that the army was able to end hostilities and maintain social order. Indeed, on 10 November, Groener and the first Chancellor of the German Republic, the Social Democrat leader Friedrich Ebert, agreed to such a focus, and Groener was to help the infant Weimar republic resist left-wing risings in 1918–19.

A German delegation crossed the front line on 7 November and met the Allied commanders under Foch in a railway carriage stationed near Compiègne. The delegation was obliged to accept largely French-dictated armistice terms, notably the handing over of much of their *matériel*, including all submarines, the evacuation of all their conquests in Western and Eastern Europe as well as Alsace-Lorraine, the Allied occupation of German territory to the Rhine and partly beyond it (a demand that originated with Foch) and the continuation of the crippling Allied blockade until peace was signed. French leaders felt that the disaster of 1870 at the hands of Germany had been revenged.

By the time of the armistice, Allied troops were crossing the battlefields of the early days of the war, noting, for example, the treatment of national contingents in the cemeteries.[78] However, with the exception of part of Upper Alsace seized by the French in 1914, the Germans were still on Allied territory. The armistice was signed at 5.10 a.m. on the morning of 11 November, and at 11 a.m. that day the armistice came into force and the guns fell silent. When the news of the armistice reached British troops at Le Quesnoy, there was 'no noise except from band and drums as nobody believed it'.[79]

A phrase pregnant with significance on which to end, but then Alan Thomson wrote that day that, having had a trumpeter sound the ceasefire: 'I then called for three cheers for King George and the many troops who had assembled in the courtyard responded right heartily. It was a stirring moment'.[80]

CHAPTER 7

Struggle Reviewed

How I wish I could only have some of these D---d [damned] politicians out from England who are running the war, and let them see what a night or two in the trenches means in midwinter ... I am very weary of it all. It's like some hideous nightmare from which there is no awaking ever.

Tom Gurney to his wife, 7 January 1918.[1]

Casualty figures for the war were extreme: 9.45 million men died, and millions more were badly injured. Individual countries lost particularly heavily: about two million Germans died, as did about 1.81 million Russians, 1.4 million French, 1.3 million Austrians, 745,000 British, 600,000 Italians, 335,000 Romanians and 116,000 Americans. Turkish casualties are uncertain, but the Bulgarians had about 90,000 war dead. Including 61,400 Indians, 56,119 Canadians, 58,460 Australians (among the 332,000 Australians who served overseas) and 16,697 New Zealanders, confirmed British and British empire military dead came to just below one million. Belgium and Serbia each had about 44,000 war dead.

Moreover, casualty rates were high: 27 per cent of all French men between the ages of 18 and 27 died in the war, with 3.5 per cent of the total population dying in battle; while of the eight million soldiers mobilized by Austria, 1,106,000 died. Alongside the deaths there were the wounded and the prisoners: 2.4 million Russians were taken prisoner. Male deaths led to a marked increase in the number of single or widowed women. In the English county of Kent, the sex ratio rose from 1,063 females per 1,000 males in the 1911 census to 1,106 in that of 1921: the excess of females over males rising from 31,851 to 57,490.[2] For many states, including France and Britain, the casualties were greater than in the Second World War (and indeed a higher percentage of the British and French male populations served in the Great War[3]), although that was not the case for Germany, the Soviet Union or America, let alone Japan and China. The latter lost about 2,000 men from the Chinese Labour Corps on the Western Front, due to bombardment and disease.

There was also the massive civilian loss caused by the destruction, disruption and disease brought by war, including large-scale flight as well as the psychological traumas of occupation, although there are no accurate figures for civilian losses in Eastern Europe and the Turkish empire.[4] Britain lost 23,500 civilians killed by enemy action, although again civilian losses were far greater in the Second World War. Figures for direct expenditure on the war vary upward from $180 billion 1914 American dollars, and were possibly about $210 billion.

The devastation of the Great War was unprecedented and intense, leading to the immediate physical shock arising from the nature of the battlefield, specifically the way in which the scale of the devastation seemingly dwarfed any opportunities for heroism. The direct exposure of large numbers to the conflict was accentuated by its impact on others via reporting and photography. The length of the conflict, the numbers involved and the fact that so much of it occurred in Europe ensured that the war could not be treated as a distant spectacle. Travelling the Bapaume Road, close to the Western Front, on 20 October 1918, Edward Heron-Allen, a visiting British civilian, wrote in his diary, 'The whole landscape seen on either side ... was a scene of complete desolation. As far as one can see to the horizon, blasted woods and ruined villages'. Two days later, he reached Ypres:

> I thought I had seen absolute devastation and ruin at
> Bapaume and Péronne, but Ypres by comparison is
> as the Sahara to a sand dune. I could not realize that

we were approaching –much less in – the outskirts of Ypres, when, passing through some mounds of rubbish, I asked where we were and was told, 'This is Ypres', it absolutely turned me cold. Even the streets are obliterated ... there were not even bases of walls to show where houses had begun and left off ... 'The Hinterland of Hell' is the only phrase that in any way describes the road and the surrounding country between Ypres and Menin. Hitherto the desolation and devastation has seemed mournful – tragic – here it is fierce and absolutely terrifying. The whole landscape is ploughed up into 'hummocks' like pack ice in the Arctic Floe-mounds and crevasses of blackened earth, dotted about with English and German graves, the entrances to dug-out leading apparently into the bowels of the earth ... shell holes and mine craters of every size.

Retribution appeared the order of the day to Heron-Allen: 'A flight of [British] aeroplanes which passed overhead in battle-formation, off on a road to the east [toward German targets], seemed a fitting commentary upon the ghastly desolation'.[5] Retribution of a different form was a lasting legacy as farmers still plough up unexploded munitions from the war.

The dominant popular image of the war today is of this desolation, of the horrors of intractable trench warfare and of a command failure to appreciate and overcome the problems it posed. An unnecessary war, fought badly, and leading to a vindictive peace, is a frequent theme, and one that contrasts with the impression held of the Second World War.

In the inter-war years, there was criticism of the conflict, especially of the secret diplomacy that had led to the war, while the terms of the Peace of Versailles (1919) were rejected as overly harsh by many commentators. The war was denigrated wholesale by the Bolsheviks, for whom it symbolized the destructive nature of the old system that they had overcome in Russia and sought to overthrow elsewhere.

These critical themes went into abeyance with the Second World War which made it easier to understand and appreciate roles in the earlier conflict, although the Great War was also disparaged by comparison with the supposedly more moral, purposeful and better-conducted Second World War, and this contrast has proved damaging to this day.

The disruption of the Second World War, and the danger of German air attack, ensured that Armistice Day was cancelled in Britain in 1939. It is interesting to speculate what the commemoration of that war would have looked like had the Germans won the Second World War. In occupied France from 1940 to 1944, the commemoration of wars with Germany was disturbed by the occupation authorities, not least because of their unhappiness about processions involving large numbers of people.

In and from the 1960s, there was a revival and strengthening of inter-war anti-war beliefs, a strengthening that very much reflected the concerns and political issues of the period. The 1960s' views were ones that largely shaped subsequent popular notions, including those of the present day. For Britain, the combination of the end of national service (conscription), the culture of the 1960s, anti-Vietnam War sentiment, the impact of the Campaign for Nuclear Disarmament and the declining national significance of Armistice Day were all potent. In 1962, Benjamin Britten combined several of Wilfred Owen's poems with the Latin mass for the dead in his evocative *War Requiem*.

Anti-war culture became more insistent and two-dimensional as visual replaced literary images which themselves also had been misleading. The photographs and film used by the BBC in its popular and visually compelling 1964 television series *The Great War* conveyed a grimness that was perceived as demonstrating a futile struggle even though that was not the intention of the scriptwriters.[6] A. J. P. Taylor's *First World War, An Illustrated History* (1963) also captured the visual grimness of the conflict. It was the first popular history of the war to show corpses and some of the full horrors of the struggle. The war also served as a clear indicator of folly, if not worse, in comic literature, and attracted satirists. Thus, in Alan Coren's *Golfing for Cats* (1975), the risible, and troubling, fictional nationwide broadcast by a British military *junta* that had emulated General Pinochet's recent coup in Chile, promised the public

> only glory and a return to those great days of our common heritage that gave us Passchendaele and the Somme, to the firm purpose that put us in the forefront of contemporary hanging, to the resolve that took Africa away from the unenlightened hottentot and put it in Threadneedle Street where it belonged.[7]

The standard images of the war, both literary and visual, have been ably criticized by military historians, notably Ian Beckett and Brian Bond, who have taken up the resistance, earlier mounted by John Terraine, to distorted 'instant' history.[8] They and other scholars have pointed out the problems created by a very selective reading of a misleading literary legacy, notably of works largely published in 1928–30.[9] Memoirs are often unreliable as history, but they are what the public and the media tend to rely on for their history because they offer triumph over adversity, as well as futility and pathos as themes, whereas straightforward scholarship is considered too dull.

Beckett has offered appropriate and blunt criticisms of error, lies and cliché in the film *Gallipoli* (1963), the play and later film *Oh! What a Lovely War* (1969), the novel *Regeneration* (1991) and the British television series *The Monocled Mutineer* (1986) and *Blackadder Goes Forth* (1989). In light of such comments, it is highly disappointing to see the prominent historian Norman Stone recently praise as a 'scene of genius' a misleading image from the film *Oh! What a Lovely War* of red tape wound around war graves stretching all over the screen, which he inaccurately employs as a description of a far more complex reality in the closing weeks of the war.[10] The play of that title is still regularly performed, including in nearby Plymouth in 2010.

Brian Bond criticized the grave limitation both of the visual medium, in his case the *Blackadder* series, 'truly the representative popular image of the Western Front for the 1990s', and also of much that was, and is, written at the popular level.[11] This image of the Great War reflects in part a disenchantment with war as a whole, both understood as a pursuit of state interest and as fighting. Critical visual images continue to appear, as in the trench warfare that was the improbable setting for Kenneth Branagh's anti-war version of Mozart's opera *The Magic Flute* (2006), for which Branagh and Stephen Fry, an actor in *Blackadder Goes Forth*, were the screenwriters. 'The utter devastation of the First World War'[12] was picked out by the reviewer as a theme in the 2002 film of James Hilton's 1934 novel *Goodbye, Mr Chips*, a novel that actually presented the terrible losses as a central aspect of its theme about service and selflessness.

In addition, popular military history has long struck a familiar note, one of wilfully incompetent generals being responsible for pointless slaughter. This approach, taken in Alan Clark's popular historical work *The Donkeys* (1961), a work that inspired Joan Littlewood, producer of the play *Oh! What a Lovely War*, has had a lengthy sway, as has his phrase 'lions led by donkeys', although the authenticity of his use of this phrase has been questioned. It was certainly a phrase employed at the time of the Crimean War (1854–56).

In his book *The First World War* (1998), the prominent popular military historian John Keegan wrote of the British landing at V Beach in the Gallipoli campaign on 25 April 1915: 'The columns on the gangplanks, packed like cattle ranked for slaughter in an abattoir'.[13] Of course, the men were not intended for slaughter nor to be eaten, and the image is totally misplaced, but the very fact that such an inappropriate phrase can be employed is indicative of a wider failure to understand the conflict, although, to be fair, cattle images were used by some participants, including Stanley Green who offered a description of being moved with a chilling anticipation of the Second World War: 'crowded like cattle into the cattle trucks and goods vans of a war-stricken French railway'.[14] In his *Anthem for Doomed Youth*, Wilfred Owen asked 'What passing bells for these who die as cattle?'. Moreover, some French troops moving up to the frontline trenches at Verdun in 1916 bleated as if lambs to the slaughter.

To return to Keegan, on the final page of the text, he declared, 'the First World War is a mystery. Its origins are mysterious. So is its course' – remarks that were surprising given the wealth of scholarship on both. Again:

> Why, when the hope of bringing the conflict to a quick and decisive conclusion was everywhere dashed ... did the combatants decide nevertheless to persist ... and eventually to commit the totality of their young manhood to mutual and existentially pointless slaughter ... the principle of the sanctity of international treaty, which brought Britain into the war, scarcely merited the price eventually paid for its protection.[15]

As before, this passage told us more about the values of a later age than those of the 1910s. Not that Keegan would have gone in that direction, but the anti-militarism his book possibly unintentionally echoed had, as a consequence, not only values of restraint that were/ are often applauded, but also the defeatist collaboration that followed the German defeat of France in 1940. A sense of the obsolescence of warfare could be seen in Keegan's works of the 1990s, especially his *A History of Warfare* (1993) and *War and Our World* (1998), but this response to the potential of nuclear weaponry offered a limited guide to earlier conflict.

The 'Lost Generation' and the futility of the Great War are myths so deeply embedded in popular consciousness that they have become irrefutable facts, as well as folk memory passed down through families, as television programmes on ancestors make clear; and any attempt to disabuse believers is treated with hostility. Given that the grief is scarcely immediate now, this situation is very different to the struggle to come to terms with the mass bereavement of the conflict that played such a major role in inter-war collective memory.[16]

A key issue is a lack of understanding today of the values of the age, both those that surrounded the outbreak and early stages of the war and those that helped to sustain the grim and costly effort. The war saw all the combatants draw on a patriotic historiography as they sought to sustain the enthusiasm of mass armies and of the crucial civilian workforce. Past military heroes and victories, such as Horatio Nelson and the battle of Trafalgar (1805), were held up for emulation, in this case to underline British confidence in naval calibre and success in a more troubling maritime environment that included challenges, such as submarines, that Nelson had not faced. In addition, past ideas and images of heroism and self-sacrifice, for example those of medieval chivalry, were extensively employed, and this process contributed to an acceptance, at least on the part of numerous non-combatants, of the death of many in the war. Moreover, academic historians produced efforts to justify war goals.

After the war, there was an immediate need for historical resource in the commemoration of the struggle, most obviously in the design of cemeteries and war memorials and the staging of anniversaries. Taking forward the practicalities of treating unprecedented numbers of dead people,[17] these issues provided an opportunity to underline national identity by offering a history of sacrifice that was, at the same time, a call for the sacrifice not to be in vain. Thus, past, present and future were linked.

Such values struck a powerful resonance at the time, but have become harder to grasp over the last half-century. Belief in the wrongness of killing has made it difficult to understand the values of combatants including service, patriotism and 'chivalry's vision of love, its camaraderie, concern, and self-sacrifice',[18] values taken up in the medievalism that was important to the cultural resonance of the war.[19] The reading of evidence in the light of subsequent interpretations is also a problem:

> In 1930, it was possible to read many texts that would later be entirely associated with the disillusional view of the war as, in fact, positive alternatives to that interpretation. It was only as the controversy simplified and the disenchantment solidified that the lines of debate were shifted and polarised, in ways that modern readers take for granted but which would have surprised many 1930 reviewers.[20]

A focus on soldiers as victims rather than as killers is also an issue, not only in terms of the surviving material but also how it is perceived.[21] Moreover, aside from the problems of reading texts, there is also the issue of which texts to read and there is a regrettable tendency when citing contemporary comments to fail to emphasize the variety of response. As an instance of this diversity, Captain P. L. Wright and Private J. T. Darbyshire of the First Buckinghamshire Battalion of the Oxfordshire and Buckinghamshire Light Infantry left very different accounts in both tone and content. For example, for October 1917: 'the condition of the ground was such as to render the chances of a successful attack exceedingly small, if not impossible, but the progress made actually was considerably greater than expected, though casualties were high' (Wright). In contrast, 'At 4 a.m., Oct 9 we were relieved by the Woster Regt who went "over the lid". We raced like hares along the duck board to try to get away before the barrage opened, but we were caught in it and several of the fellows who had been in England training with me met their end "God rest their souls in peace" left in the land of desolation' (Darbyshire).[22]

Nevertheless, allowing for differences in perception, there was still much about trench life and warfare that was ghastly, and this despite the ability of armies to improve the circumstances of their troops once they were in fixed entrenchments. Photographs can provide as grim an image as that offered by critical artists such as Paul Nash's painting *We are Making a New World* (1918), a product of his experiences at Ypres in 1917.

In practice, the circumstances of trench life varied, in particular with surface geology and weather: in some soils, it was easy to dig deep in order to gain cover, and in others, for example the stony soils of Champagne, it was not. Moreover, some soils and terrains were free-draining and others were not. The British frequently found trenches in the soil of Flanders and nearby areas of northern France, such as the Somme Valley, difficult to keep dry. Lieutenant Aubrey Harris noted: 'We've been up and down in the mud two feet deep and water deeper still … I cannot explain the state I am in. Working parties are trying to mend the trenches, they are all falling in'. At Ypres troops were 'up to the waist in slug [sludge] and water'.[23]

Wet weather increased exposure to vermin and to trench conditions such as trench foot and frostbite. Letters from the Western Front commented frequently on such weather,[24] as well as on the dread created by a forthcoming winter.[25] Several of the winters were indeed very bad, notably those of 1916–17 and 1917–18, and their severity hit both the troops and the home fronts, especially farming. The constraints of the seasons and the weather affected conflict so that, despite description in terms of industrial and/or total warfare, the war was not fought in the relentless manner of an industrial machine which is never allowed to halt. Instead, operations were limited in the winter. The rain could also be a problem in the summer, Roland, 'Ged', Garvin, a British army officer, complaining in August 1915 'the trenches became a mere glutinous mass underfoot'.[26]

At the same time units were rotated out of the front line, while, in the latter, in part due to a system of live and let live, there were long periods without attacks.[27] These periods, however, could still be hazardous as a result of shell fire, sniping and raids, especially night raids. Exposure to sniping encapsulated the randomness of fate that so many soldiers recorded. The First Battalion of the London Rifle Brigade recorded in its War Diary for 29, 30 and 31 December 1914, when it was in the line at Ploegsteert, 'Quiet day and little sniping', but, for 3 January 1915, 'Usual sniping and intermittent shelling'. The Christmas Truce of 1914 played a role, and the entry for 2 January 1915 noted orders from Second Army headquarters that 'truce with the enemy was to cease and any officer or NCO found having initiated one would be tried by court martial'. Yet, variations in danger continued. For 1 March, 'Practically no sniping all day' but, for the following day, 'Ploegsteert shelled rather heavily. A six inch incendiary shell came through Headquarters doing considerable damage', with, for 3 March, being shelled both morning and afternoon.[28]

Although, in 1916, Haig pushed a policy of raids in order to maintain the pressure on the Germans, the frequency of raids should not be exaggerated.[29] Moreover, the need to conserve shells for major offensives ensured that fire between these was restricted. In June

1916, Monash wrote from the Western Front, where he commanded the 3rd Australian Division: 'compared with Anzac [Gallipoli], the people here don't know what war is. It is true they get an intensive bombardment now and then, and that is pretty bad for anyone who gets in its way, but in between time you'd hardly know there was a war on at all'.[30]

Even at Gallipoli, circumstances varied. Alan Thomson, an artillery officer, contrasted his quarters, which had an earth floor that it was impossible to drain, with the hut vacated by a French officer into which he moved: 'It is built entirely of "75" shell boxes ... with a projecting roof and an empty cartridge case hung up in front on a gong ... It has a wooden floor!' Later in the month, he recorded playing bridge in the evenings. Yet, Thomson also noted the affects of rainy nights on his men who were bereft of roofing material.[31] Damp and cold, more generally, ensured that soldiers and officers were keen to obtain warm clothing, notably gloves, boots, socks and drawers.[32]

The consistency of conflict on the Western and Eastern Fronts did not match that on the Eastern Front in 1941–45 or the Western Front in 1944–45, as in the First World War the fronts were relatively quiet other than during offensives, which were episodic and restricted to sections of the front. Edward Southcomb wrote in July 1917 of the Germans 'sometimes he is quiet, sometimes troublesome'.[33]

There were also differences for the better between the Great War and earlier conflicts, not least in the area of medical care. This varied, being more successful for example for the British on the Western Front and Palestine than in Mesopotamia,[34] but, on the whole, there were improvements in both European and imperial spheres of operation. In part, this improvement reflected the need to provide care so that wounded troops could be returned to the front. The military infrastructure could also ensure plentiful rations, at least for the forces of the Western Allies. Both medical care and food supplies were better than those that many of the soldiers had experienced in civilian life, although this was far less true of the 'housing' offered in trench systems. Edward Southcomb, a young officer on the Western Front, was troubled by incessant rain in April 1917, so that 'all round my tent is a regular mud swamp', but he was warm and, at times, the accommodation seemed very good. In May, he noted 'The last two days I am in a topping billet, very clean and comfy and some pretty French lasses'. Food for this officer was reasonable: 'Our rations *generally* consist of bacon, meat, bread, margarine, tea, sugar, marmalade, and vegetables the latter are very scarce. There is always heaps of "bully beef"', although he had not seen potatoes for three weeks.'[35] Ordinary British troops are less well, but there was enough food.

As a reminder that military life, while very hazardous, was not otherwise necessarily worse for all soldiers than the civilian counterpart, the arbitrary nature of untimely death was already a common feature of civilian life, as was exposure to hardship at work.[36]

British troops benefited from frequent rotation out of the frontline, and from organized rest and recreation while out of it. French troops were not treated as well, although Pétain introduced important reforms, especially in the leave system. There were particular problems for the Allies in ensuring leave where the front lacked depth, most obviously at Gallipoli,[37] but this was unusual. On the Western Front, German trench facilities tended to be superior to those of the Allies, although the Germans came to suffer more from food shortages.

In Eastern Europe, where the front was more fluid, and the Russians and Austrians lacked the resources of Britain and France and did not have access to those of the New World, supplies were less plentiful and disease was more of a problem. The Italians also suffered from very poor care accompanied by harsh discipline. For all armies, the availability and quality of troops proved key issues, while, on the part of the troops, there were frequent grumbles about military discipline.

In the British army, the discontent of many soldiers led to thousands of court-martials, while what was described as shell shock affected large numbers including the war poet Wilfred Owen. Yet, it is necessary to note a more complex situation and, as ever with both scholarly and public discussion of the past, there are issues of emphasis. For example, in the 2000s there was much stress on the executions of those judged guilty of cowardice and desertion in the British army and considerable pressure for an official pardon.[38] The campaign succeeded in 2006 and was an acknowledgement of the failure during the war to appreciate the impact of post-traumatic stress disorder, but also, to a certain extent, the product of a present-day ahistorical unwillingness to understand the practices and values of the period, and, instead, of the abuse of history for the sake of therapy. Moreover, the relatively exceptional nature of the British executions received insufficient attention. There were 361 during the war, far fewer, for example, than those in the Italian army, which had at least 700, and they were primarily motivated by considerations of discipline, including dealing with criminal behaviour.[39] The British army, nevertheless, executed more men than the Germans, who executed 46, or than the British army in the Second World War, which executed nobody.

Just as the need for troops may have led to a relaxing of the physical requirements for recruits,[40] so a determination to return soldiers to the front line affected the diagnosis and treatment of the large numbers suffering from often complex symptoms.[41] In practice, the stress of war led to much somatization, with fear and stress presenting in terms of physical conditions, while there were also psychological conditions including depression and post-traumatic stress disorder. The war led to a change of perception by some doctors who were treating psychiatric disorders, and, with hysteria rethought among medical experts (going from a woman's disease to a common reaction to ceaseless bombardment and the omnipresent fear of death), the awareness of psychiatric pressures in wartime increased.[42] This was an important instance of the relationship between the war and modernity.[43]

Rather than being specifically linked to that particular conflict, however, there was often a rise of such disorders, known by different names at different times, during and immediately after war. Furthermore, shell shock was not the fate of the majority of soldiers in the Great War. Indeed, the morale of much of the British army seems to have been pretty good throughout,[44] and that also appears to have been the case with the German army until the summer of 1918. Moreover, the experience of terrible casualties in 1914–16 did not stop the French army from fighting: the disobedience in 1917 arose from a particular crisis, and morale recovered quickly after Pétain took command.

Many veterans after the war turned to extreme and often violent political movements, notably in Germany (the *Freikorps* who crushed Communist uprisings) and Italy (the *Squadristi*). In part, this tendency reflected political and economic strains, rather than the war itself, but the traumatizing experiences of war and defeat helped encourage a desire for violent retribution against supposed domestic and foreign enemies, notably in Germany, Austria, Hungary and Turkey.[45] Yet, many who were politically committed did not turn to such movements, and most veterans reintegrated into civil society, albeit a society changed by the experience of war. In Britain, Haig, who became President of the new veterans' organization, the British Legion, in 1921, helped to keep it apolitical.[46]

More generally, it is important to distinguish between the horrors of suffering and loss, for instance the French corpses 'glistening and rotting in the sun and smelling nauseous and vile' noted by Stanley Green,[47] and the degree to which the conflict was not a mindless slaughter. The frequent failure to distinguish is such that the war can claim to be the most misunderstood major conflict in history, which reflects, not only a governmental propaganda neglect of the Western Front victories in 1918 at the time,[48] but, more profoundly, a powerful disenchantment with war understood both as a pursuit of state interest and as fighting.[49] In turn, this image of the war then affects the perception of other conflicts, for example the American Civil War.

The horror of what appeared to be military futility in the Great War has distracted attention from the important and worthwhile issues at stake in the conflict and from the effectiveness of the European military system. The former was very much the case as far as the French and Belgians affected by invasion in 1914 were concerned, as well as for the British who sought to protect international law and stability by intervening. In the face of the German invasion, and, later, of the German unwillingness to consider peace unless they made significant territorial gains, this was a war fought by the British for national identity in legal and civilized international conduct. These were themes understood at the time and in the 1920s, but largely lost sight of from the 1930s.[50]

Despite the nature of the conflict on the Western Front, the war was not an impasse created by similarities in weapons systems, while it would be unwise to present an inability to end the war rapidly as a consequence of tactical stasis. The stalemate of the Western Front was due to a combination of factors (including geographical ones), no one of which by itself would have led to stalemate. The firepower of the pre-war armies was not understood in 1914, and the consequences of escalating that firepower as happened during 1915 and 1916 were not anticipated either. Tactics of manoeuvre and of attack did not take into account the effect of massed artillery, nor indeed, of modern rifles. The evolution of munitions, with significant innovations in not only grenades and mortars but also ammunition and gunnery systems, changed the nature of warfare, a process that was stoked by the evolution of defence networks. The stalemate was not stasis since tactics and munitions continually evolved, as part of an unresolved conflict between defence and attack in terms of tactics and technology.

Thus, trench warfare was not unique to the Great War but was, instead, on a continuum, and what set the war apart from previous wars in which trench warfare had occurred was the tactical and technological response to it which led to a new mode of warfare. Indeed, both sides learned from initial experiences and developed more flexible attack and defence doctrines; and there was an important degree of flexibility, not least in response to the introduction of what has been termed 'machine warfare', which the British have been seen to had developed in the Somme offensive in 1916. Alongside an emphasis on the tactical innovations seen in 1917 and 1918, it is also worth noting the comment of Paddy Griffith:

> British tactics on the Somme were already in essence the same as those used by both sides in their decisive manoeuvres of 1918. The exclusive charmed circle which is conventionally drawn around the Great War's 'tactical innovators' – whether Germans, Anzacs or tankies – turns out to be quite illusory, since tactical innovation was a game that almost

> everyone was playing, even including the woolly old
> cavalry generals themselves .... By the beginning of
> 1917 the whole shape of modern infantry tactics had
> been settled.[51]

This broadening out of the process of innovation reflected a characteristic integral to modern war, as the pressures of adapting peacetime forces and doctrines to the exigencies of combat and victory drove change forwards. The ability of both sides to sustain the struggle forced a mobilization of resources on a scale that differed from preceding conflicts, which returns attention to why neither side was willing to compromise to avoid, or end, the war.

Focusing on the strength and resilience of the two sides captures the contingent nature of developments as in the Italian and American decisions to enter the war, and thus the extent to which wartime policies were a response to the problems posed by the opposing alliance. For this reason, it is misleading to see the nature of the conflict as largely the culmination of pre-war thought, planning and preparations. Most wars do not develop as anticipated, but this was particularly true of the Great War. As in Britain's last conflict with a European power, the Crimean War (1854–6), only a brief conflict was expected by all the powers, and there were no adequate preparations for a more lengthy struggle, not least in strategic, operational and tactical doctrine, as well, more famously, for the care of the troops and the support of the deployment. Whereas Britain and her allies, France, Turkey and Piedmont, had benefited in the Crimean War from the multiple weaknesses of Russia as a military power, Germany 60 years after proved a more formidable opponent. In contrast, helped by the nearness of France and the strength and mobilization of the British economy, it proved easier than during the Crimean War to overcome the problems of care and support. The improvised character of the 1914 campaign and the first winter of operations was replaced, although in part this improvement was eased by the lack of mobility as the war became more static.

Across Europe, the cult of the offensive, which had led to the deliberate underestimation of the impact of firepower in pre-war manoeuvres,[52] is too readily read forward into the course of the conflict. There is a failure to note the degree to which pre-war planning saw attacks as an aspect of manoeuvre warfare and, indeed, urged the value of mobile defence; while, far from following a simple cult of the offensive, wartime experience forced a rethinking of the attack as the way to overcome static warfare, specifically the impasse of trench conflict. This process led not only to a number of expedients, but also to a rethinking of combined-arms operations. The emphasis on strong firepower support reflected a need to suppress defences that were stronger than those generally anticipated prior to the conflict. This need gave point to interest in new technology, particularly (but not only) gas, aircraft and tanks. If a tactical and operational perspective is thus taken, then the shift towards a new type of warfare occurred during the war, not with its outbreak. Innovation was not restricted to tactics and technology, important as it was in both respects. For the British, the Somme offensive 'marked the beginning of a learning curve, in command and control …. Mission command was extended further down the command chain, giving the brigade commanders and even more junior leaders considerable discretion in their conduct of the battle'.[53]

More generally, the co-ordination necessary to defend large trench complexes suggested the means to break them, which, in turn, helped lead to the development of the capabilities that eventually led armies out of the trenches. This was because the size of the armies, the proliferation of new weapons and the extent of entrenchment forced leaders to start thinking about the co-ordination in time and space of fire, manoeuvre, obstacles, reserve positions and so on, largely sight unseen, and accomplishing such co-ordination by topographic maps, aerial photography, electronic communications and a common knowledge of the time of day. These were essential first in the defence, but also provided the elementary skills and infrastructure that allowed offensive ideas to grow. Thus, the Germans evolved from a decentralized defence in depth to a similarly decentralized offensive capability. The allies similarly displayed a process of development. The co-ordination of manoeuvre with artillery was very important, and this explained the significance of maps, watches and telephones.

Much synchronization had to take place to carry an army through an enemy's defences.

Alongside innovation came decisiveness. The Western Front, in particular, was not merely a site of stasis; it was also the stage for the decisive actions of the war. The blocking of German offensives in 1914, 1916 and 1918 was the essential precondition of Allied victory, and in 1918 the Germans were dramatically driven back in the theatre of operations where their strength was concentrated.

Allied fighting success, including solving the tactical and operational problems of trench warfare, was accompanied by serious deficiencies in German strategy. The Germans failed in the West in 1914, and did so as the result of a plan that brought Britain into the war. This was not their sole questionable judgement on the Western Front. Although the scale of Russia, both distances and manpower, posed a major problem, the Verdun offensive of 1916 seems surprising given that there was then a better prospect of knocking Russia out of the war (and thus also helping Austria and Turkey), and also because the pursuit of a policy of attrition when Germany had fewer troops can appear maladroit. In 1918, moreover, Ludendorff badly mishandled the advantage in troop numbers gained by victory against Russia. These problems suggest a need for caution before accepting the customary arguments about the superiority of German strategic insight and staff methods, a point also valid for the Second World War.[54] The benefit the Germans had gained from being able to launch the war in the West in 1914, and against vulnerable Belgium, as well as from the weakness of Russia, could not counteract the deficiencies in their military system and international position.

The heavy casualties of the Great War reflected not so much the futility of war, or of this war, but, rather, the determination of the world's leading industrial powers to continue hostilities almost at any cost. More specifically, casualties were high because of the strength of counter-tactics: the advantage weapons technology gave the defence and the value of defence in moderate depth, given the contemporary constraints on offensive warfare, and the numbers of troops available for the defence. Moreover, casualty rates were scarcely low in many other conflicts, including the Second World War.

The contrast between operations on the Western and Eastern Fronts of the Great War highlighted the importance of the number of troops. Although more than density of defending troops was involved in this contrast, it was a key factor: as trench lines were longer on the Eastern Front, there were fewer defenders per mile. In addition, the greater length of trenches helped ensure that they were less well prepared than on the Western Front, creating tactical opportunities for the attacker.[55] Indeed, it is worth considering how far our image of the Great War would be different if the Eastern Front received equivalent scholarly attention to the Western, or if the ratio of past and current scholarship on the two had been reversed. The stress might be much more on the possibility, despite the deployment of vast forces, of achieving a decisive result, and of the ability of armies to achieve operational freedom; although the Germans won eventually on the Eastern Front principally because of internal Russian collapse. The Eastern Front showed that tactical problems did not preclude operational and strategic mobility. Furthermore, the key problems in Eastern Europe were operational and strategic rather than tactical, specifically the decision where to mount offensives, how best to distribute forces between widely separate areas of the front and how to move from success in battle to victory. The ability to sustain an advance was a crucial operational issue. In Eastern Europe, cavalry played a greater role than on the Western Front, although this role increased the logistical problem of providing sufficient fodder.

The high-technology elements seen on the Western Front could best be sustained there. Elsewhere, as aspects of the decidedly uneven nature of the learning curve, there was a tendency towards an, at least, relative demodernization of war-making, except for in Palestine and Mesopotamia and there only towards the end of the war. The British were then able to deploy the products of their war economy, such as planes or the vans used as troop carriers in Mesopotamia when it became too hot for the cavalry's horses.

Drawing attention to the possibility of differing analyses of the war depending on which Front is stressed is valid but less significant than the nature of much recent academic study of the war-making involved. Improvements in British fighting techniques, in particular, have attracted scholarly attention, although, as with the comparable academic emphasis on the challenge posed by German aggression and expansionism, this work has had scant impact on popular views.[56] As a result, the conflict continues to be one of the most misunderstood of all major wars.

CHAPTER 8

The Impact of War

We have just barely escaped a repetition of this holocaust, I, for one, thank you Mr Chamberlain and thank God for Mr Chamberlain. The man that to some degree 'understood' for a repetition of the following is rather more than I for one can sanely contemplate – read the following pages and see if after all, I am not justified in this aversion.(30 September 1938)

Curse Mr. C (and Baldwin and Co). War again is here. (1940)

Manuscript annotations inside the grim typescript of the Great War memoirs of Private Stanley Green of the 17th London Regiment.[1]

The Great War had major and largely unexpected consequences.[2] The profound political results included the fall of the Austrian, German, Russian and Turkish empires which created long-term instability across much of Eurasia, as successor regimes struggled to establish themselves and sought to benefit from opportunities for expansion. However much they were already weakened by pre-war strains, the collapse of the Austrian and Turkish empires led to long-term political problems in the Balkans and the Middle East respectively, while the Communist Soviet Union helped create a bitter ideological struggle across the world. The Cold War really dates from the aftermath of the Great War and was possibly its most pernicious consequence.

In addition, the unprecedented mobilization of resources during the war had serious economic and financial results for all the combatants as well as for many neutrals. Social consequences were also significant, while, in the industrial nations of Europe, there was a major loss of confidence in political orders, Providence and the future of mankind. However, in other nations newly freed from foreign control as a result of the war, such as Poland, there was probably great optimism, while in the Soviet Union there was some genuine optimism alongside the coerced support for the new order. The war also prompted a patriotism of national exceptionalism in both Britain and Germany. In Britain, it was based on the eventual victory, which seemed to show that, despite her inter-war economic problems, Britain was exceptional in punching above her weight. In Germany, in contrast, the exceptionalism was based on the myth that Germany had not been defeated and on the idea of betrayal from within. Both these national exceptionalisms set the scene for later events.

The war and the peace settlement took the Western empires to their height and thus, at the global level, suggested that the pre-war order was strengthened by the conflict. During the conflict, Western imperial power expanded, and markedly in the Islamic world, notably with the British conquest of the hostile sultanate of Darfur (in modern Sudan) in 1916. Moreover, Egypt was made a British protectorate in 1914, while, in 1916, Qatar became independent from Turkish rule under British protection. Farther south, in Jubaland, where the British had established a post at Serenle in 1910 and mounted an expedition in 1913–14 to increase their power, the local Awlihan clan attacked Serenle in 1916, killing the British official and most of his garrison. In response, in 1917, a punitive expedition defeated the Awlihan, seized most of their firearms and captured most of their elders. This expedition benefited from the support of the Italians in Somaliland. Jubaland was part of British East Africa, the basis of Kenya, but, in 1924, it was ceded to Italy, and added to Italian Somaliland,

More generally, the deployment of British power in Africa was helped by the extent to which most of the continent was ruled by allies in the world war: France and Belgium from 1914, Italy from 1915 and Portugal from 1917. The war led to an intensification of European military control in their colonies, particularly in and near areas of conflict, as imperial forces manoeuvred in the interior. Forces were also available to enforce imperial authority against opponents not linked to the war, as with the British expedition of 1918 against the Turkana people of Kenya.

The Great War was followed not by a retreat of Western empire, but by its advance. The imperial ethos remained strong, and the British, in particular, saw the war as reflecting the value and appeal of empire; indeed the empire helped give Britain the strength to withstand Germany in 1940. The defeat of Germany and its allies ensured that Western control over the world's surface reached its maximum extent. The redistribution of Germany's colonies resulted in Japan gaining Tsingtao in China, and the Mariana, Palau, Caroline and Marshall islands in the western Pacific islands, which, in turn, became American after the Second World War. Yet, the remainder of the German empire in Africa and the Pacific passed under the control of France, Belgium, Britain and the British Dominions of Australia, New Zealand and South Africa. Moreover, the partitioning of the Turkish empire led, in 1920, to League of Nations mandates that entailed British rule over Palestine, Transjordan and Iraq, and French rule over Syria and Lebanon.

The allocation of the German empire ensured that the war represented the last stage of the partition of Africa, and certainly led to an intensification of European control there. The distribution of German territories, however, did not always match military events. For example, French strategy in West Africa was designed to ensure that France gained more of Cameroon than the extent of French operations justified. British concern to satisfy France there ensured that this goal was realized: by off-setting advantages, Africa served to permit the furtherance of European goals. In this, Africa involved a multiplicity of players, including initially neutral Portugal, as well as the variety of imperial interests implied by the term Britain, notably South Africa and India.

These territorial gains were seen as part of a more general

strengthening of empire, one in which client states also played a role. In May 1918, Arthur Balfour, then British Foreign Secretary, had argued the value of indirect imperial sway:

> Though the establishment of an Arab kingdom in the Hejaz [part of Saudi Arabia], of an autonomous Arab protected state in Mesopotamia [Iraq] and of an internalised Jewish 'home' in Palestine will not increase the territories under the British flag, they will certainly give increased protection to British interests, both in Egypt and in India ... 'buffer states', of all the greater value to us because they have been created not for our security but for the advantage of their inhabitants.[3]

Moreover, throughout the colonial world in the late 1910s and the 1920s, there was a deepening of imperial control as areas that had been often only nominally annexed were brought under at least some colonial government. Thus, in southern Sudan, posts were established by Arab troops under British officers and military patrols were launched, while, in the more favourable terrain of northern Sudan, the armoured cars of the machine-gun batteries in the (British) Sudan Defence Force were found effective as a means of maintaining control. On India's North-West Frontier, road-building improved the British position.[4]

There was a willingness to defend imperial interests. In response to Afghan attacks in 1919 in the Third Afghan War, the RAF bombed Jalalabad and Kabul. In British Somaliland, Mullah Sayyid Muhammad was routed in 1920 by a combination of the Somaliland Camel Corps and the RAF's Z Force, supported by the Royal Navy. Here, force and mobility were combined in a campaign that revealed British versatility: the Dervish stronghold at Taleh was bombed, and the Mullah fled into the Ogaden in Ethiopia whence he was dislodged by a British-approved attack by tribal 'friendlies', the Isaqs, and fled again, soon dying of illness. Opposition to Britain in Somaliland collapsed without his charismatic leadership.

Yet, exhausted by the war, although not sufficiently to prevent Britain and France from intervening in the Russian Civil War, the European imperial powers began to sense that they had overreached themselves, particularly in the Islamic world. Britain had hoped to match traditional strategic goals both to the volatility created by the collapse of the Turkish empire and to the new form of Russian threat to British influence posed by Communism. However, revolts in Egypt (1919) and Iraq (1920–21) led to Britain granting their, in practice limited, independence in 1922 and 1924 respectively. Moreover, British influence collapsed in Persia in 1921 and the confrontation with Turkey in the Chanak Crisis of 1922 caused a political upset in London that precipitated the fall of Lloyd George and led to the abandonment of the British position in Constantinople.[5] This was a key episode in the failure of the Western powers to enforce their post-war settlement on Turkey. In particular, the Turks defeated Greek attempts to subordinate them. A Greek advance on Ankara was blocked by Kemal Atatürk at the battle of the Sakkaria (24 August – 16 September 1921), and the Greeks were driven right out of Anatolia by the Turks in 1922: Smyrna fell to Atatürk on 9–13 September.

Opposition to, and uprisings against, imperial powers testified to the more general problems created by the steady growth of anti-imperial feeling and, sometimes, by the more positive emergence of national identity. The global diffusion of Western notions of community, identity and political action, and of practices of polit-icization, helped give the colonized new tools to challenge the West's own imperial structures, and President Wilson's Fourteen Points, more specifically the doctrine of self-determination, had an impact on anti-colonial movements.[6] However, it is important not to underrate indigenous notions of identity and practices of resistance, many of them central to a pre-industrial culture of non-compliance. The Indian National Congress had been founded in 1885, followed, in 1897, by the Egyptian National Party.

During the war, nationalism was encouraged by enemies as a way to incite opposition within rival empires. The Germans sought to do this in the Islamic world, in particular trying to undermine the British in Egypt and India. Indeed, in 1918, Allenby, the British commander in Palestine, was concerned about the loyalty of Muslim soldiers in units newly arrived from India. The Allies tried, with far more success, to elicit Arab support against the Turks, and also to tap disaffection within the Austrian empire, Russia recruiting Serb and Czech divisions from among its many prisoners.

These by no means exhausted the range of options. The Germans also tried to weaken rival empires, proclaiming an 'independent' kingdom of Poland in November 1916 in an attempt to raise Poles for service against Russia. This device proved far less successful than when used by Napoleon I, but also reflected his pattern of trying to regulate conquests by creating new monarchical states and forwarding his dynastic interests. In 1918, as the Germans contemplated entrenching a new order in the former Russian empire, they planned new monarchical states there.

The Germans also tried to arm Irish nationalists, who were ready to seek their support, which helped explain the firmness of the British response to rebellion there in 1916. One of those court-martialled and shot, Patrick Pearse, the Commander-in-Chief of the insurgents, who was proclaimed President of the Provisional Government, had appealed to Ireland's 'gallant German allies'.[7] Such statements revived long-standing fears of Ireland as a backdoor to Britain, fears which were particularly pressing as Britain was involved in a difficult war and short of troops.

In 1917, the Germans also trained Finns in preparation for an attack on Finland, then part of the Russian empire, while, in 1915, an Allied intelligence report recommended attempting to stimulate an Armenian rising and then landing British troops to exploit the situation.[8] Support for the idea of a Jewish national home in Palestine was linked to British attempts to win Zionist backing in what were believed to be numerous and important communities in Europe and America.[9]

The foreign encouragement of nationalist pressure did not bring down the combatants. If such pressure, indeed, greatly weakened Austria in 1918, that reflected not so much external intervention as the military, political and economic problems created by the length of a disastrous war and the extent to which, in a political vacuum, these problems were confronted increasingly by those advocating nationalist solutions. Similarly, Turkey was vulnerable to the idea of national self-determination, as some Arabs, Armenians and Kurds sought nationhood, but the Turks from 1918 to 1923 were far more exposed to the international ambitions of the victorious powers, in their case the Greeks, Italians, French and British.[10]

In the closing stages of the war and thereafter, the Russian Communists sought to encourage anti-imperialism elsewhere, hosting a Congress of Peoples of the East at Baku in 1920. Such activity was a product of another aspect of the post-war crisis for the Western powers. The Russian Civil War, which finished in 1922, was the largest struggle in the years after the Great War. The Whites (or conservatives) played a major role in opposition to the Bolsheviks (Communists) from late 1918, with Admiral Kolchak taking power in Siberia. The failure of the Whites owed much to political and strategic mismanagement, notably divisions between their generals and an inability to match the ruthless Bolshevik mobilization of resources for the war effort, as well as to the Bolshevik advantages of a central position, control over the key industrial areas, and greater troop numbers.

The defeat of the Whites helped make foreign intervention in Russia redundant. Very much encouraged by Churchill, the Secretary of War, British forces were sent to the Baltic, the Black Sea, the Caspian, and to Archangel and Murmansk in northern Russia,[11] repeating some of the deployments seen during the Crimean War (1854–56). In addition, the Americans and, in particular, the Japanese deployed forces in Siberia, and the French in the Baltic and Black Seas and northern Russia. Other participants included Canadians, Italians and Serbs in northern Russia, former Czech prisoners of war to the east of the Soviet zone, and Finns, Latvians, Estonians, Poles and Romanians to the west. Although these forces were important in particular areas, they did not make a decisive impact. Post-war demobilization and the financial burdens left by the Great War placed obvious limits on interventionism, and the forces committed were mostly very small, although they were significant at sea. However, the key reason for this lack of decisive impact was the extent to which, aside from their inability to help determine the campaigning other than in particular areas, where they enjoyed local support, such as the Baltic Republics, foreign troops could not direct the flow of political advantage.

The Russian Civil War was a key instance of the way in which the closing stages of the Great War led directly into a post-war period also defined by struggle. The fighting in Europe from November 1918, and in the former Russian empire from the Bolshevik coup in 1917, was far more confusing than that during the conflict. In place of clear-cut adversaries came shifting alignments and uncertain interventions, for example those of Britain in the Baltic republics, and instead of the regular forces, readily apparent command structures and clearly demarcated front lines of the Great War, there were irregulars, complex relations between civil and military agencies and goals, and fluid spheres of operations. Pre-war disputes, for example between nationalities in the Austrian empire, became post-war clashes, with Czech forces advancing into Slovakia in November 1918, while the Romanians moved into Transylvania. As the number of 'players' in conflict rose, the notions of a clear-cut definition of military forces, and of war as the prerogative of the state, were put under severe strain. This obliged regular militaries to confront situations in which goals and opponents were far from clear, and atrocities, terrorism and terror became more than the small change of war.

Nationalism was crucial in the forceful definition of frontiers after the Great War, as with the occupation in 1919 of the town of Fiume by an Italian volunteer force and the Polish seizure of Vilnius from Lithuania in 1920. Ideology played a role, as when advances by Romanian and Czech forces in July 1919 led to the fall of the Communist regime in Hungary. Ideological rivalry was also a feature of conflict in post-war Germany, as radical attempts to seize power were violently contested by right-wing paramilitaries, and in Italy with the rise of Fascists in the early 1920s. The violence of these years and the sense of anger stemming from defeat were important to the widespread German and Austrian desire for a 'recolonization' of parts of Eastern Europe which contributed to Nazi policies in the region.[12]

It was not only the defeated that faced instability at home. Britain proved unable to suppress a violent Irish nationalism that led to the creation of a self-governing Irish Free State in most of the island. Although suppressed, there were also wartime or post-war strains in parts of the empire, notably in the Punjab, Belize (British Honduras) and Trinidad. Wartime problems, moreover, helped lead to post-war instability in Portugal, another of the victors. British pressure had led the Portuguese government in 1917 to the unpopular and expensive decision to support the Allies, a measure bitterly criticized by the trade unions. The government was overthrown that year by a dicta-torship under Sidónio Pais, which responded to riots by force, only for Pais to be assassinated in 1918. The liberal republic returned, but was overthrown by an army coup in 1926 that created a conservative order that lasted until a radical army coup led to its overthrow in 1974.[13]

China also witnessed post-war problems that reflected both pre-war issues and their wartime exacerbation. The difficulties of creating a new political system and a national unity after the overthrow of the Manchu dynasty in 1911 was the key factor, but these had been accentuated during the war by the subsequent failure to create a popular and successful replacement, not least in the face of Japan's demands for gains as a result of its support for the Allies. The Japan's occupied the Shandong peninsula from 1915 while, in 1916, Japan and Russia reaffirmed their earlier division of Outer and Inner Mongolia between spheres of influence that excluded Chinese power. In the warlord period of Chinese history from 1916 to 1927, atomi-zation reflected the strength of local military figures, and this led to a spread of militarization as local communities sought ways to survive under the dominance of administration by overt force.[14]

China, moreover, saw conflict during the Great War that indicated the range of disputes involved. For example, Kham, part of eastern Tibet that had been an autonomous section of China since the eight-eenth-century expansion of the latter, had resisted greater Chinese control, with a rising in 1905 that was swiftly crushed and with renewed opposition after the overthrow of the Manchu empire in 1911, but the new republican government in Beijing reasserted its control from 1912 to 1914. In turn, Thupten Gyatson, the Dalai Lama, the ruler of Tibet, responded to this reimposition of Chinese control by sending forces to the frontier, armed with new rifles from Britain. In 1917 and 1918, they clashed with the Chinese, defeating them, which led to a rising in Kham. However, in the summer of 1918, Tibet and China negotiated a truce, leaving Kham under Chinese control.

Alongside changes in specific areas, the war was important in the shifting of power away from Europe. In part, this was a matter of the heavy human and financial costs of the conflict, which were relatively more serious than the physical devastation inflicted because, compared to the Second World War, far less of the continent served as a battlefield and far less was bombed, let alone bombed heavily. In absolute and relative terms, this shift away from Europe was partially a matter of the rise of American power and, to a lesser extent, of Japan. Relations within the Western empires also changed, with an upsurge in nationalism that influenced the nature of imperial relations. The varied strains of the war played a major role, as in Jamaica where the experience of wartime racism contributed to a rising nationalism that challenged British control.[15] The same occurred in India with the emergence of Mohandas Gandhi as an organizer of protest on a national scale from 1919.

The war also played a key role in the challenge to economic stability, a challenge for which there was no comparable pre-war instance. The journalist Norman Angell had argued in *Europe's Optical Illusion* (1909; expanded into *The Great Illusion*, 1910) that international financial interdependence would make war economically damaging for all,[16] and economic mobilization from 1914 was indeed accompanied by the overthrow of globalization. John Maynard Keynes was to reflect:

> What an extraordinary episode in the economic progress of man that age was which came to an end in August, 1914 … life offered, at a low cost and with the least trouble, conveniences, comforts, and amenities beyond the compass of the richest and most powerful monarchs of other ages. The inhabitant of London could order by telephone, sipping his morning tea in bed, the various products of the

whole earth ... he could at the same moment and by the same means adventure his wealth in the natural resources and new enterprises of any quarter of the world .... But, most important of all, he regarded this state of affairs as normal, certain, and permanent, except in the direction of further improvement, and any deviation from it as aberrant, scandalous, and avoidable.[17]

In practice, there were already significant pre-war threats to the liberal economic order, not least due to tariffs and periodic recessions, but it was to be a very dynamic capitalist world that was hit hard by the war. Aside from the destruction of manufacturing plant, there was tremendous damage to trade and economic interdependence. Alongside long-term disruption, the enforced reconfiguration of the international trading system brought considerable misery to combatants and neutrals during the war.[18] This was not simply a matter of inflationary pressures, but also of hardships stemming from the seizures of resources, the Germans notably taking millions of tons of food from Russia and Romania, as well as from the deliberate interruption of trade. On the global scale, European powers, especially, but not only, Britain, sold much of their foreign investment in order to finance the war effort.

Furthermore, the disruption of trade (and its total collapse outside Europe in the case of Germany), and the diversion, under state regulation, of manufacturing capacity to war production, ensured that the European economies were less able to satisfy foreign demand. This situation encouraged the growth of manufacturing elsewhere, not least in Latin America and in European colonies, such as India. Agriculture also benefited, although the consequences were mixed as well as long-range and long-term. The end of Britain's import of sugar beet from Germany led, for example, to an increase in sugar cane imports from Cuba where the rise of prices resulted in the eviction of peasants and the clearing of forests as land was brought into cultivation.

As another instance of the wide-ranging economic impact of the war, Japanese manufacturing output rose considerably on the base of higher exports, while the increase in trade and the pressures on Allied shipping enhanced the value of the Japanese merchant marine and ensured that, with freight and charter rates rising, net annual foreign earnings from shipping increased from Yen 41 million in 1914 to over Yen 450 million in 1918. Japanese real gross national product leapt by 40 per cent over the same period. As a result, Japan went from being a debtor nation suffering in the aftermath of the Russo-Japanese War to being a major international creditor. In effect a non-combatant, as far as the burdens and costs of the war were concerned, Japan profited not only from Western orders, but also from the decline of European competition in domestic and Asian markets.[19] American exporters benefited most of all. The British war effort was heavily dependent on America, while the Americans were well placed to replace British exports to Canada and Latin America.

Growth itself brought disruption and problems. Japan suffered from inflation and growing economic differences within the country, leading to nationwide rice riots in 1918 and rising labour and tenant disputes in the 1920s. As a neutral power close to the sphere of conflict, Spain benefited from rapid economic growth, with exports rising to the Allies, although, in turn, this growth resulted in inflation, which reached 62 per cent in 1918. Inflation led to labour problems and an increase in trade union activism, and to a sustained political crisis in 1917, with the army suppressing a general strike in August. Constitutional government in Spain proved a victim of the wartime crisis, but Spain did not develop in the same way as Russia.

The unprecedented global economic range of this war was facilitated by the extent of colonial empires. India, for example, provided large quantities of products for the British war effort, including food and textiles. Import substitution and industrial expansion were also pushed in South Africa under a consolidated tariff for the entire Union introduced in 1914. The provision of goods for the British war effort was true even for areas not well integrated into imperial economies. Food exports from the Anglo-Egyptian colony of Sudan rose to meet wartime demands, leading there, as elsewhere, to the disruption stemming from price and wage inflation.

After the war, it proved difficult to rebuild the economic order. The British sought to recreate a liberal economic system focused on free trade and a revived gold standard (fixed convertibility of sterling into gold), although it is necessary to note the self-interested nature of this commitment to internationalism, for the liberal order (as it had for the past century) very much served British interests. In the face of the economic nationalism of rivals, particularly France and America, the major problems of servicing debts to an unsympathetic America,[20] and the limitations of conventional financial and monetary concepts, the British had only limited success.[21] Communist Russia was, naturally, markedly anti-liberal, while German economic relations with the victorious allies, especially France, were far from cordial on either side. This economic nationalism at the level of the major powers interacted with an extensive opposition to market mechanisms. Instead of these mechanisms, there was a widespread state-backed and tariff-enforced emphasis on domestic industrial production that was seen, for example, in the newly independent states of eastern Europe, such as Poland.[22]

If economic liberalism faced serious problems so also did the attempt to arrange an improved post-war international order. A new body for representation, negotiation and arbitration, the League of Nations, was established in 1919, meeting first in January 1920. The League had value as a forum for international debate, and notably as a platform for the weaker powers, such as Spain, to give their views on the conduct of the Great Powers.[23] It also provided a means by which to explain and manage the division of German and Turkish colonies and territories among the victorious powers. The new colonies were League of Nations' mandates, a status of trusteeship seen as an alternative to formal colonialism, both because the mandatory powers were subject to inspection by the League's Mandates Commission and because the status was presented as a preparation for independence, as indeed happened with Iraq. The League also looked towards more broad-based diplomacy in seeking international agreement on a range of issues including disarmament, drug control and the (illegal) slave trade.

The League, however, was weakened because its founder, President

Woodrow Wilson, who won the Nobel Peace Prize in 1919 for his efforts, could not persuade the US Senate to ratify the Treaty of Versailles. The Senate sought to limit the commitment that would come from a promise to preserve the territory and independence of member states and chose, instead, to maintain Congress's role in deciding to declare war. America was never a member of the League and also refused to join the permanent Court of International Justice. By contrast, the Soviet Union joined the League, but not until 1934. Under article 10 of the League's covenant, member states agreed 'to respect and preserve ... the territorial integrity and existing political independence of all members', while article 16 provided for immediate economic and social, and possible military, sanctions against any aggressive power. Reality proved otherwise and the League encountered what ultimately proved to be fatal problems as it proved unable to respond to aggression, notably the successful Japanese invasion of Manchuria (north-east China) in 1931 and the triumphant Italian invasion of Abyssinia (Ethiopia) in 1935. Thus, the collective security offered by the League was a failure in practice.

Europe went to war in 1939, and it is easy to trace this resumption of hostilities to the failure of the Versailles peace settlement of 1919 and the deficiencies of the League, and thus to see the Second World War as the sequel of the Great War (or, as it became, First World War), a product in part of the factors that had caused and sustained that conflict and, more particularly, of the unfinished business its unsatisfactory close had left. Focus on the reparations (payments) demanded from post-war Germany as an aspect of its war guilt proved a particular source of liberal (and German) criticism in the 1920s and 1930s. This criticism ignored German reparations from France after earlier victories and, instead, encouraged the view that the peace settlement had been mainly retributive. It was argued that a mishandled, if not misguided, total war in 1914–18 had led to a harsh peace, the latter a consequence of the former.

This verdict, which contributed to the liberal (and German) critique of Allied diplomacy as dishonest, selfish and short-sighted, was, in fact, an inappropriate judgement of peace terms that were certainly far less severe than those to be imposed on Germany in

1945, with those terms of course not meeting comparable criticism. Germany lost territory after the Great War to Poland, (neutral) Denmark, Belgium, France and Lithuania, notably Alsace-Lorraine to France; but talk in France of a Rhineland separated from Germany led nowhere. The victors adapted to practicalities as well as to ideological concerns: Germany had not been overrun by the Allies while, as a result of her earlier defeat of Russia, she was still in occupation of large territories in Eastern Europe when the war ended. Japan was to be occupied in 1945 despite being in a similar territorial position to Germany at the time of the November 1918 armistice, at least as far as land power was concerned; although crucially not in the air, and the use of atomic bombs provided an equation of power in favour of the victors not present in 1918.

In 1918, moreover, the victorious powers were determined to try to prevent the spread of Communist revolution from Russia to Germany. Prefiguring Western discussion in 1944–45 about Germany's future, commentators warned of the ideological threat from the East. On 2 November 1918, while commanding the advance of the British First Army which captured the city of Valenciennes that day, General Horne wrote to his wife: 'I think we must not be *too* severe with Germany, in case of there being a break up there, and we shall find no government to enforce terms upon! Bolshevism is the danger. If it breaks out in Germany it might spread to France and England'.[24] Thus, the Great War and the Communist revolution created the rationale for anti-Soviet appeasement of Germany and set the Western allies up to ignore Stalin's (highly problematic) offers to help contain Nazi Germany.

The terms of the 1919 peace were designed to prevent Germany from launching new wars, and thus to provide collective security for Europe, notably Western Europe. Under the supervision of the Inter-Allied Military Control Commission, the size and equipment of the German military were seriously restricted. Germany also had to accept an occupied zone along the French and Belgian frontiers and a demilitarized zone beyond, the net effect of which was to end the possibility that the River Rhine could provide a strategic defensive frontier for Germany.

Germany was also to be punished and weakened by heavy reparations (compensation payments to the victors), and was to be stigmatized both by a war guilt clause and by the insistence that German officers be tried for war crimes, especially the treatment of Belgian civilians in 1914 and the consequences of indiscriminate submarine warfare. The Allies had wanted war criminals extradited for trial before an international tribunal but in 1920 agreed, instead, to the German request that the trials be conducted before the Supreme Court in Leipzig. A list of 853 alleged war criminals was submitted by the Allies, but, in 1921–22, only 17 were tried. In the end, only ten were convicted and neither the Germans nor the Allies were satisfied. Concerned about the honour of the German army, the Germans argued the case of military necessity for their actions in 1914.

Far from the peace settlement sowing the seeds of a new war, as was frequently claimed, the international system it established actually worked better in the 1920s (at least from the perspective of Western interests) than was generally appreciated in the 1930s. There was domestic instability and international tension in Europe, but this had also been the case prior to 1914, and the war and the collapse of the European dynastic empires had left many disputes. Moreover, the peace settlement adapted to Turkey's success, with the more accommodating Treaty of Lausanne of July 1923 replacing that of Sèvres of August 1920. The peace settlement was also followed by a series of international agreements designed to prevent conflict, notably the Locarno Agreement of 1925 which provided for a mutual security guarantee of Western Europe and, perhaps much earlier than many could have expected in 1918, re-assimilated Germany into the international system. In the 1920s, there was a strong interest among the European powers in a viable and consensual international order, with new institutions serving as the focus for multilateral diplomacy. Attendance at the meetings of the League became almost mandatory after 1925.[25] Moreover, Soviet attempts to export revolution failed; the conflicts in Europe that had followed the war ended in 1923; and the colonial empires survived the crisis of the 1920s with most of their possessions retained.

To argue from Versailles to Hitler is therefore inappropriate. Hitler rejected Versailles and the international system it sought to create, but the responsible *realpolitik* of the 1920s that entailed compromise and benefited from the idealistic currents of that decade's international relations focused on another German, one far more prominent in the period, Gustav Stresemann, the Foreign Minister from 1923 to 1929. The rejection of such concepts and agreements by the Soviet Union had been contained, as had Mussolini's bombastic dictatorship of Italy from 1922: thus a great deal of hostile rhetoric never had much actual impact. Counterfactualism always has its limits, but to subtract the failure, protectionism, misery and extremism produced by the Depression from the 1930s is to suggest that the 1920s order could have continued in part because internationalism, liberalism, democracy and free-market capitalism would have retained more appeal, with both electorates and governments.

In rejecting this order, the extremists in Europe turned to a politics of grievance based on anger with the verdict of the Great War, and its presentation thus played a prominent role in the politics of the 1930s, building on the anger already expressed in the 1920s particularly, although not only, among the defeated.[26] A sense of being betrayed was important to Hitler's arguments, while Mussolini took forward nationalist complaints that Italy had been deprived of gains it should have received. In Germany, Hitler also benefited from the Great War in the shape of the anger about reparations and the misplaced belief that Germany was guiltless of starting the war which it had then lost because of traitors at home. The priorities in the 1923 edition of the leading German school historical atlas were typical. The map of the Western Front emphasized the German advance in 1914 and ignored the retreat in 1918.[27]

At the same time that Hitler rose to prominence and then power, anti-war sentiment was becoming more vocal in Britain and France. Explaining why a career in the army had lost its popularity, Colonel Ling stated baldly at a staff conference in 1930: 'The use of war as a definite instrument of national policy is against the present state of public opinion'.[28] The previous year, Richard Aldington's anti-war novel, *Death of a Hero* (1929) made a considerable impact in Britain, as, in Germany did Erich Maria Remarque's *All Quiet on the Western Front* (1929). The French novelist, Henri Barbusse, who had fought in the war, the inspiration for *Le Feu* (1916, *Under Fire*), became a prominent pacifist.

A poet, Aldington had suffered from both gas and shell-shock during the war. Shell-shock induced a powerful sense of hopelessness not only in the individuals who suffered but also in a medical system that could not cope with the number of cases and that was affected by more general governmental financial constraints.[29] Writing in the late 1920s, Stanley Green referred to men sobbing after the pressure of fighting, to the stunned nature of survivors, to the 1929 suicide of a comrade who could not cope, to his own mind still being fixed on the war and to how 'today thousands of men rave and wear out their war-ridden minds in the padded cells of our asylums'.[30] The severely disfigured were kept out of public view, partly because of fear of upsetting people, but also because of fear of them begging. Nevertheless, there was a rise in support and rehabilitation because there were so many men who were unable to work due to disability.

Alongside the questioning of medical assumptions and practices (see p. 228), the war challenged many cultural and ideological suppositions, inducing a degree of despair,[31] although often for complicated reasons, as with the British officer and poet Siegfried Sassoon who for long was pro-war, being awarded the Military Cross, before protesting in July 1917 in 'A Soldier's Declaration' about the unnecessary prolongation of the war.[32] The conflict's direct artistic impact included not only a reiteration of Classical ideals as a way to cope with suffering,[33] but also an accentuation of the already strong Modernist assault on traditional culture; aristocratic and middle-class culture to some critics. Thus, the war challenged resistance to the reception of Modernism. Stanley Spencer, who had served as a British medical orderly on the Salonica Front, and then became an official war artist, recreated his own experiences in the murals he painted in the Sandham Memorial Chapel in 1927–32. Instead of a heroic view, there were hospital scenes depicting the mundane, but necessary, care of the shattered, as well as images of everyday army life such as *Reveille* and *Filling Water Bottles*. The scene of the front line, *Dug-out*, was one of grave-like trenches and a vegetation of barbed wire. In Germany, Otto Dix depicted casualties with harsh realism.

The widespread horror of the war and the heavy casualties stimulated in some a commitment to pacifism, internationalism and collective security through the League of Nations, but it would be misleading to discuss British or French society solely in this light and to imply that this consequence of the war facilitated the Appeasement of the dictators in the 1930s, and thus eased the path to another cataclysm.[34] A heroic account of the conflict was also actively propagated, for example in juvenile fiction.[35] There was a determination to honour the dead, and their sacrifice was presented as a national honour, as with the success of the American Legion's pilgrimage to Paris in 1927. War mothers reaffirmed military service as the noblest role for male citizens. The cult of fallen soldiers thus spoke to public celebration as well as private grief.[36] The nobility of suffering, alongside the cruelty of war, emerged in *Journey's End* (1928), a powerful play by Robert Sherriff, a veteran, and a far more accomplished work than *Oh! What a Lovely War*. Prominent memorials commemorated the fallen, as with the Vimy Memorial inaugurated there in 1936 by Edward VIII to commemorate the Canadians who had died capturing Vimy Ridge in 1917. As Prince of Wales in 1923, he had inaugurated the war memorial in Newcastle that now stands outside the Civic Centre. Photographs of the scene indicate the large numbers who attended in order to show their respects, although they were greatly outnumbered by the over 300,000 people who, on 11 November 1934, assembled on the slopes of Melbourne's Domain to witness the dedication of the Shrine of Remembrance to the men from the Australian state of Victoria who had died in the war.

There was also an unprecedented quest to identify the fallen, especially through photography which, like letters and memoirs, served as a key form of individual recollection. More was at stake than individual recollection, as the chiselled names on memorials reflected the degree to which commemoration now was democratic and inclusive in the practice of naming soldiers of all ranks, rather than the anonymity of the mass grave that had characterized many earlier wars. Illustrating the variety of forms of recollection, individual messages from the spirit world were also significant, and there was a major vogue in spiritualism after the war, reflecting the loss of faith in science and reason.

If simple lines cannot be readily drawn from the war to the world of the 1930s, this situation reflected not a lack of influence but rather the extent to which the consequences of the war suffused the post-war years yet did so in a varied way that responded to the diverse experience of the conflict. For example, in Germany, the furore over the anti-war film (of the novel) *All Quiet on the Western Front* (1930), which was swiftly banned, was a product of the strength of authoritarian, conservative, militaristic and nationalist assumptions,[37] assumptions that were linked to the failure to reintegrate trauma- tized veterans into society.[38] Although often drawing on Modernist idioms, the Fascist and Nazi glorification of war was in large part a conservative rejection of confusing and disturbing Modernism, as well as of disturbing, threatening, indeed alienating, social change. Thus, albeit in a different context, the fear of change that had helped cause the Great War was seen again in encouraging bellicosity in the 1930s. It was this social change that was one of the clearest conse- quences of the conflict: the war was a major force for social change, in Europe, and more widely. Traditional assumptions were questioned, and social practices were affected by higher inflation, greater taxation, rationing, the absence of men at the front-line, and the spread of female employment and trade unionism. The diversion of manufac- turing, transport and the world of work to the war effort devastated family life and hit living standards.

The war was financed in part by higher taxation, notably income tax as in America, but largely by borrowing, both internationally and domestically, including by means of the prominent sale of war bonds, which was also a reflection of the search for public support by governments. This borrowing was inflationary, as was the shortage of resources and labour caused by the shift to a war economy accom- panied by conscription, although, while high, inflation did not match the rise in borrowing. In Italy, for example, the national debt rose by 500 per cent in 1915–18 and inflation by over 300 per cent. The financial strain was even acute for the Americans, whose national debt went from $1 billion to $27 billion, in part because they were underwriting their allies' bills while waiting for post-war reimbursements. By November 1918, 70 cents in each dollar of American state spending was borrowed and this financial pressure was a factor in President Wilson's wish to end the war speedily. More generally, as a result of the war, the political and economic privileges and status of established elites and middle classes, notably in industrial nations, were qualified and challenged, and the stability of entire countries threatened or lost.

The situation in Britain shows how the war changed the position of women. New roles, many in industry, were filled, so that large numbers of women workers were recruited by the Ministry of Munitions from 1915 as the shell shortage was tackled. The percentage of female trade unionists rose from 7.8 in 1900 to 17 in 1918, and women received higher wages than hitherto, although their wages remained lower than men's and, in factories, women were controlled by male foremen. Work in munitions manufacture, which was frequently a cause of ill-health, if not death, due to trinitroglycerin poisoning, was a direct form of war effort as was nursing. Whereas only 72 army sisters had been employed in British military hospitals in 1898, a total of 32,000 women served as military nurses in 1914–19. In addition, women had a place in the command structure of nursing, and were able to give orders to male ward orderlies. Although there was no direct link, the establishment of the First Aid Nursing Yeomanry (FANY) in 1908 was followed by the Women's Volunteer Reserve in 1914 and the Women's Army Auxiliary Corps (WAAC) in 1917.[39] FANY was essentially a middle-class outfit, whereas the WAAC was working or lower middle class and provided clerks, cooks, drivers and storewomen.

There was also an important change in attitudes to women. In Britain, in 1918, it was possible to extend for the first time the vote to women of 30 and over, as long as they were householders, wives of householders, occupants of property worth £5 annually, or graduates of British universities. In contrast, all men over 21 were given the vote, although younger men in the forces could also vote while conscientious objectors were excluded for five years. Conscription therefore appeared to require democracy: total war and universal participation walked hand-in-hand, and the general election held on 14 December 1918 was fought under the new arrangements. It returned the Coalition (although Labour was no longer in it), with Lloyd George as Prime Minister. Labour benefited in its election campaign from the high rate of employment, which enabled the trade unions to provide generous financial support, but the unexpectedly early end to the war limited election preparations.

As a reminder of the complexity of explanation and the multiplicity of explanations, war work may have gained women the vote in Britain, but the women who did war work were predominantly without property and under 30 and thus did not gain the vote, although such a remark about war work leaves aside the tremendously important commitment involved for most women in the emotional links with sons, husbands, fathers and brothers.[40] It is probable that (some) women gained the vote because the politicians were terrified by the prospect of universal male suffrage, which, they knew, would have to come. Enfranchising women in their maturity was seen as a defensive step to lessen the impact of the proletarian male vote. The restrictions on the female vote also reflected the extent to which male casualties led to concern that the electorate would have a substantial female majority. Yet, whatever the compromises, the key change was that the war had shown that women had a national and martial spirit that was recognized in terms of citizenship.[41]

In Britain, the impact of the war years on women was not simply restricted to grief, sorrow about parting, work and the vote. In addition, new opportunities were related to increased mobility and independence, and there was a decline in control and influence over young women by their elders, both male and female. As a consequence, alongside the fidelity of many at a distance,[42] and the lonely anxieties that made the state of postal communications such an issue,[43] there was a new sexual climate. Chaperonage became less comprehensive and effective, and styles of courtship became freer; the number of illegitimate births rose to six per cent of the total in 1918.[44]

Thus, in some respects, the war prefigured the 1960s in helping precipitate a major discontinuity, both cultural and social. Yet, alongside the challenging of Victorian norms, class-based attitudes and practices pervaded other areas. These were seen, for example, in recruitment and promotion within the armed forces and also in civilian war work. Women who served near the front, such as nurses and telephonists with the American army in 1917–18, found that the military hierarchy expected them to fulfil traditional gender roles and made scant allowance for their contribution.[45] The latter was also the case of the First Russian Women's Battalion of Death established in July 1917 in an unsuccessful attempt to bolster morale. The unit, which suffered heavy casualties, was not matched by the Western Allies. More generally, assumptions about gender were deliberately not disruptive. Thus, female war workers in Britain were regarded as temporary and were not permitted to retain their jobs after the war.[46] Furthermore, the notion of a Home Front was an aspect of an affirmation of established gender concepts and roles, with women again regarded as nurturers.

Notions of masculinity were also affected by the war, not least with the reality of often crippling and/or disfiguring injury,[47] which was a counterpoint to the emphasis on conflict as fulfilling the male role.[48] This latter attitude had an obvious consequence for conscientious objectors. The tribunals that considered the latter were a striking manifestation of the marked growth in the power of the state: this growth was an important legacy of the war and a major way in which it shaped the twentieth century. As a cause and consequence of the growth in state power, regulation came to the fore and the consequences were dramatic. In July 1916, the Australian commander John Monash wrote to his wife from London:

> You can hardly imagine what the place is like. The Zeppelin scare is just like as if the whole place was in imminent fear of an earthquake. At night, the whole of London is in *absolute darkness* … All games and museums are closed – nothing but war-work everywhere … everything is at famine prices. Nothing is going on – in the ships, in the streets, anywhere – that has not a direct bearing on the war. Martial law everywhere – no private motors allowed, no

functions, no racing ... Nothing I had read conveyed
to me any idea of how the war had taken hold of the
whole British nation, and how every man, woman
and child were bent on the one sole purpose, to
prosecute the war in every form of activity.[49]

Blackouts to make targeting harder demonstrated both the consequences of the war for civilian life and the range of government. In
all the combatants, state authority increased during the war, often,
particularly in Germany, with the military playing a major role,[50]
not least in seeking to control economies, from managing resources
to dictating production priorities. Any diminution of control was
very unwelcome to military authorities, and this attitude affected
any move towards warfare outside military control. In October 1918,
the German military successfully resisted proposals within the War
Cabinet for continuing the war by staging a popular uprising.[51]

The impact of war on the societies was seen in townscapes as well
as regulations. Thus, in London, there was a growth of munitions
production and military hospitals on the edge of the city, for example
in Enfield and Edmonton respectively. These tended to be located on
new sites, although by the end of the war, the long-established Royal
Arsenal at Woolwich employed over 50,000 people. Conversely, the
pace of pre-war residential development and of the improvement of
the transport infrastructure both slowed greatly or stopped during
the war. Instructions to the British milling and baking industries led
to a dilution of wheat flour, so that bread included more barley, beans
and potatoes, and its dirty-white colour was a striking consequence
of government regulation. Licensing hours for pubs were regulated
and the government also increasingly intervened to fix wages. The
shift from laissez-faire government to interventionism was seen in
most respects, for example through the supportive reactions of the
state and the public in Britain to Belgian refugees and Belgian relief
programmes.

In France, the government controlled bread prices, and state-
supervised consortia directed the allocation of supplies in crucial
industries, and controlled pricing and profits, although the production

of munitions surprisingly was left to entrepreneurs who organized themselves through *Le Comité des Forges*. A government-directed boot and shoe industry was created for military supply, as was a chemical industry. State control was widely extended, but, unlike in Germany, there was an appropriate level of care for civilian needs, and thus morale, both civilian and military. British assistance with raw materials, food, credit and transport, was important to both French effectiveness and French administrative developments, and France ended the war owing a considerable debt to Britain. The mobilization of the war economy in Britain provided a pattern which the British insisted should be the model for intervention in the French economy, and this pattern was implemented by key administrators, notably Etienne Clémentel, the Minister of Commerce from October 1915, who directed industries other than those involved in supplying military *matériel*.[52]

Among combatants and neutrals alike, the war led to a new emphasis on centralized planning and the mobilization of national resources, as with the Council of National Defense and the War Industries Board in America. The more overt play of ideological factors in the domestic politics of states from the close of the Great War also ensured that the context within which later wartime industrial mobilization occurred was to change. If, during the war, the degree of such mobilization had already encouraged large-scale governmental and social change, this encouragement was less novel than it might appear because such change had also arisen from earlier conflicts. Thus, British participation in the French Revolutionary and Napoleonic Wars from 1793 to 1815 had led to a major increase in government activity, the results of which included an expansion in the information that it sought to deploy. The Ordnance Survey to map the country was complemented, in 1801, by the first British national census, while income tax was introduced and the rights of workers to take industrial action were curtailed. Living standards were also affected by economic problems that, in part, arose from the wars with France, although, due to the weather, the government could not control the harvests.

The economic and social context, however, was very different in the Great War because of the key role then of manufacturing, and therefore of large organized workforces. Pre-industrial forms of deference and social control, in terms of the rule and role of landlords and clerics, were no longer pertinent for the bulk of the population, although, in rural areas globally, they remained more relevant than is sometimes appreciated. The social politics of the period gave the state a greater role than a century earlier during the Napoleonic Wars, in the sense that the organization of economic mobilization was necessarily on a larger scale, and also required more central direction.

The war helped ensure that state intervention became the normal reflex to crisis to a greater extent than hitherto. There had always been that interventionist element to government, but, although not invariable, notably in 1920s' America, it became more pronounced both as far as state policy was concerned and with apparent regard to popular acceptance. As with the Second World War, claims of popular acceptance among the combatants for greater government powers should not be taken too far, as the language of national togetherness concealed a reality in which regional, class or ethnic division and anger played a major role. Nevertheless, the war contributed greatly to the direction of greater government action already seen prior to 1914 with rising concern then with social welfare which was regarded as important to national stability and thus strength. In the 1930s, one important result in democratic societies of these attitudes was a measure of greater cohesion, with an economic politics of corporatism and increased government intervention in the economy, and with politics dominated by one party, as in America, Mexico and, from 1931, in the shape of the National Government, Britain.

The general thrust during the century was for yet more intervention. From the 1920s and, even more, 1930s, until the advance of neo-liberalism in the late 1970s and 1980s, state intervention in the economy was conventionally seen in terms of reform. Planning, moreover, reflected a strong current of collectivism. The Great War was far from the sole factor in encouraging this development. Prior to that conflict, the progressive reform movements that had been so important in the late nineteenth century had enjoyed a fresh activist burst, with the 'New Liberalism' in power in Britain from 1905, and the consequent enactment of social welfare reforms, and with the Progressive Era in America. There was an ambiguous relationship, in Britain, America and elsewhere, between progressivism and the socialism that was becoming increasingly influential among the working classes of the developed world, but the reality and implications of progressivism were very much those of public responsibility and power, both expressed in government. The war put a break on the political dimension of progressivism, as in Britain where, instead, the conflict helped mould a more patriotic and popular Conservative Party,[53] but, for the combatants, the war led to a major extension of state power and enabled governments to circumvent many of the constraints and exigencies of pre-war politics.

The Great War, however, was followed by a very varied political situation. In America, there was a conservative reaction that reflected the hostility to socialism, and concern about the example of the Russian Revolution that led to a Red Scare, as well as the economic problems of the move to a peacetime economy, including inflation, strikes and recession. A reaction against wartime regulation was also significant. As a consequence, the 1920s, in America, saw an emphasis on a non-interventionist role by the state. The Republican Presidents, Warren Harding, Calvin Coolidge and Herbert Hoover, who occupied the White House between 1921 and 1933, benefited from a reaction against change, immigration and urban life.

It was not only in the Soviet Union, where wartime mobilization was made a permanent feature by the Bolsheviks,[54] that the situation was different to America. Instead, there was a more general emphasis on government regulation and intervention. This emphasis brought together varied currents, for example, in Britain, the rise of the Labour Party to political power in 1923 and 1929, but also the role of business experts in government, which was a continuation of wartime practices. Across most of the world, the Depression of the 1930s put paid to the laissez-faire state and to self-help in social welfare.

A contributory factor to state interventionism was provided by a crisis of religious belief that owed much to the war. Its heavy casualties sapped confidence in divine purpose (as well as the particular value of Western civilization), while, paradoxically, encouraging spiritualism, and the widespread disruption brought on by the war, greatly hit churchgoing. In the inter-war years, churches found it difficult to reach out successfully to the bulk of the industrial working class, much of which was indifferent to, or alienated from, all churches, in part due to Church support for the war as in national days of prayer, although the conflict also promoted religiously based pacifism, especially, in Britain, among Methodists and Anglicans. Moreover, as a result of the Great War, Church-based societies became less important and politics and government more secular. 'Reform and Welfare' in part represented the prominence of human agencies in society over spiritual responses to life.

Expressed across the world through a variety of political systems, this emphasis led to a stress on planning and on egalitarianism and community as a goal or rhetorical strategy. A willingness in government and among the public to let individuals or other agencies take responsibility and power became far less pronounced. Thus, despite differences in national circumstances, the expansion of the state was a key theme that owed much to the Great War.

Turning to military consequences, discussion about the Great War in the 1920s and 1930s focused heavily on how best to ensure victory in any subsequent conflict, and, in particular, a victory that was less costly in casualties and in social and political dislocation.[55] The German army ordered a large number of staff officers to prepare studies of the recent conflict within a context in which the weakened state of the post-war army led to an emphasis on defensive planning.[56] In Britain a framework for writing the history of the war was already established in 1915. When completed in 1948, it provided a mass of information, although with less clarity about responsibility for failures.[57] Discussion over the future character of warfare focused greatly on the supposed potential of the new weapons deployed in the Great War as the need to avoid a repetition of trench warfare affected the subsequent strategic culture of the victorious powers. There was particular interest in the capacity of air power, with a conviction in Britain and America that strategic bombing would have a major impact. The German air offensive on London was studied by British airmen interested in the strategic potential of air power.

There was also interest in tanks, although considerable uncertainty over the extent to which they should play a role in force structure and doctrine.[58] This was a problem that partly arose from differences over the assessment of their role in 1918, and this uncertainty was accentuated because Plan 1919, which had envisaged a major role for tanks, was not brought to fruition. Moreover, the extent to which large-scale tank attacks were not mounted in the last two months of the war encouraged officers who emphasized the role of more traditional weaponry, especially artillery.[59] The French also presented victory in the war as demonstrating the value of their existing military system.[60] Discussions during the 1920s and 1930s about the role of tanks in any future war led to the development of the so-called infantry tank, which was popular in Britain. The more powerfully armed battle tank was rather neglected in Britain in favour of faster, more manoeuvrable tanks which, in the event in the Second World War, proved vulnerable in combat with other tanks. Moreover, the role of the tank was not clearly assessed in inter-war Germany, which did not possess well-armed tanks until the arrival of the up-gunned MkIVs in 1942. The role of tanks changed from infantry support to tank-tank encounters during the Second World War, although the French had already developed the CharB which outgunned the German tanks of 1940.

The Great War subsequently also attracted the attention of military commentators not in government service, most prominently Basil Liddell Hart, a British army officer, who had been wounded on the Somme in 1916, turned military correspondent and ardent self-publicist. His ideas affected by his reading of the war, Liddell Hart sought to turn his perspectives into rules given credence by history. Thus, in a 1920 memorandum 'Explanation of the theory of the application of the essential principles of strategy to infantry tactics', he wrote:

> The improvements in weapons and the wide extensions enforced by them have created new conditions in the infantry fight. It has developed into what may be termed group combats; the defenders realising that a self-contained group based on a tactical point

is more effective than a trench line, the breaking of which results in the whole line falling back; the attackers countering this method of defence by endeavouring to penetrate between the centres of resistance and turn their flanks.

A bitter critic of Great War generalship, Liddell Hart was particularly keen to advocate advances that did not entail frontal attacks: the 'indirect approach' that emphasized manoeuvre, not attrition, and notably for mechanized forces bypassing the flanks of enemy armies in order to hit their communications.[61] It was claimed, not least by Liddell Hart, that his ideas influenced German *blitzkrieg* tactics in the Second World War, yet the latter were, in fact, a development not only of mechanized warfare and the offensive tactics employed by the Germans in 1917–18 but also of the effective combined arms doctrine developed under Hans von Seeckt, Commander-in-Chief of the *Reichswehr* in 1920–26, and, earlier, a staff officer on the Eastern Front and in Turkey.[62] Thus, the tactics developed to help overcome the obstacles provided by trench warfare in the Great War played a major role in the Second World War, offering a link that is less apparent if the stress, instead, is on the indecisiveness of trench warfare.

CHAPTER 9

The Making of the Modern World

> If you have the intention to really prepare for war, you must see that you have state control of everything – first conscript all the manpower of the empire, then run and manage your railways and ships so that directly war is declared you have sufficient reserves for war requirements – of course it would never pay any private company to do that, then you must see that you have adequate supplies of all metals, rubber and other materials entirely irrespective of your peace requirements ... the real need, I imagine, is that the peoples of England should work harder and that there should be less football, racing etc.
>
> Arthur Child-Villiers, August 1918.[1]

The impact of the Great War may seem, from 1939, to be swallowed up by that of the Second World War, but that is to underplay the extent to which the second conflict, its results and the post-war world all reflected not a script set in, and with, the Great War but, rather, factors that were important to the latter and, more particularly, to the world it created. This point was true of the super-powers of the Great War and the post-war world. Hitler's Germany owed much to a paranoid reading of the earlier conflict, of why Germany had lost it and of how it needed to do better. In many respects, Hitler's views represented the refraction of pre-1914 right-wing nationalist and racist views through the prism of German defeat and the disintegration of Austrian hegemony over part of Slavic Europe. He sought to expunge the memory of Germany's defeat in the war. On 21 June 1940, as victorious German forces pushed into southern France, Hitler met a French delegation under General Charles Huntziger in the same railway carriage in the forest of Compiègne where the armistice had been signed on 11 November 1918, and Huntziger was given a non-negotiable armistice convention which was signed the following day.

The British empire essentially fought the Second World War as a second account of what it had done in the Great War, with Australia, Canada, India and other parts of the empire again playing a key role in support of Britain. Indeed, these similarities were readily apparent in contrast to the very different world that followed independence for India in 1947. The similarities for Britain were enhanced by the role of Churchill, for the cabinet member of the Great War became, initially a cabinet member for the Second World War, again as First Lord of the Admiralty, and then, from 1940, as Prime Minister. Moreover, key figures had served in a minor capacity in the Great War, many in the military, for example Clement Attlee, the leader of the Labour Party and, from 1942, Deputy Prime Minister, had served in the army at Gallipoli and in Mesopotamia and France, eventually as a major. The lessons of the Great War encouraged commanders in the Second World War such as Montgomery, British commander in North Africa in 1942–43 and in Northern Europe in 1944–45, to be cautious with their troops, and also encouraged Montgomery to emphasize artillery-led tactics.[2]

The British empire, however, was ushered off the stage between 1947 and 1964 while the cohesion offered by the Dominions also disappeared. In some respects, the fate of the empire reflected long-term anti-colonial themes that owed much to the strains of the Great War as well as to the course of the Second World War. In contrast, the superpowers of the Second World War and the Cold War owed their genesis or rise to the Great War, with Soviet Communism a product of Russia's defeat by Germany as well, paradoxically, of the subsequent defeat of Germany by the Allies. America became a leading power as a result of the Great War even though it did not take the position it was subsequently to do with and after the Second World War. America was already the world's foremost industrial power by 1914, but it also became the largest creditor and thus the major international lender in the 1920s.

Yet, as in 1865 at the end of the Civil War, a large-scale post-war demobilization greatly lessened America's potential role in the post-war order. Although economic and financial strength certainly defined America as a great power in the 1920s, its strategic role and military strength were far more restricted. America continued to have one of the largest navies in the world, not least because of the handing over and destruction of the German navy; but its small army was not really combat-ready. Military weakness interacted with a lack of American policy in international relations, certainly in so far as translating vague goals into coherent planning was involved. America acted, unilaterally, as a regional power in Latin America, but, even there, the American role was restricted, with withdrawals, eventually, from Nicaragua and Haiti. The Americans played a part in European diplomacy in the 1920s,[3] but their presence in the Middle East, which was left to the control of Britain and France, was limited. Outside Latin America, America essentially took a non-interventionist part that was distinctly at odds with its powerful economy.

The American stance was very different after the Second World War, but the basis of American strength, not least relative to the other powers, owed much to the Great War. Moreover, America's dominant narrative from the Second World War became one in which a failure to sustain its Great War commitment by acting as part of the League of Nations in the 1920s, or in response to German expansionism in the 1930s, helped cause the Second World War, and thus must not be repeated. In short, the Great War became part of the rationale for American great power status.

Europe proved the central confrontation zone in the Cold War and the weakness of the European powers that this resulted from was in some respects a repeat and consequence of the Great War. Germany was defeated in both world wars and there was no Central European alternative to its power. Austria, in particular, had proved far more vulnerable than Germany to the principle of national self-determination actively pushed by President Wilson. The treaty settlements imposed on Austria by the French Revolutionaries and Napoleon had been drastic, with Austria losing the Austrian Netherlands (modern Belgium and Luxembourg) and Lombardy in 1797, Venetia (which she had gained in compensation in 1797) and Tyrol in 1805, her territories in southwest Germany in 1806, West Galicia (in Poland), Cracow and much of Carinthia and Croatia in 1809 and Salzburg in 1810. Nevertheless, Austria had retained control of Bohemia, Moravia, Slovakia, Transylvania, most of Galicia and part of Croatia. After the Great War, in contrast, all of these were lost, as were territories Austria had regained in 1814–15 and others gained subsequently: Galicia went to Poland, Transylvania to Romania, Trentino and Istria to Italy and Croatia, Bosnia and Slovenia to Yugoslavia. Bohemia, Moravia and Slovakia became the independent state of Czechoslovakia, while Hungary became fully independent.

This was a settlement without compromise, and one that not only left Central Europe vulnerable to German expansionism in the late 1930s, but also served in the Cold War to facilitate the Soviet dominance of Eastern Europe. As such, the settlement to the Great War was responsible both for much of the geopolitics of the Appeasement years but also for those of the Cold War. The end of the Cold War in 1989–91, however, suggested that the influence of the Great War was receding alongside, but even more than, that of the Second World War. In particular, the collapse of Soviet Communism appeared to mean a very different character to Russian power, and certainly led to a new historical narrative. Lenin passed into the twilight and, while Stalin's success in resisting, and then defeating, Germany remained highly significant to this narrative, this success could now be detached from Lenin and the legacy of the Great War.

Also from the 1990s, the rise in East Asian power and issues became more insistent, notably with the growing strength of China. East Asia had played a role in the Great War, with both Japan and, less meaningfully, China declaring war on Germany, and, therefore, being represented in the Paris Peace Conference. However, the key events of the war years in East Asia were not the Japanese capture of the German base of Tsingtao in 1914, but, rather, the Japanese occupation of the Shandong peninsula in 1915 and, in particular, the subsequent pressure on China which gravely compromised the government of the latter. The 'Twenty-One Demands' presented to China included an acceptance of the extension of Japanese commercial rights in Manchuria, the Japanese takeover of German interests in Shandong and an extension of the Japanese leasehold there, and the limitation of China's right to cede control of coastal areas to third powers, which would prevent equivalent gains by European powers. The Japanese also demanded in the 'Twenty-One Demands' that the Chinese government agree to use Japanese advisers in its army, police and financial administration, which would make Chinese modernization serve Japanese interests. This measure was blocked by American pressure as it was counter to America's Open Door Policy for China giving equal rights to all foreign powers, as well as being objected to by several pressure groups in America on social and military grounds.

In both China and the Russian Far East during the Russian Civil War, the war saw a new dynamism in Japanese expansionism, taking forward that seen in the 1890s and, more successfully, 1900s. As in the 1900s, alliance with Britain and Russian defeat, provided Japan with opportunities. 70,000 Japanese troops were sent to Siberia in 1918, the largest contingent of Allied troops committed in the Russian Civil War. Also in 1918, Japan signed a defence treaty with China which, under the pretext of blocking the spread of Communism from Russia, gave Japan the right to move troops through China. However, Japan was unable to sustain its presence in Shandong or the Russian Far East and had to abandon both in 1922: American pressure was important to the former check.

The key narrative for China was not that set by the Great War, but, rather, the consequences of the fall of the Manchu empire in 1911–12 and the creation, instead, of a weak republic, focused on Yüan Shih-k'ai, the general turned Prime Minister (1911), and President (1912), who proclaimed himself Emperor on 12 December 1915. This step led to rebellion across much of China and Yüan died the following June bereft of any real power. Yet, the Great War also created opportunities and revised issues for China, with the national assertion and self-determination it encouraged[4] helping foster Kuomintang (Nationalist Chinese) opposition to Western, particularly British, interests in the 1920s. Nevertheless, neither Japanese expansionism nor Chinese divisions were solely due to the war. Moreover, it is difficult to draw close links between post-1937 East Asian history and the Great War, except indirectly through the impact of some of the themes noted above including international Communism and American power-projection.

The meaning of the Great War also owed much to its very varied resonance in the national myths of the new and newly independent states created across the world from 1918, states which covered much of Eastern Europe and the Middle East by 1919 and much of South Asia and Africa as well by 1960. Many of these states downplayed their role in the Great War, and notably so if they were colonies then. During the war, Ireland was not a colony but, instead, part of the United Kingdom of Great Britain and Ireland, and its MPs played a major role in Westminster. However, from 1922, the Irish Free State (now the Republic of Ireland) defined its nationalist independence in terms of a rejection of the British empire. In the Great War, 200,000 Irish troops had fought for the British, 30,000 of whom died, including, in June 1917, Major William Redmond MP, who, that March, pleaded for Parliament 'in the name of Irish soldiers' to grant Home Rule for Ireland within the empire at once.[5] After the war, the political movement that had hoped to gain Home Rule through participation in the conflict[6] was slighted or ignored as, at the public level, were the war dead. Instead, in marked contrast to the position in Northern Ireland, where the sacrifice of many local troops at the Somme was important to Unionist identity,[7] there was an emphasis in the Republic on the Easter Rising of 1916 against British rule, which, in fact, was very much a minority effort, and on the War of Independence after the Great War.[8]

In practice, the Great War and the struggle for independence were not polar opposites. A number of Irish Republican Army commanders had served in the Great War, including Commandant Tom Barry, who shot wounded men dead in the road at the Kilmichael Ambush, men he might have been serving with a couple of years earlier. In 1918, there were crowds to welcome the troops home, yet many had voted or were about to vote for the nationalist Sinn Féin party which won 73 out of the 105 parliamentary seats in the election of 1918. Moreover, the Treaty of 1921 dividing Ireland and creating the Irish Free State was ratified by referendum in 1922. By then, support for the British empire had fallen greatly in what became the Irish Free State, and this fall led to an underplaying of the commitment in the Great War. This underplaying was seen with the National Irish War Memorial to the war dead, which was erected not in the centre of Dublin, as initially suggested, but at the more remote location of Islandbridge. Furthermore, the memorial was not formally opened until 1994.[9]

For similar reasons, states like India make scant play of the Great War. Over 800,000 Indians fought in the war, but they have been twice marginalized: by nationalist historians of India who focus on the independence struggle against Britain, and by Eurocentric accounts of the Great War itself, notably with their concentration on the Western Front.[10] Some states that were subordinated or occupied during the war also found little to commemorate, notably Persia (Iran), much of which was taken over by Britain and Russia, providing a key background to the seizure of power by Riza Khan in 1921.

The situation, however, is very different for certain states for which the conflict played a major role in aspects of their history, for example Armenia and the Armenian Massacres, and Israel and the Balfour Declaration. Each is highly contentious, with both the episode and its significance subjects for dispute. The Christian Armenians were seen by the Turkish authorities as a potentially pro-Russian fifth column and they were brutalized. Aside from large-scale killing and the expropriation of property, many were driven into an arid region where they died, a key episode in the process by which the Ottoman empire was transformed into Turkey, a state with a clearly proclaimed ethnic identity and one that broke with the multiple ethnicities of the far more cosmopolitan Ottoman system.[11] For the Turks, the war is also important, an importance greatly magnified by Turkey's neutrality in the Second World War. What to the Turks is Çanakkale, not Gallipoli, is a crucial episode in the career of Kemal Atatürk, the Father of the Nation, as well as in the freeing of the Turkish nation from foreign pressure, and the 1915 campaign is also used to explain action against the Armenians, although this action is not seen as as deadly as it is (more accurately) portrayed by the latter.

The legacy of the Great War in what became Israel is also highly contentious. For example, in October 1915, Sir Arthur Henry McMahon, the British High Commissioner in Cairo, informed Hussein ibi Ali, ruler of the Hejaz (part of modern Saudi Arabia), whose support against the Turks was being sought, that Britain was 'prepared to recognize and support the independence of the Arabs', but that districts to the west of Aleppo, Harna, Homs and Damascus should be excluded from a proposed independent Arab state on the grounds that they were not purely Arab. Zionists seized on this argument that Palestine was not therefore included in the state, and hence could be settled by Jews, but their interpretation was hotly disputed by Arab leaders, who argued that the wording referred to Lebanon alone, where there was a substantial Christian population.

Following the decision of the War Cabinet of 31 October 1917, in which the Foreign Secretary, Balfour had emphasized the favourable potential impact on the heavily pro-Zionist Jews of Russia and America,[12] the Balfour Declaration issued by the British government on 2 November expressed support for a Jewish national home in Palestine. That Declaration, however, left its borders unclear and some claims proved particularly bold, reflecting a sense that the Middle East could be redrawn with scant concern for the view of its inhabitants. That year, *The True Boundaries of the Holy Land, as Described in Numbers XXXIV: 1-12. Solving the Many Diversified Theories as to Their Location* by the recently deceased Hillel Isaacs was published in Chicago by his daughter, Jeanette Isaacs Davis. The work was published before the meeting of the American Jewish Congress in order to establish a common Jewish position before the peace conference that was expected at the end of the war. Isaacs' own map, drawn in 1916, gave Israel extensive frontiers, especially to the north where they extended to include all the coast to the Gulf of Alexandretta, in other words the coast of modern Lebanon and Syria.

This was more land than that actually sought by Zionist organizations, and reflected the extent to which the war provided opportunities for those who wished to suggest new international arrangements and boundaries.

The Arab sense of betrayal was not restricted to Palestine, but was part of a wider perception of betrayal to suit Anglo-French imperial interests. Faisal, the son of Hussein ibn Ali, ruler of the Hejaz, had joined with the British in capturing Damascus in 1918, but his ambition to rule Syria was thwarted by France, which gained a League of Nations mandate to govern it. In 1920, Faisal's forces were defeated at Maisalun, France seized Damascus, and Faisal took refuge in Iraq.

For the major combatants, however, the war has far less political resonance. Australians still cite Gallipoli, the subject of Peter Weir's iconic film *Gallipoli* (1981), alongside the 'Great Betrayal' of the Second World War, when British priorities for imperial defence clashed with Australian interests. In turn, this alleged failure to provide sufficient support for resisting Japan in 1941–42 then encouraged a further emphasis on Gallipoli as an example of British perfidy in an earlier generation. Thus, commemoration of the battle is in part an ideological project.[13] This grievance history, deeply tedious in the case of Australians, did not, however, play much of a role for Britain, France, Germany (after the Second World War), Russia or America. Instead, there was an almost elegiac quality to memorialization as the last British veterans died in 2009, while the public discussion in Britain continued to be dominated by the 1960s' theme of the Lost Generation, rather than being focused on any particular political grievance. The victory much applauded (or regretted) in, and after, 1918 appeared to be too hard-won, if not an ironic counterpoint to the horrors of trench warfare. Thus, the very fact of war, and the process of conflict itself, continued to appear a defeat, however much powerful novels, such as Pat Barker's *Regeneration* (1991) and Sebastian Faulks' *Birdsong* (1993), might present protagonists who discover themselves in the midst of the pain of battle. Loss was a key theme in many novels, as in Sébastien Japrisot's *Un Long Dimanche de Fiançailles* (1991, *A Very Long Engagement*) about the search for the truth about the death of a fiancé. What had become the dominant cultural trope of war in Western Europe was sufficiently anti-war to affect greatly the understanding of victory in 1918.

Knowledge of the Great War changed with time. In the 1960s, when British schoolchildren were force-fed Wilfred Owen and other war poets, there was much attention in Britain devoted to the conflict, and on average, eight million people saw each episode of the BBC's *Great War* series in 1964. Yet, it is ironic, now, to read the news release of 23 October 1969 for the *History of the First World War*, a lavishly illustrated weekly series published by the British Printing Company: 'It is from material such as this that Homer and Thucydides, Tolstoy and the authors of the Book of Genesis, wrought their immortal tragedies … on our side the names of Ypres and Passchendaele, Gallipoli and the Somme, Jutland, Heligoland Bight and Zeebrugge are even more a part of our national consciousness than El Alamein [1942], Kohima [1944], the Imjin River [1950] or Suez [1956].' The advertisements for the series, such as those in the *Daily Express* on 23 October and the *Daily Telegraph* the next day, stressed immediacy: 'Everywhere you will stand next to heroes'. As an instance of transience, however, battles such as Heligoland Bight (1914) and Kohima (1944) are no longer part of the British national consciousness.

In France, the memory boom of the 1980s was given a historical resonance in September 1984 when Helmut Kohl and François Mitterand, the German Chancellor and French President, jointly visited Douamont, a key fortress in the Verdun campaign of 1916. They provided a clear sign of Franco-German unity, and thus the strength of the European Economic Community (now European Union), by holding hands. This use of Verdun indicated the extent to which it could bear differing meanings. Earlier, the French Third Republic, which was overthrown by German invasion in 1940, had encouraged the idea that the battle reaffirmed a strength and greatness not seen during the Franco-Prussian War of 1870–71 and that it displayed the soul of France uniting soldiers and civilians. However, the meaning that Verdun had remained equivocal, as, alongside celebrating successful resistance, it could also be used to emphasize France's suffering and her need not to suffer again.[14] Moreover, the case of Alsace-Lorraine underscored the inter-war ambivalences within the representation of the war.[15] More recently, Verdun has been overlain as a political issue by Franco-German reconciliation, while the controversial memory of Vichy as well as the roles of de Gaulle, the Free French and the Resistance have greatly focused French attention on the second of the two world wars.

For the major combatants, popular interest in the war remains acute, especially in Britain and Australia. This process is also notable in Canada where the film *Passchendaele* was released in 2009 to great interest. The war in Afghanistan has strengthened the Canadian need for memorialization, has awakened a sense of pride among Canadians in their military past and has helped rid them of some of the myth that Canadians are only 'Peace Keepers'. Yet, as in Britain, the interest in the Great War is often genealogical or a case of social memorialization, rather than a matter of political identity, ideology or contention. More generally, the role of the family in providing the means and content of history centres on the idea of the link between the generations, and this idea, alongside a desire to recover male identity, provides the key to much of the interest in the Great War.[16] Genealogy thus complements monuments, which were very much the public commemoration of earlier generations.[17] Battlefield visits, common in the 1930s but much less so after the Second World War, revived from the late 1960s, and have become significant not as an aspect of grief but, rather, as a combination of curiosity with an affirmation of identity.[18]

Recollection replacing commemoration is part of the distancing of time, the extent to which it rewrites as well as repositions history. When not studied from the perspective of critics, wartime memorialization is now frequently treated as a sad curiosity. In London, public acceptance of the war effort was shown in the spontaneous appearance of street shrines set up to commemorate those who had died for their country or to record the names of those who had gone to serve. Such shrines were the site of a popular religiosity that indicated the strength of wartime devotion and was also seen in national prayer days, as well as in the 'Procession of Witness for God' led through London by the Bishop of London on 9 June 1917. The first shrine we know of was established in Hackney in 1916, and many others followed, particularly in the East End. A large shrine was erected in Hyde Park in August 1918, prompting 100,000 people to visit it within a week, with many leaving floral tributes there.

This contemporary sense of loss has been reawakened by genealogical work and, in particular, the extent to which television embraced it in Britain in the late 2000s. The death, on 26 July 2009, at the age of 111 of Harry Patch, the last British veteran of the Great War, as well as Britain's oldest man, was much reported. Characteristically, there was renewed talk of the futility of war, a theme that ignored why Patch and others went off to war, in his case in 1917, being wounded at Passchendaele.[19] Indeed, the sense of loss offers little as far as an understanding of the war is involved. That encourages us in the following chapter to consider briefly the likely situation in the future.

Conclusion

Saul has slain his thousands but David his tens of thousands.

> Machine Gun Corps Memorial, Hyde Park Corner,
> London

Memories change. This inscription appears on the memorial prominently erected at Hyde Park Corner, London to members of the Machine Gun Corps who fell in the Great War. David holding a sword takes central place on the memorial, but he is flanked by two machine guns wreathed in victory. Such a memorial today would seem strange, not to say bizarre, to many. Commemoration indeed changes in tone and content, and sometimes brutally so, as in 1986 when the impressive Imperial Tobacco War Memorial was demolished to make way for a branch of the supermarket ASDA. Collective memories, moreover, have altered with the passing of the last veterans.

Yet, the Great War continues to provide a grim fascination, not least because of an elegiac memorialization of an apparently less complicated, but also doomed, world. Furthermore, although it was staged behind the lines, the film footage of the conflict, notably British works such as *The Battle of the Somme* and *The Battle of the Ancre*, lends itself to television. On 12 January 2010, BBC2 broadcast a documentary about the first year of the Obama administration, in which the writer-narrator, Simon Schama, urged President Obama, both in Afghanistan and more generally, to follow the example of

President Truman whose attitudes were in part explained in terms of his record in the Great War, as a captain in the Field Artillery, a record which was illustrated with film footage of the war. Similarly, much of the anti-war literature that is frequently cited has a cinematographic quality.[1]

Looking ahead, it is unclear how far the present situation will continue. Indeed, the question may be not only how the war is memorialized but even whether it is commemorated at all. The likely breakdown or lessening, with time, of public provision in commemoration may well mean that the memorialization is most pronounced at the level of individual communities or, more likely, families whose historical memory is particularly focused on the struggle. Moreover, a probable switch in emphasis within the media from the Anglophone world, in which the American market for example helps finance British programmes, to East and South Asia, may well mean that the war becomes far less prominent, or that its emphasis is changed.

Already, the Great War does not serve the role taken by the Second World War in validating the purpose of America, Russia and Britain, while there is not a concern to draw lessons comparable to those for which Appeasement, the Holocaust, Vichy and the Second World War as a whole are mined. If a role of the past is to provide apparently clear lessons, then the Great War seems to the public only to provide that of the futility of war. Scholarship suggests the opposite and there have been valuable attempts to explain the methods, extent and significance of the Allied victory in 1918 to a wider audience,[2] but while the idea of a 'trickle-down' from academic work to the wider public is comforting to scholars, it is largely erroneous.

Moreover, local recollection of the Great War in many parts of the world will be affected by the extent to which the conflict will be reduced to, and explained in terms of, long-term trends, such as the colonial period. This recollection will be particularly important in Africa and Asia, which will downplay the effort involved in the Great War as well as its significance, both for these continents and more generally. Ultimately, some of the politics of the war's recollection in the future can be foretold from the past. There is scant serious danger of the resumption of a toxic narrative comparable to the German 'stab-in-the-back', but, instead, the problem that, yet again, revulsion at the casualty figures will combine with the laziness of moral relativism and the unwillingness to study what actually happened, in order to sustain the propagation of seriously misleading views on the politics and war-making of conflict, and notably the Great War. Such an approach draws on potent currents of sentimentality, the emotional response to problems and a populist unwillingness to grapple with difficult issues; and they combine to reflect and strengthen a form of cultural weakness that is potentially debilitating. There is a civic and professional duty for historians, a responsibility to the present and the future, as well as the past, to try to explain and discuss the war without yielding to the ease of conventional platitude.

Notes

Preface

[1] DRO, 5277M/F3/29, two (similar) accounts by Worrall, in April 1918 and October 1931.

[2] DRO, 413M Add. F1.

[3] S. Lone, *Provincial Life and the Military in Imperial Japan. The Phantom Samurai* (London, 2009), p. 105.

[4] H. Strachan, 'Towards a comparative history of World War I. Some reflections', *Militärgeschichtliche Zeitschrift*, 67 (2008), 339.

Introduction

[1] Alan to Edith Thomson, 11 November 1918, Thomson papers.

[2] M. Howard, *A Part of History. Aspects of the British Experience of the First World War* (London, 2008), intro; P. Parker, *The Last Veteran. Harry Patch and the Legacy of War* (London, 2009).

Chapter 1

[1] E. H. Moorhouse, *1588 to 1914. Album-Atlas of British Victories on the Sea. 'Wooden Walls to Super-Dreadnoughts'* (London, 1914).

[2] M. Paris, *Warrior Nation: The Representation of War in British Popular Culture, 1850–2000* (London, 2000).

[3] C. E. Forth, *The Dreyfus Affair and the Crisis of French Manhood* (Baltimore, Maryland, 2004).

4   A. Gat, *A History of Military Thought from the Enlightenment to the Cold War* (Oxford, 2001), p. 343.

5   P. W. Schroeder, 'A. J. P. Taylor's international system', *International History Review*, 23 (2001), 25.

6   M. Howard, *The Franco-Prussian War* (London, 1961), pp. 220–1.

7   D. N. Collins, 'The Franco-Russian Alliance and Russia's Railways, 1891–1914', *Historical Journal*, 16 (1973), 777–88.

8   M. S. Seligmann, 'A View from Berlin: Colonel Frederick Trench and the Development of British Perceptions of German Aggressive Intent, 1906–1910', *Journal of Strategic Studies*, 23 (2000); and *Spies in Uniform: British Military and Naval Intelligence on the Eve of the First World War* (Oxford, 2006).

9   A. Mombauer, *Helmuth von Moltke and the Origins of the First World War* (Cambridge, 2001).

10 T. G. Otte, '"What we desire is confidence": The search for an Anglo-German naval agreement, 1909–1912', in K. Hamilton and E. Johnson (eds), *Arms and Disarmament in Diplomacy* (Edgware, 2007), p. 47; M. S. Seligmann (ed), *Naval Intelligence from Germany: The Reports of the British Naval Attachés in Berlin, 1906–1914* (Aldershot, 2007).

11 J. W. Steinberg, *All the Tsar's Men: Russia's General Staff and the Fate of Empire, 1898–1914* (Battimore, Maryland, 2010).

12 W. D. Godsey, 'Officers vs diplomats: bureaucracy and foreign policy in Austria-Hungary, 1906–1914', *Mitteilungen des Österreichischen Staatsarchiv*, 46 (1998), 43–66.

13 R. F. Hamilton and H. H. Herwig (ed), *Decisions for War, 1914–1917* (Cambridge, 2004); W. Mulligan, *The Origins of the First World War* (Cambridge, 2010).

14 R. R. McLean, *Royalty and Diplomacy, 1890–1914* (Cambridge, 2001).

§5 K. Neilson, *Britain and the Last Tsar: British Policy and Russia, 1894–1917* (Oxford, 1996).

16 K. Wilson, 'The Channel Tunnel question at the Committee of Imperial Defence, 1906–1914', *Journal of Strategic Studies*, 13 (1990).

17 T. G. Otte, '"The method in which we were schooled by experience":

British strategy and a continental commitment before 1914', in K. Neilson and G. Kennedy (eds), *The British Way in Warfare: Power and the International System, 1856–1956* (Farnham, 2010), pp. 318–19.

18 T. G. Otte, 'Neo-revisionism or the emperor's new clothes: some reflections on Niall Ferguson on the origins of the First World War', *Diplomacy and Statecraft*, 11 (2000), 285.

19 F. McDonough, *The Conservative Party and Anglo-German Relations, 1905–1914* (Basingstoke, 2007).

20 K. Wilson (ed), *Decisions for War, 1914* (London, 1996).

21 D. Showalter, 'From deterrence to doomsday machine: the German way of war, 1890–1914', *Journal of Military History*, 64 (2000), pp. 708; A. Mombauer, *Helmuth von Moltke and the Origins of the First World War* (Cambridge, 2001).

22 A. Offer, 'Going to war in 1914: a matter of honour?', *Politics and Society*, 23 (1995), pp. 213–41.

23 R. H. Macdonald, *Sons of the Empire: The Frontier and the Boy Scout Movement, 1890–1918* (Toronto, 1993); G. Dawson, *Soldier Heroes. British Adventure, Empire and the Imagining of Masculinities* (London, 1994).

24 A. J. Echevarria, *Imaging Future War: The West's Technological Revolution and Visions of War to Come, 1880–1914* (Westport, Connecticut, 2007).

25 Hamilton, British Adjutant General, report on Saxon exercises 1909, LH, Hamilton papers 4/2/9, p. 60a.

26 BL, Add. 50101 fols 8–21; A. J. Echeverria, 'A crisis in warfighting: German tactical discussions in the late nineteenth century', *Militargeschichtliche Mitteilungen*, 55 (1995), 51–68.

27 NA, WO, 33/2816, p.43, 2819, p.26.

28 NA, WO, 33/2/822, p.93.

29 R. M. Ripperger, 'The development of French artillery for the offensive, 1890–1914', *Journal of Military History*, 59 (1995), 599–618.

30 G. C. Cox, 'Of aphorisms, lessons, and paradigms: comparing the British and German official histories of the Russo-Japanese wars', *Journal of Military History*, 66 (1992), 389–401.

31 BL, Add. 50344, p.3; M. Howard, 'Men against fire: the doctrine of the offensive in 1914', in P. Paret et al. (eds), *Makers of Modern Strategy from Machiavelli to the Nuclear Age* (Princeton, New Jersey, 1986), pp. 510–26.

32 D. G. Herrmann, *The Arming of Europe and the Making of the First World War* (Princeton, New Jersey, 1996); D. Stevenson, *Armaments and the Coming of War: Europe, 1904–14* (Oxford, 1996).

33 M. Epkenhans, 'Military-industrial relations in imperial Germany, 1870–1914', *War in History*, 10 (2003), pp. 1–26.

34 D. Stevenson, 'War by timetable? The railway race before 1914', *Past and Present*, 162 (1999), pp. 163–94.

35 N. Lambert, 'Transformation and technology in the Fisher era: the impact of the communications revolution, 1904–1910', *Journal of Strategic Studies*, 27 (2004), pp. 272–97.

36 A. Whitmarsh, 'British army manoeuvres and the development of military aviation, 1910–1913', *War in History*, 14 (2007), 325–46.

37 *Daybook*, 12, 3 (2008), p. 16.

38 W. M. McBride, 'Strategic determinism in technology selection: the electric battleship and US naval-industrial relations', *Technology and Culture*, 33 (1992), p. 249.

39 R. F. Hamilton and H. H. Herwig (eds), *War Planning 1914* (Cambridge, 2010), pp. 253–6.

40 P. Gatrell, *Government, Industry and Rearmament in Russia, 1900–1914* (Cambridge, 1994); J. M. B. Lyon, '"A peasant mob": the Serbian army on the eve of the Great War', *Journal of Military History*, 61 (1997), p. 493.

41 H. Strachan, 'The First World War', *Historical Journal*, 43 (2000), p. 893.

42 P. Kennedy (ed), *The War Plans of the Great Powers, 1880–1914* (London, 1979),

43 J. C. Arnold, 'French tactical doctrine, 1870–1914', *Military Affairs*, 42 (1978), 64; D. Porch, *The March to the Marne: the French Army, 1871–1914* (Cambridge, 1981).

44 R. A. Doughty, 'French strategy in 1914: Joffre's own', *Journal of Military History*, 67 (2003), p. 453.

45   S. Manning, *Evelyn Wood. Pillar of Empire* (Barnsley, 2007), p. 229.

46   E. M. Spiers, 'Reforming the infantry of the line, 1900–1914', *Journal of the Society for Army Historical Research*, 59 (1981), p. 94.

47   T. Travers, 'The offensive and the problem of innovation in British military thought, 1870–1915', *Journal of Contemporary History*, 13 (1978), 546.

48   R. C. Hall, *The Balkan Wars, 1912–13: Prelude to the First World War* (London, 2000), p. 134.

49   J. T. Sumida, 'The quest for reach: the development of long-range gunnery in the Royal Navy, 1901–12', in S. D. Chiabotti (ed), *Military Transformation in the Industrial Age* (Chicago, Illinois, 1996), pp. 49–96.

50   Sumida, 'A matter of timing: the Royal Navy and the tactics of decisive battle, 1912–1916', *Journal of Military History*, 67 (2003), 131–2.

Chapter 2

1   E. Blunden, *Undertones of War* (1928; University of Chicago edition, 2007) p. 19.

2   Horne to his wife, Kate, in S. Roberts (ed), *The First World War. Letters of General Lord Horne* (Stroud, 2009), p. 276.

3   BL, Add. 50287 fol.71.

4   G. Wawro, *The Franco-Prussian War: The German Conquest of France in 1870–1871* (Cambridge, 2003), pp. 264–5, 288–9.

5   J. Horne and A. Kramer, *German Atrocities in 1914: Meanings and Memory of War* (New Haven, Connecticut, 2001); J. Lipkes, *Rehearsals: The German Army in Belgium, August 1914* (Leuven, 2007).

6   I. V. Hull, *Absolute Destruction: Military Culture and the Practices of War in Imperial Germany* (Ithaca, New York, 2005).

7   T. Zuber, *The Battle of the Frontiers: Ardennes 1914* (Stroud, 2007).

8   N. Gardner, *Trial by Fire: Command and the British Expeditionary Force in 1914* (Westport, Connecticut, 2003).

9   H. H Herwig, *The Marne, 1914: The Opening of World War I and the Battle that Changed the World* (New York, 2009).

10   J. A. Sanborn, 'Unsettling the empire: violent migrations and social disaster in Russia during World War I', *Journal of Modern History*, 77 (2005), 296.

11   D. Showalter, *Tannenberg: Clash of Empires* (Hamden, Connecticut, 1991).

12   I. F. W. Beckett, *Ypres: The First Battle* (London, 2004).

13   Child-Villiers to his father, Victor, 7th Earl of Jersey, 14 November 1914, LMA, ACC/2839/D/002.

14   E. W. Osborne, *The Battle of Heligoland Bight* (Bloomington, Indiana, 2006).

15   N. Black, *The British Naval Staff in the First World War* (Woodbridge, 2009).

16   J. W. Coogan, *The End of Neutrality: The United States, Britain, and Maritime Rights, 1899–1915* (Ithaca, New York, 1981); A. Offer, *The First World War: An Agrarian Interpretation* (Oxford, 1989); P. G. Halpern, 'World War I: the blockade', in B. A. Elleman and S. C. M. Paine (eds), *Naval Blockades and Seapower* (Abingdon, 2006), p. 94.

17   W. Wegener, *The Naval Strategy of the World War*, edited by H. H. Herwig (Annapolis, Maryland, 1989).

18   G. Kennedy, 'Intelligence and the blockade, 1914–1917: a study in friction, administration and command', *Intelligence and National Security*, 22 (2007), 699–721.

19   C. McKee, *Sober Men and True: Sailor Lives in the Royal Navy, 1900–1945* (Cambridge, Massachusetts, 2002), p. 113.

20   M. Aksakal, *The Ottoman Road to War in 1914: The Ottoman Empire and the First World War* (Cambridge, 2008).

21   C. B. Burdick, *The Japanese Siege of Tsingtau* (Hamden, Connecticut, 1976); E. Drea, *Japan's Imperial Army: Its Rise and Fall, 1853–1945* (Lawrence, Kansas, 2009), pp. 138–44. On the Japanese army, M. Kennedy, *The Military Side of Japanese Life* (London, 1924). Kennedy was a British army officer attached to a Japanese regiment.

22   R. Anderson, *The Battle of Tanga* (Stroud, 2002).

23   BL, Add. 49714 fol. 28.

24   A. Brew, *The History of Black Country Aviation* (Stroud, 1993).

25 H. H. Herwig, 'Admirals vs generals: the war aims of the imperial German navy, 1914–1918', *Central European History*, 5 (1972), pp. 208–33.

26 D. Djokic, *Nikola Pašić and Ante Trumbić. The Kingdom of Serbs, Croats and Slovenes* (London, 2010), p. 37.

Chapter 3

1   Reproduced by kind permission of Hugh Orr-Ewing's grandson. Orr-Ewing won the Military Cross in 1916 and survived the war.

2   Alan to Edith Thomson, 1 October 1915, Thomson papers.

3   A. Krell, *The Devil's Rope. A Cultural History of Barbed Wire* (London, 2002).

4   LMA, CLC/521/MS 24718, pp. 14–15, quote, p. 13.

5   Robert to Earl Fortescue, 9 November 1915, DRO, 1262M/FC60.

6   Alan to Edith Thomson, 3 November 1915, Thomson papers.

7   BL, Add. 49703 fol.43.

8   18 (not 28 as in catalogue) August 1915, LH. Fuller papers, IV/3/155.

9   BL, Add. 49703 fol. 42.

10 T. Travers, *The Killing Ground: The British Army, the Western Front and the Emergence of Modern Warfare, 1900–1918* (London, 1987).

11 G. Phillips, 'Douglas Haig and the development of twentieth-century cavalry', *Archives*, 28 (2003), 161; G. Mead, *The Good Soldier: The Biography of Douglas Haig* (London, 2007).

12 G. Sheffield and D. Todman (eds), *Command and Control on the Western Front: The British Army's Experience, 1914–1918* (Staplehurst, 2004).

13 BL, Add. 49703 fols 137–8.

14 K. O. Morgan, 'Lloyd George and Germany', *Historical Journal*, 39 (1996), 759.

15 C. Gray, *Modern Strategy* (Oxford, 1999), p. 189.

16 A. Bucholz (ed), *Delbrück's Modern Military History* (Lincoln, Nebraska, 1997), esp. pp. 12–20; R. Foley (ed), *Alfred von Schlieffen's Military Writings* (London, 2001).

17 Smith-Dorrien to Robertson, 27 April 1915, DRO, 1262M/FH 94.

18   T. Cook, *No Place to Run* (Vancouver, 1999).

19   P. G. Halpern, *The Naval War in the Mediterranean, 1914–1918* (London, 1987).

20   G. Nekrasor, *North of Gallipoli: The Black Sea Fleet at War, 1914–17* (Boulder, Colorado, 1992).

21   M. Wilson, 'Early submarines', in R. Gardiner (ed), *Steam, Steel and Shellfire: The Steam Warship 1815–1905* (London, 1992) pp. 147–57.

22   BL, Add. 49714 fol. 29.

23   C. V. Reed, 'The British naval mission at Constantinople: an analysis of naval assistance to the Ottoman empire, 1908–1914' (doctoral dissertation, Oxford, 1995).

24   E. J. Erickson, *Ordered to Die: A History of the Ottoman Army in the First World War* (Westport, Connecticut, 2001) and *Ottoman Army Effectiveness in World War I: A Comparative Study* (London, 2007).

25   *Notes on the Turkish Army* (London, 1915), pp. 3, 5.

26   Birdwood to General Callwell, 15 May 1915, AWM, 3 DRL/3376, 11/4.

27   Birdwood to Maxwell, 8 June 1915, AWM, 3 DRL/3376, 11/4.

28   T. Travers, *Gallipoli* (Stroud, 2001), p. 310. See also J. MacLeod (ed), *Reconsidering Gallipoli* (Manchester, 2004).

29   Godley to Birdwood, 27 February 1915 AWM, 3 DRL/3376, 11/4; Travers, *Gallipoli,* p. 176.

30   Monash to wife, 16, May 1915, AWM, 3 DRL/2316, 1/1 p. 64.

31   AWM, 3 DRL/3376, 11/4.

32   Monash to wife, 30 May 1915, AWM, 3 DRL/2316, 1/1 p. 72.

33   Alan to Edith Thomson, 4 September 1915, Thomson papers.

34   Alan to Edith Thomson, 24 September, 7 October, 20 November 1915, Thomson papers.

35   D. Massam, 'British maritime strategy and amphibious capability, 1900–40' (doctoral dissertation, Oxford, 1995).

36   C. Duffy, *Through German Eyes. The British and the Somme, 1916* (London, 2006), p. 328.

37   B. C. Busch, *Britain, India and the Arabs* (London, 1971).

38   Maxwell to Kitchener, 19, 23 May 1915, NA, PRO 30/57/65, nos 906, 949.

39   P. A. Mohs, *Military Intelligence and the Arab Revolt: The First Modern Intelligence War* (Abingdon, 2007).

40   Kitchener to Balfour, 6 November 1915, NA, PRO 30/57/66.

41   I. C. Badesi, 'West African influence on the French army of World War One', in G. W. Johnson (ed), *Double Impact: France and Africa in the Age of Imperialism* (Westport, Connecticut, 1985); R. S. Fogarty, *Race and War in France. Colonial Subjects in the French Army, 1914–1918* (Baltimore, Maryland, 2008).

42   Birdwood to C. in C. India, 3 December 1915, AWM, 3 DRL/3376, 11/4.

43   N. M. Zehfuss, 'From stereotype to individual: World War I experiences with *Tirailleurs Sénéglais*', *French Colonial History*, 6 (2005), pp. 140–6.

44   T. Tai-Yong, 'An imperial home-front: Punjab and the First World War', *Journal of Military History*, 64 (2000), 371–410.

45   B. C. Busch (ed), *Canada and the Great War* (Montréal, 2003).

46   R. Anderson, *The Forgotten Front: The East African Campaign, 1914–1918* (Stroud, 2004); H. Strachan, *The First World War in Africa* (Oxford, 2004); E. Paice, *Tip and Run: The Untold Tragedy of the Great War in Africa* (London, 2007).

47   D. Killingray, 'Labour exploitation for military campaigns in British colonial Africa, 1870–1945', *Journal of Contemporary History*, 24 (1989), pp. 483–9.

48   T. J. Stapleton, *No Insignificant Part: The Rhodesia Native Regiment and the East Africa Campaign of the First World War* (Waterloo, Ontario, 2006).

49   B. Nasson, *Springboks on the Somme: South Africa in the First World War* (Johannesburg, 2007).

50   A. Samson, *Britain, South Africa and the East Africa Campaign, 1914–1918. The Union Comes of Age* (London, 2006).

51   W. A. Renzi, *In the Shadow of the Sword: Italy's Neutrality and Entrance into the Great War, 1914–15* (New York, 1988).

52   Kitchener to Asquith, 5 November 1915, NA, PRO 30/57/66; D. J. Dutton, 'The Balkan campaign and French war aims in the Great

War', *English Historical Review*, 94 (1979), 97–113; R. A. Prete, 'Imbroglio par excellence: mounting the Salonika campaign, September–October 1915', *War and Society*, 19 (2001), esp. pp. 68–70.

53   D. J. Dutton, *The Politics of Diplomacy: Britain and France in the Balkans in the First World War* (London, 1998).

54   W. Weston to Earl Fortescue, 24 July 1915, DRO, 1262 M/FC 60.

55   F. Dickinson, *War and National Reinvention: Japan in the Great War, 1914–1919* (Cambridge, Massachusetts, 1999).

56   Birdwood to C. in C. India, 3 December 1915, AWM, 3 DRL/3376, 11/4.

57   W. Weston to Earl Fortescue, 24 July 1915, DRO, 1262M/FC60.

58   G. Hartcup, *The War of Invention* (London, 1983); J. A. Johnson, *The Kaiser's Chemists: Science and Modernization in Imperial Germany* (Chapel Hill, North Carolina, 1990).

59   BL, Add. 49715 fol. 5, cf. fol.6.

60   S. R. Grayzel, '"The souls of soldiers": civilians under fire in First World War France', *Journal of Modern History*, 78 (2006), 588–622, esp. pp. 597–600, 621.

61   Alan to Edith Thomson, 3 November 1915, cf. 24 September 1915, Thomson papers.

62   BL, Add. 49703 fols 184–9.

63   Callwell to Birdwood, 31 March 1915, AWM, 3 DRL/3376, 11/4.

64   Alan to Edith Thomson, 5, 7 October 1915, Thomson papers.

65   W. Weston to Earl Fortescue, 24 July 1915, DRO, 1262 M/FC 60.

66   D. French, *British Strategy and War Aims, 1914–16* (London, 1986).

Chapter 4

1   D. Omissi, *Indian Voices of the Great War: Soldiers Letters, 1914–18* (Basingstoke, 1999), p. 32.

2   N. Grundy, *W. L. Wyllie, R. A.: the Portsmouth Years* (Portsmouth, 1996).

3   LMA, CLC/533/MS 09400.

4   L. V. Smith, *The Embattled Self: French Soldiers' Testimony of the Great War* (Ithaca, New York, 2007).

5   R. Foley, *German Strategy and the Path to Verdun: Erich von Falkenhayn and the Development of Attrition, 1870–1916,* (Cambridge, 2009).

6   R. B. Bruce, 'To the last limits of their strength: the French army and the logistics of attrition at the battle of Verdun', *Army History* 45 (1988), 9–21.

7   R. A. Prete, 'Joffre and the origins of the Somme: a study in Allied military planning', *Journal of Military History*, 73 (2009), pp. 447–8.

8   Child-Villiers to his mother, Margaret, 24 July 1916, 7 May 1917, LMA, Acc/2839/D/001–2.

9   S. D. Badsey, '*Battle of the Somme*: British war propaganda', *Historical Journal of Film, Radio and Television*, 3/2 (1983), 99–115; R. Smither, '"A wonderful idea of the fighting": the question of fakes in *The Battle of the Somme*', *Imperial War Museum Review*, 3 (1986), pp. 4–16.

10   P. H. Liddle, *The British Soldier on the Somme, 1916* (Camberley, 1996), pp.31–2.

11   LMA, GL MS 9400.

12   G. Stamp, *The Memorial to the Missing of the Somme* (London, 2006).

13   Horne to wife, 16 January 1917, Roberts (ed), *Horne*, p. 205.

14   LMA, GL MS 9400.

15   Alan to Edith Thomson, 8 September, 5 November 1916, Thomson papers.

16   I have benefited from the advice of Anthony Saunders. See also his *Trench Warfare 1850–1950* (Barnsley, 2010), p. 118.

17   P. Hart, *The Somme* (London, 2005), pp. 487–8.

18   J. Schindler, 'A hopeless struggle: Austro-Hungarian cryptology during World War I', *Cryptologia*, 24 (2000), 339–50 and 'Steamrollered in Galicia: the Austro-Hungarian army and the Brusilov offensive, 1916', *War in History*, 10 (2003), 27–59; T. Dowling, *The Brusilov Offensive* (Bloomington, Indiana, 2008).

19   P. von Wahlde, 'A pioneer of Russian strategic thought: G. A. Leer, 1829–1904', *Military Affairs*, 35 (1971), 148–53.

20   P. Kenez, 'The Russian Officer Corps before the Revolution: the military mind', *Russian Review*, 31 (1972), 226–36.

21 K. Hitchins, *Romania 1866–1947* (Oxford, 1994), p. 265.

22 G. E. Torrey, 'Romania in the First World War: the years of engagement', *International History Review*, 14 (1992), pp. 462–79.

23 Kitchener to Balfour, 6 November 1915, NA, PRO 30/57/66.

24 N. J. M. Campbell, *Jutland: An Analysis of the Fighting* (London, 1986).

25 A. Gordon, *The Rules of the Game: Jutland and British Naval Command* (London, 1996), pp.514–15.

26 P. Beesley, *Room 40, British Naval Intelligence, 1914–1918* (London, 1984).

27 R. Guilliatt and P. Hohnen, *The Wolf: How One German Terrorised The Allies in the Most Epic Voyage of World War One* (New York, 2010).

28 BL, Add. 49714 fol 145.

29 BL, Add. 49715 fol 210.

30 C. P. Vincent, *The Politics of Hunger: The Allied Blockade of Germany, 1915–1919* (Athens, Georgia, 1985).

31 R. J. Q. Adams, *Arms and the Wizard: Lloyd George and the Ministry of Munitions* (London, 1978).

32 G. Feldman, *Army, Industry and Labor in Germany, 1914–1918* (Princeton, New Jersey, 1966).

33 A. Mitrović, *Serbia's Great War, 1914–1918* (London, 2007).

34 J. E. Gumz, *The Resurrection and Collapse of Empire in Habsburg Serbia, 1914–1918* (Cambridge, 2009); L. Bencze, *The Occupation of Bosnia and Herzegovina in 1878* (New York, 2005).

35 L. H. Siegelbaum, *The Politics of Industrial Mobilization in Russia, 1915–17: A Study of the War Industries Committees* (New York, 1984); N. Stone, 'Organizing an Economy for War: The Russian Shell Shortage, 1914–1917', in G. Best and A. Wheatcroft (eds), *War, Economy and the Military Mind* (London, 1976).

36 J. F. Godrey, *Capitalism at War: Industrial Policy and Bureaucracy in France, 1914–1918* (Oxford, 1987).

37 E. Greenhalgh, 'The archival sources for a study of Franco-British relations during the First World War', *Archives*, 27 (2002), 158–9.

38 E. Greenhalgh, 'Technology development in coalition: the case

of the First World War tank', *International History Review*, 22 (2000), 835–6.

39 R. Bessel, 'Mobilizing German society for war', in R. Chickering and S. Förster (eds), *Great War, Total War: Combat and Mobilization on the Western Front, 1914–1918* (Cambridge, 2000), p. 444.

40 BL, Add. 49703 fol. 109.

41 M. Stibbe, 'The internment of civilians by belligerent states during the First World War and the response of the International Committee of the Red Cross', *Journal of Contemporary History*, 41 (2006), 5–19; P. Panayi, *The Enemy in Our Midst: Germans in Britain during the First World War* (New York, 1991); S. O. Müller, 'Who is the enemy? The nationalist dilemma of inclusion and exclusion in Britain during the First World War', *European Review of History*, 9 (2002), 63–83.

42 N. Stargardt, *The German Idea of Militarism: Radical and Socialist Critics, 1866–1914* (Cambridge, 1914).

43 A. Marron, *The Last Crusade: The Church of England and the First World War* (Durham, North Carolina, 1985).

44 K. Grieves, *The Politics of Manpower, 1914–1918* (Manchester, 1988); W. G. Natter, *Literature of War, 1914–1940: Representing the 'Time of Greatness' in Germany* (New Haven, Connecticut, 1999); J. Verhey, *The Spirit of 1914: Militarism, Myth and Mobilization in Germany* (Cambridge, 2000).

45 J. Vellacott, *Pacifists, Patriots and Vote: The Erosion of Democratic Suffragism in Britain during the First World War* (Basingstoke, 2007).

46 G. Dallas and D. Gill, *The Unknown Army* (London, 1985).

47 Alan to Edith Thomson, 25 December 1916, Thomson papers; J. G. Fuller, *Troop Morale and Popular Culture in the British and Dominion Armies, 1914–1918* (Oxford, 1990).

48 K. Naumann, 'Teaching the world: globalization, geopolitics, and history education at U. S. universities', *GHI Bulletin of the German Historical Institute (Washington): Supplement*, 5 (2008), 128–9.

49 A. Gregory, *The Last Great War: British Society and the First World War* (Cambridge, 2008).

50 J. L. Thompson, *Politicians, the Press and Propaganda: Lord*

Northcliffe and the Great War, 1914–1919 (Kent, Ohio, 1999); J. F. Williams, *Anzacs, the Media and the Great War* (Sydney, 1999).

51 BL, Add. 40714 fols 48–55.

52 Alan to Edith Thomson, 7 October 1915, Thomson papers.

53 P. Spinks, '"The war courts": the Stratford-on-Avon borough tribunal, 1916–18', *Warwickshire History*, 11 (2000–1), pp. 150–8.

54 S. Kudryashev, 'The revolts of 1916 in Russian Central Asia', in E. J. Zürcher (ed), *Arming the State. Military Conscription in the Middle East and Central Asia, 1775–1925* (London, 1999), p. 142.

55 J. Fisher, 'Major Norman Bray and Eastern unrest in the British Empire in the aftermath of World War I', *Archives*, 27 (2002), pp. 41–2.

56 P. Crowley, *Kut 1916* (Stroud, 2009), p. 272.

57 J. Fisher, *Curzon and British Imperialism in the Middle East, 1916–19* (London, 1999).

58 D. Bloxham, *The Great Game of Genocide: Imperialism, Nationalism, and the Destruction of the Ottoman Armenians* (Oxford, 2005) and *Genocide, The World Wars and the Unweaving of Europe* (London, 2008), pp. 19–98; T. Akçam, *A Shameful Act: The Armenian Genocide and the Question of Turkish Responsibility* (London, 2007).

59 R. Gingeras, *Sorrowful Shores: Violence, Ethnicity, and the End of the Ottoman Empire, 1912–1923* (Oxford, 2009).

60 B. Cartledge, *Mihály Károlyi and István Bethlen* (London, 2009), p. 25.

61 J. Watson, *W. F. Massey* (London, 2010), p. 49.

62 Alan to Edith Thomson, 8 September 25 November 1916, Thomson papers.

63 LMA, ACC/1360/556/4.

64 A. Kramer, *Dynamic of Destruction: Culture and Mass Killing in the First World War* (Oxford, 2007).

65 M. Stibbe, *German Anglophobia and the Great War, 1914–1918* (Cambridge, 2001).

66 E. R. May, *The World War and American Isolation, 1914–1917* (Cambridge, Massachusetts, 1966).

Chapter 5

1   Child-Villiers to his mother, 29 April 1917, LMA, ACC/2839/D/003.

2   L. H. Barnardiston 3/4, 7–8 December 1917.

3   F. J. Romero Salvadó, 'Spain and the First World War: the structural crisis of the liberal monarchy', *European History Quarterly*, 25 (1995), 544–5 and *Spain 1914–1918: Between War and Revolution* (London, 1999).

4   M. Stibbe, *German Anglophobia and the Great War, 1914–1918* (Cambridge, 2001); R. Scheck, *Alfred von Tirpitz and German Right-Wing Politics, 1914–1930* (Atlantic Highlands, New Jersey, 1998).

5   R. MacGinty, 'War cause and peace aim? Small states and the First World War', *European History Quarterly*, 27 (1997), pp. 46–7.

6   B. Albert, *South America and the First World War: The Impact of the War on Brazil, Argentina, Peru and Chile* (Cambridge, 1988); P. Martin, *Latin America and the War* (Baltimore, Maryland, 1925); M. Streeter, *Central America and the Treaty of Versailles* (London, 2010), pp. 61–7; M. Streeter, *South America and the Treaty of Versailles* (London, 2010), pp. 72–9.

7   X. Guoqi, 'The Great War and China's military expedition plan', *Journal of Military History*, 72 (2008), pp. 124–38.

8   M. Frey, 'Trade, ships, and the neutrality of the Netherlands in the First World War', *International History Review*, 19 (1997), pp. 541–62; M. M. Abenhuis, *The Art of Staying Neutral: The Netherlands in the First World War, 1914–1918* (Amsterdam, 2006).

9   N. Black, *The British Naval Staff in the First World War* (Woodbridge, 2009), pp. 181–2.

10 J. Winton, *Convoy: The Defence of Trade, 1890–1990* (London, 1983); J. Terraine, *Business in Great Waters: The U-Boat Wars 1916–45* (London, 1989).

11 W. N. Still, *Crisis at Sea: The United States Navy in European Waters in World War 1* (Gainesville, Florida, 2007).

12 P. E. Dewey, *British Agriculture in the First World War* (London, 1989).

13 D. Juniper, 'Gothas over London', *RUSI* 148 No. 4 (2003), pp. 74–80.

[14] Tom Gurney to wife, 16 October 1917, 8 February 1918, LMA, ACC/1360/556/9, 21.

[15] M. B. Barrett, *Operation Albion: The German Conquest of the Baltic Islands* (Bloomington, Indiana, 2008).

[16] M. Rendle, 'The Officer Corps, professionalism, and democracy in the Russian Revolution', *Historical Journal*, 51 (2008), 921–42; and *Defenders of the Motherland: The Tsarist Elite in Revolutionary Russia* (Oxford, 2010).

[17] P. Kenez, 'Changes in the social composition of the Officer Corps during World War 1', *Russian Review'* 31 (1972) pp. 369–75; D. R. Jones, 'The imperial Russian Life Guards Grenadier Regiment, 1906–17: the disintegration of an elite unit', *Military Affairs*, 33 (1969), 289–302; A. Wildman, 'The February revolution in the Russian Army', *Soviet Studies*, 22 (1970), pp. 3–23.

[18] R. S. Feldman 'The Russian General Staff and the June 1917 offensive', *Soviet Studies*, 19 (1968), pp. 526–43.

[19] A. D. Harvey, 'Trotsky at Halifax, April 1917', *Archives*, 22 (1997), pp. 170–4.

[20] M. Ferro, 'The Russian Soldier in 1917: undisciplined, patriotic and revolutionary', *Slavic Review* 30, (1971) pp. 483–512; G. Katkov, *Russia 1917, the Kornilov Affair, Kerensky and the Breakup of the Russian Army* (London, 1980); R. A. Wade, *The Russian Revolution, 1917* (2nd edn. Cambridge, 2005), pp. 264–5.

[21] L. H. Benson papers, A/7, pp. 1–2, 5; B. Gudmundsen, *Stormtroop Tactics: Innovation in the German Army 1914–1918* (New York, 1989).

[22] S. M. Di Scala, *Vittorio Orlando* (London, 2010), pp. 99–100.

[23] Southcomb to aunt Connie, 18 April 1917, DRO, 413M add F1.

[24] Coke to Husey, 16 February 1917, LMA, CLC/533/MS 09400.

[25] J. Sheldon, *The German Army on the Somme, 1914–1916* (Barnsley, 2005), p.398.

[26] B. Rawling, *Surviving Trench Warfare: Technology and the Canadian Corps, 1914–1918* (Toronto, 1992).

[27] Den Fortescue to Earl Fortescue, 15, 17 April 1917, DRO, 1262M/ FC/62a.

28   Southcomb to aunt Connie, 18 April 1917, DRO, 413M add. F1.

29   LMA, ACC/1360/556/4.

30   DRO, 5277M/F3/26.

31   Gurney to wife, 13 April 1917, LMA, ACC/1360/556/3.

32   Child-Villiers to his mother, 3 June 1917, LMA, ACC/2839/D/001.

33   L. V. Smith, *Between Mutiny and Obedience: The Case of the Fifth Infantry Division during World War 1* (Princeton, New Jersey, 1994); A. Loez, *14–18. Les Refus de la Guerre. Une Histoire des Mutins* (Paris, 2009).

34   I. Passingham, *Pillars of Fire: The Battle of Messines Ridge, June 1917* (Stroud, 1999).

35   G. Sheffield and J. Bourne (eds) *Douglas Haig: War Diaries and Letters, 1914–1918* (London, 2005), p. 37.

36   R. Prior and T. Wilson, *Passchendaele: the Untold Story* (New Haven, Connecticut, 1996).

37   P. Dennis and J. Grey (eds), *1917: Tactics, Training and Technology* (Loftus, 2008).

38   I. M. Brown, *British Logistics on the Western Front, 1914–1919* (Westport, Connecticut, 1998).

39   Information provided by Anthony Saunders, and see also his *Trench Warfare 1850–1950* (Barnsley, 2010), p. 146.

40   Coke to Husey, 17 February 1917, LMA, CLC/533/MS 09400.

41   LMA, CLC/533/MS 09400.

42   LMA, CLC/533/MS 09400.

43   BL, Add. 49703 fols 128–9.

44   T. Pidgeon, *The Tank at Flers* (Cobham, 1995).

45   13, 14 September 1916, LMA, CLC/533/MS 09400; Child-Villiers to his mother, 26 September 1916, LMA, ACC/2839/D/002.

46   B. Hammond, *Cambrai 1917: The Myth of the First Great Tank Battle* (London, 2008).

47   A. Syk, 'The 1917 Mesopotamia Commission. Britain's first Iraq inquiry', *RUSI Journal*, 154/4 (2009), pp. 94–101.

48   B. M. Linn, *The Echo of Battle. The Army's Way of War* (Cambridge, Massachusetts, 2007), p. 113.

49   P. Brigden, *The Labour Party and the Politics of War and Peace,*

1900–1924 (Woodbridge, 2009); P. Ward, *Red Flag and Union Jack. Englishness, Patriotism and the British Left, 1881–1924* (Woodbridge, 1998).

50   C. Wrigley, *David Lloyd George and the British Labour Movement: Peace and War* (Brighton, 1976).

51   L. L. Farrar, *Divide and Conquer: German Efforts to Conclude a Separate Peace, 1914–1918* (New York, 1978).

52   A. Hoover, *God, Germany and Britain in the Great War: A Study in Clerical Nationalism* (New York, 1989).

53   E. P. Kelcher, 'Emperor Karl and the Sixtus affair', *Eastern European Quarterly*, 26 (1993), pp. 163–84.

54   A. Lentin, *General Smuts* (London, 2010), p. 41.

55   R. McNamara, *The Hashemites. The Dream of Arabia* (London, 2009), p. 75.

56   R. L. Nelson, '"Ordinary men" in the First World War? German soldiers as victims and participants', *Journal of Contemporary History*, 39 (2004), pp. 425–35.

57   R. Gerwarth, *The Bismarck Myth. Weimar Germany and the Legacy of the Iron Chancellor* (Oxford, 2005), p. 28.

58   D. J. Dutton, '"Private" papers: the case of Sir John Simon', *Archives*, 31 (2005), p. 79.

59   M. Healy, *Vienna and the Fall of the Habsburg Empire: Total War and Everyday Life in World War I* (Cambridge, 2004).

60   A. Offer, *The First World War: an Agrarian Interpretation* (Oxford, 1989); J. Winter and J.-L. Robert (eds), *Capital Cities at War: London, Paris, Berlin, 1914–19* (Cambridge, 1997).

61   R. Chickering, *The Great War and Urban Life in Germany: Freiburg, 1914–1918* (Cambridge, 2007).

62   L. Sondhaus, 'Planning for the endgame: the Central Powers, September 1916–April 1917', in I. F. W. Beckett (ed), *1917: Beyond the Western Front* (Leiden, 2009), p. 23.

Chapter 6

1   Alan to Edith, 11 November 1918, Thomson papers.

2   BL, Add. 49699, fols 53–5.

3   C. Alston, '"The suggested basis for a Russian Federal Republic":

Britain, anti-Bolshevik Russia and the Border States at the Paris Peace Conference, 1919', *History*, 91 (2006), p. 31.

4 Child-Villiers to his mother, 2 March 1918, LMA, ACC/2839/D/001.

5 V. Liulevicius, *War Land on the Eastern Front: Culture, National Identity and German Occupation in World War I* (Cambridge, 2000).

6 P. J. Weindling, *Epidemics and Genocide in Eastern Europe, 1890–1945* (Oxford, 2000).

7 D. Showalter, "'The East gives nothing back': the Great War and the German army in Russia', *Journal of the Historical Society*, 2 (2002), 1–19, esp. 15–16.

8 Sidney Rogerson, DRO, 5277M/F3/34.

9 M. Middlebrook, *The Kaiser's Battle, 21st March 1918: The First Day of the German Spring Offensive* (London, 1978).

10 LMA, CLC/521/MS 24718, pp. 124–6.

11 Ebrington to Earl Fortescue, 10 May 1918, DRO, 1262M/FC 61.

12 Gurney to wife, 18 April 1918, LMA, ACC/1360/556/32.

13 Child-Villiers to his mother, 1 April 1918, LMA, ACC/2839/D/001.

14 Haig, Memorandum on operations on the Western Front, BL, Add 52460, pp. 56–7.

15 H. Strachan, *The First World War* (London, 2003), p. 289.

16 DRO, 5277M/F3/29.

17 M. S. Neiberg, *The Second Battle of the Marne* (Bloomington, Indiana, 2008).

18 N. Maurice, *The Maurice Case* (London, 1972); D. Woodward, *Lloyd George and the Generals* (Newark, Delaware, 1983); D. French, *The Strategy of the Lloyd George Coalition, 1916–18* (Oxford, 1995); E. Greenhalgh, 'David Lloyd George, George Clemenceau, and the manpower crisis', *Historical Journal*, 50 (2007), 397–421.

19 D. J. Dutton (ed), *Paris 1918: The War Diary of the British Ambassador, the 17th Earl of Derby* (Liverpool, 2001).

20 B. Morton, *Woodrow Wilson* (London, 2008), p. 124.

21 K. D. Stubbs, *Race to the Front. The Material Foundations of Coalition Strategy in the Great War* (Westport, Massachusetts, 2002) is far bolder than D. Trask, *The A. E. F. and Coalition*

Warmaking, 1917–1918 (Lawrence, Kansas, 1993); J. Mosier, *The Myth of the Great War: A New Military History of World War 1* (New York, 2002) exaggerates the American role. For the context of an individual unit, P. F. Owen, *To the Limits of Endurance: A Battalion of Marines in the Great War* (College Station, Texas, 2007).

22   K. Burk, *Britain, America and the Sinews of War, 1914–1918* (London, 1984).

23   R. S. Cameron, *Mobility, Shock, and Firepower: The Emergence of the U. S. Army's Armor Branch, 1917–1945* (Fort McNair, DC., 2008).

24   D. Horn, *The German Naval Mutinies of World War One* (New Brunswick, New Jersey, 1969); N. Hewitt, "'Weary waiting is hard indeed": the Grand Fleet after Jutland' in I. F. W. Beckett (ed), *1917 Beyond the Western Front* (Leiden, 2009), p. 69.

25   B. Singer, *Maxime Weygand* (Jefferson, North Carolina, 2008), pp. 35–8.

26   M. A. Yockelson, *Borrowed Soldiers: Americans Under British Command, 1918* (Norman, Oklahoma, 2008).

27   R. H. Ferrell, *Collapse at Meuse Argonne: The Failure of the Missouri-Kansas Division* (Columbia, Missouri, 2004); M. Grotelueschen, *The AEF Way of War: the American army and combat in World War I* (New York, 2007).

28   G. Martin, 'German strategy and military assessments of the American expeditionary force', *War in History*, 1 (1994), 160–96.

29   B. Neumann, 'A question of authority: reassessing the March–Pershing "feud" in the First World War', *Journal of Military History*, 73 (2009), 1135–8.

30   Child-Villiers to his mother, 13 June 1918, LMA, ACC/2839/D/001.

31   G. Harper, *Dark Journey: Three Key New Zealand Battles of the Western Front* (Auckland, 2007).

32   J. Black, 'Open Season', *Standpoint*, 16 (2009), p. 25.

33   R. J. Crampton, *Aleksandŭr Stamboliĭski* (London, 2009), pp. 64–5.

34   B. W. Harvey and C. Fitzgerald (eds), *Edward Heron-Allen's Journal: The Great War: From Sussex Shore to Flanders Fields* (Lewes, 2002), p.244.

35 2. AWM, 3 DRL/6643, 5/27.

36 DRO, 5277M/F3/29.

37 D. J. Childs, *A Peripheral Weapon? The Production and Employment of British Tanks in the First World War* (Westport, Connecticut, 1999).

38 Report on operations, AWM, 3 DRL/6643, 5/27.

39 Child-Villiers to his mother, 12, 15 (quote) August 1918, LMA, ACC/2839/D/001.

40 DRO, 5277M/F3/30, 31 August 1918.

41 R. Martel, *French Strategic and Tactical Bombardment Forces of World War I*, edited by S. Suddaby (Lanham, Maryland, 2007).

42 Child-Villiers to his mother, 26 September 1918, LMA, ACC/2839/D/002.

43 M. Cooper, *The Birth of Independent Air Power* (London, 1986).

44 G. K. Williams, *Biplanes and Bombsights: British Bombing in World War 1* (Maxwell, Air Force Base, Alabama, 1999).

45 Alan to Edith Thomson, 11 November 1918, Thomson papers.

46 Child-Villiers to his mother, – October 1916, LMA, ACC/2839/D/001.

47 J. Bailey, *The First World War and the Birth of the Modern Style of Warfare* (Camberley, 1996).

48 D. V. Johnson and R. L. Hillman, *Soissons 1918* (College Station, Texas, 1999).

49 J. S. Murray, 'The face of Armageddon', *Mercator's World* 1/2 (1996), 30–7; M. Heffernan, 'Geography, cartography and military intelligence: the Royal Geographical Society and the First World War', *Transactions of the Institute of British Geographers*, 21 (1996), pp. 504–33.

50 A. Palazzo, 'The British Army's counter-battery staff office and control of the enemy in World War I', *Journal of Military History*, 63 (1999), 55–74; D. Jenkins, 'The other side of the hill: combat intelligence in the Canadian Corps, 1914–1918', *Canadian Military History* 10 (2001).

51 M. Occleshaw, *Armour Against Fate: British Military Intelligence in the First World War* (London, 1989); J. M. Ferris, *The British Army*

and Signals Intelligence During the First World War (London, 1992).

52 J. Bailey, 'The First World War and the birth of modern warfare', in M. Knox and W. Murray (eds), *The Dynamics of Military Revolution, 1300–2050* (Cambridge, 2001), p. 132.

53 DRO, 5277M/F3/30, 20 August 1918.

54 Alan to Edith Thomson, 11 November, commander of 33rd Infantry Brigade to Thomson, 12 November 1918, Thomson papers.

55 A. Palazzo, *Seeking Victory on the Western Front: The British Army and Chemical Warfare in World War One* (Lincoln, Nebraska, 2000).

56 DRO, 5277M/F3/30, 28 September 1918.

57 S. B. Schreiber, *Shock Army of the British Empire: The Canadian Corps in the Last 100 Days of the Great War* (Westport, Connecticut, 1997); P. Dennis and J. Grey (eds), *1918: Defining Victory* (Canberra, 1999); P. Harris, *Amiens to the Armistice: The BEF in the Hundred Days' Campaign* (London, 1999); T. Cook, *Shock Troops: Canadians Fighting the Great War, 1917–1918* (Toronto, 2008).

58 DRO, 5277M/F3/30.

59 A Clayton, *Paths of Glory: The French Army, 1914–18* (London, 2003); R. Doughty, *Pyrrhic Victory: French Strategy and Operations in the Great War* (Cambridge, Massachusetts, 2005).

60 B. Millman, *Pessimism and British War Policy, 1916–1918* (London, 2001).

61 AWM, 3 DRL/6643, 5/27.

62 P. Griffith (ed) *British Fighting Methods in the Great War* (London, 1996).

63 R. C. Hall, *Balkan Breakthrough, the Battle of Dobro Pole 1918* (Bloomington, Indiana, 1918).

64 Y. Sheffy, *British Military Intelligence in the Palestine Campaign, 1914–1918* (London, 1998).

65 M. Hughes, 'General Allenby and the Palestine Campaign, 1917–18', *Journal of Strategic Studies*, 19 (1996), p. 82.

66 G. Dyer, 'The Turkish Armistice of 1918', *Middle Eastern Studies*, 8 (1972), pp. 143–52.

67 M. Cornwall, *The Undermining of Austria-Hungary: The Battle for Hearts and Minds* (Basingstoke, 2000).

68 G. E. Rothenberg, *The Army of Francis Joseph* (West Lafayette, Indiana, 1998); M. Cornwall (ed), *The Last Years of Austria-Hungary* (2nd edn, Exeter, 2002).

69 R. Chickering, *Imperial Germany and the Great War, 1914–1918* (Cambridge, 1998).

70 W. Diest, 'The military collapse of the German empire: the reality behind the stab-in-the-back myth', *War in History*, 3(1996), 186–207; H. Strachan, 'The morale of the German army, 1917–1918', in H. Cecil and P. Liddle (eds), *Facing Armageddon: The First World War Experienced* (Barnsley, 1996), pp. 383–98; A. Watson, *Enduring the Great War: Combat, Morale and Collapse in the German and British Armies, 1914–1918* (Cambridge, 2008).

71 Child-Villiers to his mother, 24 Aug., 8 September 1918, LMA, ACC/2839/D/001, though for concern about the rain, letter of 6 September 1918.

72 Horne to his wife, 18, 24 October 1918, Roberts (ed), *Horne*, pp. 266, 270.

73 AWM, 3 DRL/6643, 5/27.

74 Alan to Edith Thomson, 11 November 1918, Thomson papers.

75 Fortescue to Earl Fortescue, 3 November 1918, DRO, 1262M/FC62a.

76 Alan to Edith Thomson, 11 November 1918, Thomson papers.

77 B. Lowry, *Armistice 1918* (Kent, Ohio, 1966); A. J. Ryder, *The German Revolution of 1918: A Study of German Socialism in War and Revolt* (Cambridge, 1967); H. Goemans, *War and Punishment: The Causes of War Termination and the First World War* (Princeton, New Jersey, 2000).

78 Den Fortescue to his father, Earl Fortescue, 11 November 1918, DRO, 1262M/FC/62a.

79 DRO, 5277M/F3/30.

80 Alan to Edith Thomson, 11 November 1918, Thomson papers.

Chapter 7

1   LMA, ACC/1360/556/17.

2   M. Rawcliffe, 'Population', in N. Yates (ed), *Kent in the Twentieth Century* (Woodbridge, 2001), p. 12.

3   I. F. W. Beckett, 'The soldier's documents of the Great War and the military historian', *Archives*, 23 (1998), p. 67.

4   H. McPhail, *The Long Silence: Civilian Life under the German Occupation of Northern France, 1914–1918* (London, 1999).

5   B. W. Harvey and C. Fitzgerald (eds) *Edward Heron-Allen's Journal of the Great War* (Lewes, 2002), pp.253–5.

6   A. Danchev, 'Bunking and debunking: the controversies of the 1960s', in B. Bond (ed), *The First World War and British Military History* (Oxford, 1991), pp. 263–88.

7   A. Coren, *Golfing for Cats* (London, 1975), p. 72.

8   J. Terraine, 'Instant history', *RUSI Journal*, 107 (1962), pp. 140–5, and *The Smoke and the Fire: Myths and Anti-Myths of War, 1861–1945* (London, 1980); G. Sheffield, 'John Terraine as a military Historian', *RUSI Journal*, 149 (2004), pp 70–5. See also G. Brayborn (ed), *Evidence, History and the Great War: Historians and the Impact of 1914–18* (London, 2003).

9   C. Barnett, 'The Western Front experience as interpreted through literature', *RUSI Journal*, 148, no. 6 (2003), pp. 50–6; P. Parker, *The Old Lie. The Great War and the Public-School Ethos* (London, 2007).

10   I. F. W. Beckett, *The Great War 1914–18* (Harlow, 2001); S. Badsey, '*Blackadder Goes Forth* and the "Two western fronts" debate', in G. Roberts and P. M. Taylor (eds), *The Historian, Television and Television History* (Luton, 2001), pp. 113–25; G. D. Sheffield, '"Oh! What a Futile War": representations of the Western Front in modern British media and popular culture', in I. Stewart and S. L. Carruthers (eds), *War, Culture and the Media: Representations of the Military in 20ᵗʰ Century Britain* (Trowbridge, 2006), pp. 54–74; N. Stone, *World War One, A Short History* (London, 2007), p. 178.

11   B. Bond, *The Unquiet Western Front. Britain's Role in Literature and History* (Cambridge, 2002), quote p. 86, see also Bond, *Survivors of a Kind. Memoirs of the Western Front* (London, 2008) and (ed), *The First World War and British Military History* (Oxford, 1991);

S. Andoin-Rouzeau and A. Becker, *14–18:Understanding the Great War* (New York, 2002); D. Todman, *The Great War. Myth and Memory* (London, 2007).

12   *Times Playlist*, 1–7 May 2010, p. 30.

13   J. Keegan, *The First World War* (1998: London, 1999 edn), p. 264.

14   LMA, CLC/533/MS 24718, pp. 7–8.

15   J. Keegan, *The First World War*, p. 456.

16   J. F. Vance, *Death So Noble: Memory, Meaning, and the First World War* (Vancouver, 1997) and 'Remembering Armageddon', in D. Mackenzie (ed), *Canada and the First World War* (Toronto, 2005), pp. 409–33.

17   L. Capdevila and D. Voldman, *War Dead: Western Societies and the Casualties of War* (Edinburgh, 2006).

18   A. J. Frantzen, *Bloody Good. Chivalry, Sacrifice, and the Great War* (Chicago, Illinois, 2004), p. 265.

19   S. Goebel, *The Great War and Medieval Memory: War, Remembrance and Medievalism in Britain and Germany, 1914–1940* (Cambridge, 2007).

20   J. S. K. Watson, *Fighting Different Wars. Experience, Memory, and the First World War in Britain* (Cambridge, 2004), p. 311. For Canadian memory, D. Williams, *Media, Memory and the First World War* (Montréal, 2009).

21   H. Strachan, 'The war to end all wars? Lessons of World War I Revisited', *Foreign Affairs*, 82/1 (2003), p. 150.

22   M. Hardy, "Be cheerful in adversity": views from the trenches, 1917–1918, Buckinghamshire Records Office, *Annual Report and List of Accessions, 1995*, p. 13.

23   Tameside, Manchester Regiment Archives, MB2/25/21, undated; B. Lamin, *Letters from the Trenches* (London, 2009), p. 120.

24   Alan to Edith Thomson, 5, 25 November 1916, Thomson papers; Gurney to wife, 7 January 1918, LMA, GLRO. ACC/1360/556/17.

25   Gurney to wife, 16 October 1917, LMA, GLRO. ACC/1360/556/9.

26   Ged to his mother, Christina, 18 August 1915, M. Pottle and J. G. G. Ledingham (eds), *We Hope To Get Word Tomorrow. The Garvin Family Letters* (London, 2009).

[27] Gurney to wife, 7 January 1918, LMA, GLRO. ACC/1360/556/17; T. Ashworth, *Trench Warfare 1914–1918: the live and let live system* (London, 1980).

[28] LMA, GL MS 9400.

[29] J. Ellis, *Eye-Deep in Hell: Trench Warfare in World War I* (New York, 1976).

[30] Monash to wife, 20 June 1916, AWM, 3 DRL/2316, 1/1, p. 195.

[31] Alan to Edith Thomson, 1, 26 October 20 November 1915, Thomson papers.

[32] Eg. LMA, GLRO. ACC/1360/556/3, 4, 16. For a valuable published account of soldiers' experiences, P. Hart, *1918: A Very British Victory* (London, 2008).

[33] Southcomb to aunt Connie, 25 July 1917, DRO, 413M add F1.

[34] M. Harrison, *The Medical War: British Military Medicine in the First World War* (Oxford, 2010).

[35] DRO, 413M add F1.

[36] J. Winter, 'Army and society: the demographic context', in I. F. W. Beckett and K. Simpson (eds), *A Nation in Arms: A Social Study of the British Army in the First World War* (Manchester, 1985), pp. 193–209.

[37] M. Hughes, 'The French army at Gallipoli', *RUSI Journal*, 150, no. 3 (2005), p. 65.

[38] A. Babington, *For the Sake of Empire* (London, 1983); J. Putkowski and J. Sykes, *Shot At Dawn* (London, 1989).

[39] G. Oram, *Military Executions during World War I* (London, 2003).

[40] G. Phillips, 'An army of giants: height and medical characteristics of Welsh soldiers, 1914–1918', *Archives*, 22 (997), p. 143.

[41] G. Thomas, *Treating Trauma of the Great War: Soldiers, Civilians and Psychiatry in France, 1914–1940* (Baton Rouge, Louisiana, 2009).

[42] B. Shephard, *A War of Nerves: Soldiers and Psychiatrists, 1914–1994* (London, 2000).

[43] M. S. Micale and P. Lerner (eds), *Traumatic Pasts: History, Psychiatry, and Trauma in the Modern Age, 1870–1930* (Cambridge, 2001).

44 For example, J. Jackson, *Private 12768: Memoir of a Tommy* (Stroud, 2004); M. Walsh (ed) *Brothers in War: one family's ultimate Great War sacrifice* (London, 2010).

45 R. Gerwarth, 'The Central European counter-revolution: paramilitary violence in Germany, Austria and Hungary after the Great War', *Past and Present*, 200 (2008), pp. 175–209.

46 J. Kissely, 'Douglas Haig and veterans', *RUSI Journal*, 155 no. 1 (2010), p. 90; N. Barr, *The Lion and The Poppy: British Veterans, Politics, and Society* (Westport, Connecticut, 2005).

47 LMA, CLC/521/MS 24718, p. 23.

48 S. Badsey, *The British Army in Battle and Its Image 1914–1918* (London, 2009), p. 187.

49 R. Prior and T. Wilson, 'Paul Fussell at war', and D. Englander, 'Soldiering and identity: reflections on the Great War', *War in History*, 1 (1994), pp. 63–80, 300–18.

50 S. Audoin-Rouzeau and A. Becker, *14–18. Understanding the Great War* (New York, 2002).

51 P. Griffith, *Battle Tactics of the Western Front: The British Army's Art of Attack, 1916–1918* (New Haven, Connecticut, 1994), p. 193.

52 L. Sondhaus, *Franz Conrad von Hötzendorf: Architect of the Apocalypse* (Boston, Massachusetts, 2000), p. 92.

53 G. Sheffield, 'British High Command in the First World War: an overview', in Sheffield and G. Till (eds), *Challenges of High Command in the Twentieth Century* (Camberley, 1999), p. 23.

54 D. Stahel, *Operation Barbarossa and Germany's Defeat in the East* (Cambridge, 2009).

55 J. Winter, G. Parker and M. Habeck (eds), *The Great War and the Twentieth Century* (New Haven, Connecticut, 2000).

56 For a perceptive review, B. Schwarz, 'Was the Great War necessary?', *Atlantic Monthly* (1999), pp. 118–28.

Chapter 8

1 LMA, CLC/521/MS 24718.

2 J. Winter and B. Baggett, *The Great War and the Shaping of the Twentieth Century* (New York, 1996).

3   BL, Add. 49699 fol. 85.

4   P. M. Holt and M. W. Daly, *A History of the Sudan* (5ᵗʰ edn, Harlow, 2000), p. 103; NA, WO, 33/2764, p. 257; General Rawlinson, Commander-in-Chief India, to General Montgomery-Massingberd, the Deputy Chief of General Staff, India, 8 November 1922, LH, MM 8/27.

5   J. Darwin, *Britain, Egypt and the Middle East: Imperial Policy in the Aftermath of War, 1918–1922* (London, 1981); J. R. Ferris, *Men, Money and Diplomacy: The Evolution of British Strategic Policy, 1919–1926* (Ithaca, New York, 1989).

6   E. Manela, *The Wilsonian Moment: Self-Determination and the International Origins of Anticolonial Nationalism* (New York, 2007).

7   R. R. Doerries, *Prelude to the Easter Rising: Sir Roger Casement in Imperial Germany* (London, 2000).

8   Intelligence report by Lieutenant H. Pirie-Gordon, 13 November 1915, AWM, 3 DRL/3376, 11/4.

9   G. Lewis, *Balfour and Weizman, The Zionist, the Zealot and the Emergence of Israel* (London, 2009).

10 W. W. Haddad and W. Ochsenwald (eds), *Nationalism in a Non-National State: The Dissolution of the Ottoman Empire* (Columbus, Ohio, 1977); D. Quataert, *The Ottoman Empire, 1700–1922* (2ⁿᵈ edn, Cambridge, 2005), pp. 191–2.

11 C. Kinvig, *Churchill's Crusade. The British Invasion of Russia, 1918–1920* (London, 2006).

12 R. Gerwarth and S. Malinowski, 'Hannah Arendt's Ghosts: Reflections on the Disputable Path from Windhoek to Auschwitz', *Central European History*, 42 (2009), p. 299.

13 F. Ribeiro de Meneses, *Portugal 1914–1926: From the First World War to Military Dictatorship* (Bristol, 2004).

14 E. A. McCord, 'Civil war and the emergence of warlordism in early twentieth century China' *War and Society*, 102 (1992), pp. 35–56.

15 R. Smith, *Jamaican Volunteers in the First World War: Race, Masculinity and the Development of National Consciousness* (Manchester, 2004).

16 M. Ceadel, *Living the Great Illusion: Sir Norman Angell, 1872–1967* (Oxford, 2009).

17 John Maynard Keynes, *The Economic Consequences of the Peace* (London, 1919)

18 S. Broadberry and M. Harrison (eds), *The Economics of World War I* (Cambridge, 2005).

19 P. Duus (ed), *The Cambridge History of Japan VI. The Twentieth Century* (Cambridge, 1988), p. 438.

20 R. Self, *Britain, America, and the War Debt Controversy: The Economic Diplomacy of an Unspecial Relationship, 1917–41* (London, 2006).

21 D. P. Silverman, *Reconstructing Europe after the Great War* (Cambridge, Massachusetts, (1982); R. W. D. Boyce, *British Capitalism at the Crossroads, 1919–1932: A Study in Politics, Economics, and International Relations* (Cambridge, 1987).

22 A. Eeichova and P. L. Cottrell (eds), *International Business and Central Europe, 1918–1939* (Leicester, 1983).

23 R. Henig, *The League of Nations* (London, 2010), p. 187; J. Yearwood, *Guarantee of Peace: The League of Nations in British Policy, 1914–1925* (Oxford, 2009).

24 Horne to wife, 2 November 1918, Roberts (ed), *Horne*, p. 273.

25 Z. Steiner, *The Lights that Failed: European International History, 1919–1933* (Oxford, 2005).

26 S. Dimitrova, "'My war is not your war": the Bulgarian debate on the Great War', *Rethinking History*, 6 (20002), pp. 15–34.

27 *F. W. Putzgers Historischer Schul-Atlas* (Bielefeld, 1923), p. 137.

28 L. H. Adam 2/1 p.23.

29 P. Leese, 'Problems returning home: the British psychological casualties of the Great War', *Historical Journal*, 40 (1997), 1066–7; M. Tyquin, *Madness and the Military: Australia's Experience of the Great War* (Loftus, 2006).

30 LMA, CLC/521/MS 24718, pp. 2–3, 6–7, 15, 22.

31 J. T. Stuart, 'The question of human progress in Britain after the Great War', *British Scholar*, 1 (2008), 53–78; R. J. Overy, *The Morbid Age: Britain between the war* (London, 2009).

32   J. M. Wilson, *Siegfried Sassoon: The Making of a War Poet* (London, 1998).

33   A. Caiden-Coyne, *Reconstructing the Body. Classicism, Modernism, and the First World War* (Oxford, 2009).

34   M. L. Siegel, *The Moral Disarmament of France: Education, Pacifism, and Patriotism, 1914–1940* (Cambridge, 2004).

35   M. Paris, 'A different view of the trenches: juvenile fiction and popular perceptions of the First World War', *War Studies Journal*, 3 (1997), pp. 32–45.

36   L. M. Budreau, 'The politics of remembrance: the Gold Star mothers' pilgrimage and America's fading memory of the Great War', *Journal of Military History*, 72 (2008), 409–10 and *Bodies of War. World War I and the Politics of Commemoration in America, 1919–1933* (New York, 2010); G. L. Mosse, *Fallen Soldiers: Reshaping the Memory of the World Wars* (Oxford, 1990).

37   W. Wette, 'From Kellogg to Hitler, 1928–1933: German public opinion concerning the rejection or glorification of war', in W. Deist (ed), *The German Military in the Age of Total War* (Leamington Spa, 1985), pp. 88–93.

38   J. Crouthamel, *The Great War and German Memory. Society, Politics and Psychological Trauma, 1914–1945* (Exeter, 2009), p. 224.

39   L. Noakes, *Women in the British Army: War and the Gentle Sex, 1907–1948* (London, 2006).

40   M. Roper, *The Secret Battle: Emotional Survival in the Great War* (Manchester, 2009).

41   N. F. Gullace, *'The Blood of Our Sons': Men, Women, and the Renegotiation of British Citizenship during the War* (Basingstoke, 2002).

42   Alan to Edith Thomson, 9 February 1916, Thomson papers.

43   Alan to Edith Thomson, 12 October, 10, 21 November 1915, 25 December 1916, Thomson papers.

44   I. D. Thorn, *Nice Girls and Rude Girls: Women Workers in World War One* (London, 1999).

45   S. R. Grayzel, *Women's Identities at War: Gender, Motherhood, and Politics in Britain and France during the First World War*

(Chapel Hill, North Carolina, 1999); S. Zeiger, *In Uncle Sam's Service: Women Workers with the American Expeditionary Force, 1917–1919* (Ithaca, New York, 1999).

[46] G. Braybon and P. Summerfield, *Out of the Cage: Women's Experiences in Two World Wars* (London, 1987).

[47] J. Bourke, *Dismembering the Male: Men's Bodies, Britain, and the Great War* (London, 1996).

[48] T. Tate, *Modernism, History, and the First World War* (Manchester, 1998).

[49] Monash to wife, 18 July 1916, AWM, 3 DRL/23/6, 1/1, pp. 201–2.

[50] I. V. Hull, *Absolute Destruction: Military Culture and the Practices of War in Imperial Germany* (Ithaca, New York, 2004).

[51] D. Moran and A. Waldron (eds), *The People in Arms: Military Myth and National Mobilization since the French Revolution* (New York, 2003).

[52] J. F. Godfrey, *Capitalism at War: Industrial Policy and Bureaucracy in France, 1914–1918* (Oxford, 1987).

[53] N. Keohane, *The Party of Patriotism. The Conservative Party and the First World War* (Farnham, 2010).

[54] P. Holquist, *Making War, Forging Revolution: Russia's continuum of Crisis, 1914–1921* (Cambridge, Massachusetts, 2002).

[55] E. A. Hueller, *The 'Casualty Issue' in American Military Practice: The Impact of World War I* (Westport, Connecticut, 2003).

[56] M. Strohn, *The German Army and the Conduct of the Defensive Battle, 1918–1939* (Cambridge, 2010).

[57] A. Green, *Writing the Great War: Sir James Edmonds and the Official Histories, 1915–1948* (London, 2003).

[58] B. Bond, *British Military Policy between the Two World Wars* (Oxford, 1980).

[59] T. Travers, *How the War Was Won: Command and Technology in the British Army on the Western Front, 1917–1918* (London, 1992).

[60] E. C. Kiesling, *Arming Against Hitler: France and the Limits of Military Planning* (Lawrence, Kansas, 1996).

[61] LH, Liddell Hart papers, 7/1920/167; A. Danchev, *Alchemist of War: The Life of Basil Liddell Hart* (London, 1998).

[62] J. S. Corum, *The Roots of Blitzkrieg: Hans von Seeckt and German Military Reform* (Lawrence, Kansas. 1992); R. M. Citino, *The Path to Blitzkrieg: Doctrine and Training in the German Army, 1920–1939* (Boulder, Colorado, 1999).

Chapter 9

[1] Child-Villiers to his mother, 27 August 1918, LMA, ACC/28391/D/001. cf. 7 May 1917, /002.

[2] S. Hart, *Montgomery and Colossal Cracks: The 21st Army Group in Northwest Europe, 1944–5* (Westport, Connecticut, 2000).

[3] P. O. Cohrs, *The Unfinished Peace after World War I. America, Britain and the Stabilisation of Europe, 1919–1932* (Cambridge, 2008).

[4] X. Guoqi, *China and the Great War: China's Pursuit of a New National Identity and Internationalization* (Cambridge, 2005).

[5] T. Denman, *A Lonely Grave; the Life and Death of William Redmond* (Blackrock, 1995).

[6] J. Horne (ed), *Our War: Ireland and the Great War* (Dublin, 2008).

[7] R. S. Grayson, *Belfast Boys. How Unionists and Nationalists Fought and Died Together in the First World War* (London, 2009), pp. 167–77.

[8] T. W. Moody, 'Irish history and Irish mythology', *Hermathena* (1978–9), pp. 7–25; C. Brady (ed), *Interpreting Irish History: The Debate on Historical Revisionism* (Dublin, 1994); R. Foster, *The Irish Story: Telling Tales and Making It Up in Ireland* (Oxford, 2002).

[9] A. Dolan, *Commemorating the Irish Civil War: History and Memory 1923–2000* (Cambridge, 2003); T. Denman, *Ireland's Unknown Soldiers: The 16th (Irish) Division in the Great War* (Blackrock, 1992).

[10] S. Das, 'India and the First World War', in M. Howard (ed), *A Part of History. Aspects of the British Experience of the First World War* (London, 2008), pp. 63–4.

[11] T. Akçam, *A Shameful Act: The Armenian Genocide and the Question of Turkish Responsibility* (London, 2007).

[12] T. G. Fraser, *Chaim Weizmann. The Zionist Dream* (London, 2009), p. 62.

13 M. Connelly, '*Gallipoli* (1981): "a poignant search for national identity"', in J. Chapman, M. Glancy and S. Harper (eds), *A New Film History: Sources, Methods, Approaches* (Basingstoke, 2007), pp. 41–53.

14 I. Ousby, *The Road to Verdun. France, Nationalism and the First World War* (London, 2002).

15 S. Goebel, 'Intersecting memories, war and remembrance on twentieth-century Europe', *Historical Journal*, 44 (2001), p. 857.

16 J. Winter, 'The generation of memory; reflections on the "memory boom" in contemporary historical studies', *Bulletin of the German Historical Institute, Washington*, 27 (2000), pp. 80–2.

17 G. L. Mosse, *Fallen Soldiers: Reshaping the Memory of the World Wars* (Oxford, 1990); J. Winter, *Sites of Memory, Sites of Mourning: the Great War in European Cultural History* (Cambridge, 1995); B. Scales, *A Place to Remember. A History of the Shrine of Remembrance* (Cambridge, 2009); P. H. Hoffenberg, 'Landscape, memory and the Australian war experience', *Journal of Contemporary History*, 36 (2001), pp. 111–31.

18 T. Skelton and G. Gliddon, *Lutyens and the Great War* (London, 2008), p. 154; B. Scales, *Return to Gallipoli: Walking the Battlefields of the Great War* (Cambridge, 2006).

19 H. Strachan, 'Into History', *RUSI Journal*, 154/4 (2009), p. 5.

Conclusion

1 D. Williams, *Media, Memory and the First World War* (Montréal, 2009).

2 G. Sheffield, *Forgotten Victory: The First World War – Myths and Reality* (London, 2001); C. Messenger, *The Day We Won the War* (London, 2008).

Selected further reading

The emphasis here is on recent works. Earlier scholarship can be approached through these valuable studies.

Beckett, I. F. W. (2001), *The Great War 1914–1918*.

Berghahn, V. (1995), *Germany and the Approach of War in 1914*.

Bond, B. (2002), *The Unquiet Western Front. Britain's Role in Literature and History*.

Carver, M. (2001), *The Turkish Front*.

Chickering, R. and Förster, S. (eds), (2000), *Great War, Total War: Combat and Mobilization on the Western Front, 1914–1918*.

Clayton, A. (2005), *Paths of Glory: The French Army 1914–1918*.

Dickinson, F. (1999), *War and National Reinvention: Japan in the Great War, 1914–1919*.

Erickson, E. J. (2001), *Ordered to Die: A History of the Ottoman Army in the First World War*.

Ferguson, N. (1998), *The Pity of War*.

Foley, R. (2005), *German Strategy and the Path to Verdun: Erich von Falkenhayn and the Development of Attrition, 1870–1916*.

Fromkin, D. (2004), *Europe's Last Summer: Who Started the War in 1914*.

Galántai, J. (1989), *Hungary in the First World War*.

Gordon, A. (1996), *The Rules of the Game*.

Gregory, A. (2008), *The Last Great War: British Society and the First World War*.

Herwig, H. (1997), *The First World War: Germany and Austria-Hungary 1914–1918*.

— (2009), *The Marne, 1914*.

Horne, J. (ed) (2010), *A Companim to World War I*.

Howard, M. (2002), *The First World War*.

Joll, J. (1992), *The Origins of the First World War*.

MacMillan, M. (2003), *Peacemakers: The Paris Conference of 1919*.

Mombauer, A. (2002), *Origins of the First World War*.

Morrow, J. H. (2004), *The Great War. An Imperial History*.

Neiberg, M. S. (ed) (2006), *The World War I Reader*.

Prior, R., and Wilson, T. (2001), *The First World War*.

— (2005), *The Somme*.

Sheffield, G. (2004), *The Somme*.

Showalter, D. (1991), *Tannenberg*.

Stevenson, D. (2004), *1914–1918: The History of the First World War*.

Stone, N. (2007), *The Eastern Front 1914–1917*.

— *World War One. A Short History*.

Strachan, H. (2001), *The First World War, I: To Arms*.

Taylor, A. J. P. (1966), *The First World War*.

Thompson, M. (2008), *The White War. Life and Death on the Italian Front, 1915–1919*.

Todman, D. (2005), *The First World War: Myth and Memory*.

Travers, T. (2001), *Gallipoli*.

— (2003), *The Killing Ground*.

Williams, D. (2009), *Media, Memory and the First World War*.

Winter, J. (1995), *Sites of Memory, Sites of Mourning*.

Winter, J. and Prost, A. (2005), *The Great War in History: Debates and Controversies, 1914 to the Present*.

Index

Index